Theories of trade unionism

Theories of trade unionism:

A sociology of industrial relations

Michael Poole

Senior Lecturer in Industrial Relations
University of Wales Institute of Science and Technology

ROUTLEDGE & KEGAN PAUL

London, Boston and Henley

First published in 1981
by Routledge & Kegan Paul Ltd
39 Store Street,
London WC1E 7DD,
9 Park Street,
Boston, Mass. 02108, USA, and
Broadway House,
Newtown Road,
Henley-on-Thames,
Oxon RG9 1EN
Set in IBM Press Roman by Columns
and printed in Great Britain by
Biddles Ltd, Guildford, Surrey
© M.J.F. Poole, 1981

British Library Cataloguing in Publication Data

Poole, Michael
    Theories of trade unionism.
    1. Trade-unions
    I. Title
    331.88'09   HD6483   80-41561

ISBN 0 7100 0695 0

Contents

Tables

Figures

Preface

The principal objective of this volume is to fashion a comprehensive text on the development of trade union theory from which both the student and specialist may enhance their understanding of this rapidly expanding field of inquiry. In consequence, the foremost concern is to integrate, in comprehensive vein, that corpus of classical and contemporary literature which has been directed towards advancing our analytical appreciation of the aims and workings of modern associations of labour. Yet our goal is not merely to produce a bibliographic review (although, in the absence of such a treatise, this would be a laudable intention) but rather, to embark upon the formulation of a higher order synthesis of the main schools of thought and to generate a number of original propositions and integrating frameworks.

In the account itself, we have drawn upon a rich vein of approaches and, in consequence, have extended the examination well beyond the confines of Anglo-Saxon scholarship. To be sure, as will become apparent, in respect of substantive theories (i.e. generalizations with specific reference to trade unionism) the bulk of the formulations have originated from British and American literature because these twin tributaries still remain the most influential sources of the various contributions to labour theory. However, in terms of analytical precepts and explanatory categories, it is the continental European heritage which is generally ascendant.

A prefatory note is also invaluable for recording the many debts which all writers accumulate during the course of their work. Undoubtedly my prime obligation is to my wife who not only shouldered the usual burdens of an author's spouse, but whose own professional expertise also contributed greatly to improvements in both the content and style of the manuscript itself. In formulating my ideas I also drew heavily upon the experiences of trade unionists whose views I have been recording for a number of years. Professor Dorothy Wedderburn suggested that I should concentrate on producing a sociological framework for this analysis and this undoubtedly proved to be useful advice. In various communications with Professor

Malcolm Warner I became aware of the saliency of organizational variables for the study of trade unionism and a decision to devote a whole chapter to this theme was undoubtedly influenced by his own impressive researches in this area. Professor Roger Mansfield read through an earlier draft of the book and helped to erase a number of deficiencies of presentation and substance. Moreover, I should like also to record my indebtedness to Dr Arun Sahay, an erstwhile colleague at the University of Sheffield, whose recognition of the sociological significance of values ultimately caused me to reconsider my own. At Routledge & Kegan Paul, David Stonestreet was a model of competence and efficiency. But, above all, for Peter Hopkins I hope that this book will be a tribute to his native Wales since much of the inspiration during the course of composition was occasioned by my move to the Principality.

It is also with gratitude that my debts to the following copyright holders for permission to quote from their respective works are acknowledged since, without such goodwill, the process of scholarship would become exceedingly constrained. A. P. Watt agreed to allow the production of Figure 5.2 of the current volume from their text *Social Stratification and Trade Unionism* by G. S. Bain, D. Coates and V. Ellis, while the British Sociological Association and J. Child, R. Loveridge and M. Warner behaved likewise in the respects of Figures 7.2 and 7.3 that had earlier appeared in the article, 'Towards an Organizational Study of Trade Unions', *Sociology* (vol. 7, no. 1, 1973). The authorities of the *British Journal of Industrial Relations*, the *Industrial Relations Journal* and the *Sociological Review* granted permission to reprint respectively: Figure 2.3, Table 2.1, the representations of 'Dependent and independent variables in industrial and labour relations systems' (p. 31), and of 'The effect of personality on processes in labour relations' (p. 40) from A. N. J. Blain's and J. Gennard's article 'Industrial Relations Theory – A Critical Review' (vol. 8, no. 3, 1970); Figure 2.2 from R. Singh's 'Systems Theory in the Study of Industrial Relations: Time for a Reappraisal?' (vol. 7, no. 3, 1976); and Figure 5.1 from J. H. Goldthorpe's and D. Lockwood's paper 'Affluence and the British Class Structure' (vol. 11, 1963). And finally, the Industrial Relations Research Association, Collier-Macmillan and the Open University allowed Figure 2.1 to be reprinted from A. Craig's 'A Framework for the Analysis of Industrial Relations Systems' which appears in *Industrial Relations and the Wider Society*.

The manuscript itself was expertly and efficiently typed by Stevie Burges, who, I regret to add, endured some very indifferent handwriting but did so with remarkable resilience and good humour. In the latter stages, her unstinting efforts were valuably complemented by those of Kath Hollister. Jane Sparks of the Friary Library of the University of

Wales Institute of Science and Technology helped me greatly in the preparation of the bibliography. Finally, however, it is of course incumbent upon me to add the usual rider that the responsibility for the contents of this book rests entirely with the author.

Point of departure

The gradual transformation of industrial societies from their earliest elemental foundations has been accompanied by a phenomenon of great
moment: the rise of associations of labour to a position of considerable
prominence in the institutional structure of modern communities. Hence
although of course there were a wide variety of unions of working men
and women that substantially pre-dated the industrial revolution, until
recently, their impact upon national policy and the day-to-day management of the enterprise had generally been circumscribed. But, in the
modern era, the power of union officer and lay representative has without
question become an issue of paramount concern and, however legitimate
such consternation may appear to be, it would seem symbolic of a progressive evolution in the formal as well as in the less structured patterns of
influence which now obtain in a wide range of occupational and industrial
milieux.

Accompanying this ongoing adaptation in social institutions there has
been a noticeable quickening of attention in academic circles themselves in
the formulation of systematic models of trade union growth, structure and
policy. As a corollary, therefore, not only has the collation of empirical
data proceeded apace, but more especially, a growing conceptual sophistication has been manifest in the delineation of forces producing this meta-
morphosis. This is, for instance, particularly evident in the isolation of
factors affecting union growth[1] and in the understanding of the weights
to be attached to the appropriate variables in the interpretation of the
modes of government and internal administration of leading trade unions.[2]
Moreover, despite the somewhat crab-wise pattern of intellectual progress,
there has been a clear tendency for increasingly sophisticated analytical
models to be deployed in the interpretation of trade union action and
behaviour and for these to have evidently emanated from one or more of
the main social science disciplines.

Notwithstanding the multiplicity of volumes which have now appeared
on the trade union question, however, there have been remarkably few

1

attempts to draw together the main strands of classical and modern approaches to labour theory and to integrate these conceptions into the propositions which have informed the basic categories deployed by the founding fathers of modern sociology. In an attempt, therefore, to eradicate this major lacuna in existing knowledge two objectives will be uppermost in the following analysis: first, it will be our concern to review the principal debates on the theory of trade unions within the cognate fields of inquiry of industrial relations and industrial sociology respectively; and second, of no less importance will be our endeavour to advance existing theoretical propositions by a detailed assessment of the saliency of (a) the distribution of power (b) structural, institutional and organizational variables and (c) culture, values and perception in the overall explanatory equation. Furthermore, within the compass of this volume we shall attempt to secure a balance of classical and modern perspectives by deploying the criterion of quality of contribution as the main yardstick for inclusion of any major item in the text itself. After all, although in conceptual terms some of the earliest approaches to generalizing about labour movements were conspicuously rudimentary and often exhibited a 'rule of thumb' character in their application to specific problems, equally, they displayed an unmistakable clarity of vision and perspicacity which were in no way vitiated by the boldness of their underlying assumptions.

Our general survey of approaches to labour theory appropriately begins, therefore, by an examination of the main tributaries of contemporary analytical thought. Indeed, these have generally been understood to have derived from five principal sources: first, the 'ethical' or 'moral' school in which primacy of emphasis was placed upon the role of cultural variables in shaping union growth and character; second, the revolutionary appraisal in which the consequences of union organization and action for the fermentation of radical politico-economic changes were variously assessed; third, the defensive or conservative conception in which unions were understood as agencies for the protection of members' interests, and as producing a form of 'communism of opportunity' in which job regulation and control were paramount concerns; fourth, the 'economic implications school' in which the saliency of economic forces in the formation and later development of trade unions and in occasioning predominantly instrumental purposes was emphasized; and fifth, the political perspective in which the role of unions in industrial government and in power struggles between unions, management and the state was envisaged.[3]

As we shall observe at several points in the ensuing analysis, these first approximations to a theory of labour still have remarkably durable lines of filiation with contemporary perspectives. Nevertheless, in respect of the history of trade union thought, a fundamental and abrupt change in analytical focus accompanied the publication of John T. Dunlop's *Industrial Relations Systems*.[4] After all, this ushered in an analytical breadth based on Parsonian structural-functionalism and it foreshadowed a new disciplinary base for the interpretation of industrial and labour relations themselves. Yet, as a consequence of the widespread diffusion of a range of system models, trade unions as such ceased to be a central focus for analysis since undoubtedly Dunlop himself endeavoured to analyse broader patterns of industrial relations than those encapsulated in collective bargaining institutions. Hence, trade unions were now construed as only one major party amongst the general ensemble of actors in the industrial relations system, concerned primarily with rule-making and being constrained in their activities by a number of environmental exigencies (market and budgetary, technical, and the distribution of power in the larger society).

Nevertheless, in mainstream industrial relations and sociological theory in the UK, trade unions retained a position of analytical dominance. Indeed, the interest in collective bargaining remained particularly central to the preoccupations of the so-called 'liberal-pluralist', 'voluntarist', or 'Oxford' school.[5] But despite a shared concern for rule-making the epistemological and theoretical origins of this approach differed markedly from system formulations, for these were grounded primarily in the historiographical researches and substantive theories of the Webbs coupled with Durkheimian sociological precepts. Moreover, although Allan Flanders was unquestionably the principal architect of this school of thought, its significance has been compounded latterly by the adoption of his ideas, particularly by Clegg and Bain, in their subsequent and ongoing theoretical analyses.[6]

Meanwhile, amongst industrial sociologists, and more recently amongst radically inclined industrial relations scholars, the relationship between social stratification and trade unionism has been persistently emphasized.[7] In conceptual terms, the basic premises of this approach may be clearly traced to Weberian and Marxian precepts but, in the last few years, partly as a consequence of the disavowal of the crudest versions of the social inequality thesis (i.e. that which involves *direct* links between stratification and trade unionism), a degree of integration would appear to be consequential upon the recognition of the centrality of power in union-management relations *per se*. Certainly the focus on control has now become part of the general currency of debate and, in recent years, in terms of conceptual and operational measurement, some fundamental breakthroughs in technique have been recorded.[8]

But, although by convention the principal modes of contemporary labour theory have been classified into 'system', 'Oxford', and 'industrial sociological' or 'radical' schools respectively, there are many interpenetrating cross-currents which make the rigid pigeon-holing of these approaches increasingly difficult to sustain. Hence, in the latter part of this volume, a more advanced synthesis will be undertaken in order that the relevant contributions from the early theories of labour, together with the critical insights of these contemporary schools of thought, may be extended as part of a wider encompassing analytical matrix. As a result, after acknowledging the saliency of power for understanding trade unionism (and the basic requirement of incorporating 'resource' as well as 'exercise' approaches) our discourse proceeds to a higher analytical level by focusing upon structural constraints upon action, the role of institutional and organizational variables and the impact of cultural and subjective forces in the general theoretical composition of strategic explanatory dimensions.

In the first place, then, modern structuralist accounts of trade unions will be acknowledged to have diverse roots, with the main progenitors of current formulations being structural-functionalism and Durkheimian and Marxian premises respectively. But, as we shall see, for analytical purposes it is vital not only to include an historical dimension, but also the notions of levels of structure and of structural differentiation. That is to say, although structural forces should be regarded ultimately as *constraints* upon and not as *determinants* of action, they may be analysed at a number of levels. Indeed, these include both the familiar macro-micro distinction and also the notion of deep or primary and surface or secondary structures. The latter dimension incorporates various correlates of union action and behaviour (such as the size of the enterprise) but involves the further analysis of antecedent and logically more fundamental structures (such as politico-economic movements and technical change). Similarly, as we shall record, structural differentiation is a fundamental aspect of the overall conception since it tends to produce ever more complex patterns within the division of labour and thus not only to operate against the development of integrated trade union movements, but also to affect patterns of long-term trade union evolution itself.

Yet while few analysts of trade unionism would wish to contest the proposition that power and structural change have far-reaching consequences for action and behaviour, the inclusion of institutional and organizational variables is, on the face of it, more controversial. But although the main dimensions of organizational structure are properly regarded as mediating variables between broad societal forces and membership action, their analytical utility is particularly evident in the explanations for the durability of traditional customs and practices, and in the varying emphases upon administrative and democratic rationales within trade unions themselves.

Such an approach, however, in turn forms the prelude to the most advanced components of the integrative model which depend upon the recognition of the ultimately decisive consequences of cultural and value premises in shaping trade union action. Again, at more specific levels, the perceptions and orientations of trade union members, representatives and officials are distinguished as crucial variables in accounting for union character. Drawing principally upon Weberian methodological and theoretical postulates,[9] then, the final part of our discourse will be concerned with an examination of such fundamental questions as the role of culture in international comparative researches, the significance of 'party' as an analytical construct (this has particular poignancy in the British case, of course, in view of the historical link between trade unions and the Labour Party), the proposition that control only has importance as a pre-condition for creation, and finally the formal elaboration of action categories to encompass 'end', 'value', 'affectual' and 'traditional' rationality.

The upshot, therefore, will be the development of a conceptual or categorical system which is more advanced than that obtaining in current formulations.[10] Naturally, during the course of this endeavour, we shall aim to incorporate the insights from existing analytical frameworks but these we shall seek to transcend by means of a higher order synthesis. The general effect should, therefore, be a contribution of interest to the theoretically inclined student and specialist in a field of inquiry which has become a focal point of research among scholars from a wide range of social science disciplines.

1 Early theories of the labour movement

In recent years the dearth of systematic theories of union action and behaviour has been lamented. Thus, in *Trade Unionism under Collective Bargaining*, Hugh Clegg not only identified such a problem but also drew attention to the paradoxical nature of this situation in a period when unions have come to be regarded as among 'the most powerful forces shaping our society and determining our future'.[1] Yet, although we would in no way wish to dispute the uneven quality of much of contemporary theory, or to infer that any universally accepted model of trade union growth, structure and policy has any real prospect of emerging in the near future, at the same time, it is essential to recognize the long-standing tradition of interest in generalizations about trade union and labour movements. Indeed, in many instances, the germs of contemporary debates may be traced back to accounts of upwards of a century ago.

The principal objective of this chapter, then, will be to focus upon early theories of the labour movement and to locate the origins of many of the foremost of present contributions in these classical traditions. For our major categories we have based the analysis upon the classification of Mark Perlman deployed in his seminal contribution, *Labor Union Theories in America*[2]; although this has been adapted, of course, to take into account the distinctive British cultural context and to incorporate primarily British material. Furthermore, although it is not our view 'that writing a study covering theoretical material after 1933' is 'essentially impossible because the latter period (until now) just simply failed to produce veins of theoretical material rich enough to warrant mining,'[3] equally, the comprehensiveness and impressive stature of the forerunners of modern theory are undoubtedly worthy of emphasis.

But the original attempts at theorizing were far from homogeneous and undoubtedly reflected the severances of discipline, methodology, ethics and political conviction familiar today. In particular, it was possible even in the earliest accounts to discern a major disunity between 'idealist' scholars who placed great weight upon the salience of ethical values in determining union growth and character, and those who adopted an 'administrative' or 'structuralist' position and who thereby emphasized the conditioning effects of organizational and external environmental variables respectively.[4] Again, such basic differences of approach were magnified by a number of strident polemical tracts which straddled disciplinary boundaries and academic divisions between, for example, economists and behavioural scientists. This latter 'bifurcation of interest and perspective' was thus remarked upon by Galenson and Lipset who recognized that whereas the first approach stressed that the labour market was 'merely one of a number of different types of markets, all subject to the same economic laws', the institutional analysis of the trade union and the employment relationship fell largely within the province of the behavioural scientist.[5]

To make some sense of these variations, however, Mark Perlman established five basic interpretations of trade unionism each of which was associated in its formation 'with characteristics or premises peculiar to a particular academic discipline or a particular general social movement'.[6] These were the conceptions, respectively, of trade unions as 'moral' institutions, as part of a revolutionary tradition, as a 'psychological' or defensive reaction to early conditions of industrialism, as institutions shaped by economic forces and essentially 'business' or welfare in outlook, and finally as political organizations in the two senses of being part of the democratic process and of reflecting strategic changes in the balance of power between working people, employers and government. Moreover, the five major social movements or academic disciplines encapsulated in each perspective were (1) Protestant Christian Socialist and the Roman Catholic Christian social movements (2) the Marxian social movements (3) the environmental psychology discipline (4) the neo-classical economics discipline and (5) the legal history or jurisprudential history discipline.[7]

Of course, in so far as the construction of *modern* theories of trade unionism is concerned, there are a number of obvious problems in this classification. In the first place the ethical-political and disciplinary roots of the main theories are conflated and so are not logically resolved into their principal differences of type. Moreover, a wider set of antecedent disciplines should really be acknowledged (the omission of sociology being of obvious importance); while the ethical and ideological origins of the main controversies on, say, union character are more diverse than is implied in the Perlman classification. In addition, whereas in his original treatise, Perlman explicitly adopted a positivist approach, in the introduction to the 1976 edition he acknowledged a certain sympathy with a normative perspective.[8] None the less, for an outline of *classical* approaches to trade union theory the basic framework of this approach is of proven utility and, therefore, with modifications, it constitutes a valuable point of reference for our own account.

MORAL AND ETHICAL THEORIES OF TRADE UNIONISM

In the first perspective on trade union growth and character, then, unions were conceived of as the offspring of advancing ethical and moral values in the nineteenth century and thus as products of evolutionary developments in the wider *culture* of which an emerging opposition to the patent injustices and poverty of the period was an obvious manifestation. This approach to trade unionism focused attention, therefore, upon a series of independent ethical, idealist and religious factors[9] which were seen as critical to the formation of British trade unions and, in particular, as determinants of aspects of its essential character.

Pre-eminent amongst these was Nonconformism, the role of which has been immortalized in the familiar epithet that the trade unions and Labour Party owe far more to Methodism than to Marxism. In the nineteenth century, too, the role of Christian Socialists cannot be ignored, for they expounded a belief in the 'brotherhood of man and the consequent development of mutual obligations'.[10] Indeed, Ludlow, Maurice and Kingsley all called for moral responsibility, the support of trade unions, and the encouragement of the producer co-operative movement (for these forms of organization were seen to permit a more just distribution of wealth), the full realization of the energies and resources of weaker members of the population and the fostering of 'initiative, self-confidence, self-restraint, self-government and the capacity for democracy'.[11] More latterly, too, G. K. Chesterton remarked upon the parallels between Christian and Socialist collectivism which both arose from compassion for the unfortunate and from the belief that evil in society emanates from incessant accumulation of riches and from interpersonal competition.[12]

None the less, it is a commonplace to argue that as the twentieth century has advanced the overt expression of religious belief has waned; but, be this as it may, the concern for justice within the labour movement appears to be more perennial. Such a phenomenon is also evident in the work of contemporary moral philosophers such as Rawls who espoused, in *A Theory of Justice*, objectives which have traditionally aroused considerable support within the British trade union movement. And, above all, of course, he advanced the claim that 'social and economic inequalities are to be arranged so that they are both: (a) to the greatest benefit of the least advantaged . . . and (b) attached to offices and positions open to all under conditions of fair equality of opportunity'.[13] Moreover, the general conception of justice here is that:[14]

> All social primary goods — liberty and opportunity, income and wealth, and the bases of self-respect — are to be distributed equally unless an unequal distribution of any or all of these goods is to the advantage of the least favored.

Such values, too, were echoed by Durkheim in the *Division of Labour in Society* where he observed that the central task of advanced industrial societies is a 'work of justice' because the ideal of modern society is 'to involve our social relationships with even greater equity in order to ensure the free development of all socially useful potentialities'.[15]

An essentially 'idealist' view of world history which has underpinned the moral or ethical approach to unionism therefore finds a modern counterpart in the emphasis on justice as a driving force of unionism and as an indispensable bulwark against the extremes of 'business unionism' and of revolutionary socialism respectively. Flanders, in particular, thus noted the salience of justice to the long-run capacity of trade unions to survive both hostile public reaction and the indifference of the membership as a whole.[16]

> The trade union movement deepened its grip on public life in its aspect as a sword of justice. When it is no longer seen to be this, when it can no longer count on anything but its own power to withstand assault, it becomes extremely vulnerable. The more so since it is as a sword of justice rather than a vested interest that it generates loyalties and induces sacrifices among its own members, and these are important foundations of its strength and vitality.

Of course Flanders was to acknowledge that socialism had traditionally represented the conscience of the British trade union movement but argued that this variety of socialism, which evolved organically from working people's actions, was conceived as 'a set of ideals, as a moral dynamic not as a blueprint for an economic and social system'.[17] Moreover, his remarks on the significance of the pursuit of justice and on the vulnerability of the union movement when conceived merely as 'a vested interest' would appear in retrospect to have been remarkably prescient in the modern context.

In theoretical terms, too, the role of Methodism, in particular, in shaping the character of early British trade unionism has been the subject of frequent comment and certainly Halévy,[18] Semmel,[19] Thompson[20] and, more recently, Moore,[21] all emphasized its salience. Thus Halévy pointed out that, in contrast with her continental neighbours, Britain experienced a generally peaceful transition from an agricultural to an industrial society and owed this, in his judgment, almost entirely to the effects of Methodism in tempering revolutionary aspirations.[22] This viewpoint has been echoed by Semmel who accredited to Wesley a direct and indirect contribution towards 'making England a Liberal and not a "totalitarian" democracy'.[23] But by contrast, of course, Thompson, in his classic study, *The Making of the English Working Class*, regarded Methodism as a form of 'psychic exploitation', for, in his view, the harsh disciplines imposed within working-class communities turned the labourer 'into his own slave driver' and helped to ensure a commitment to hard and, above all, to disciplined work that was essential for manufacturing enterprise.[24]

A more balanced view of the role of Methodism, however, was proffered in *Pit-men, Preachers and Politics*, where Moore suggested that Methodism did indeed obscure the salience of class conflict in mining communities of the Durham region, and as a consequence of its ethical rather than economic or political character, inhibited the growth of class consciousness.[25] But, at the same time, although Methodists did not articulate and pursue class interests, they still represented a source of working-class leadership from within local communities. And furthermore, because of their emphasis upon traditional and communal values and activities, in practice the harsh doctrines of Methodism made less of an impression upon the fabric of community life than is frequently supposed.[26] Indeed, Methodism was wedded to, and would appear actively to have fostered, traditional bonds of sociability.

None the less, other writers have cast doubt upon the role of Methodism in this respect, particularly in terms of its being a decisive determinant of early union organization and character. The Hammonds, for example, contended that Methodism was less extensive in its impact than both its supporters and opponents would claim, and above all, they noted that this creed and its moderating influence was largely absent from communities of the urban poor.[27] Hobsbawm, too, took the view that Methodism made only a supplementary contribution to trade union formation, class consciousness and general social outlook in the early part of the nineteenth century and that other forces of a more structural character were ultimately of far greater effect in framing the contours of unionism, such as the changes in the distribution of occupations.[28]

Indeed, whatever the impact of Methodism and of other ethical values in shaping early union character in Britain, it is clear that as a general theory it is by no means satisfactory as a result of being grounded in a one-sided idealist view of world history. Hence, not only are wider structural constraints on action (such as occupational changes, enterprise size, the business-cycle and so on) entirely omitted from the analysis but also the significance of power in enabling ideals to come to fruition is also by and large disregarded. And yet, as Pelling has observed, this latter factor was undoubtedly paramount in occasioning the fitful development of early trade unions themselves.[29]

> the greatest obstacle to the development of trade unionism arose from the hostility of the employers of labour. They were usually well aware that their interests, in the short term at least, were bound to suffer as a result of collective instead of individual wage bargaining . . . and early in the nineteenth century it was not uncommon for employers to try to force all their workers to abjure unionism altogether.

Moreover, there were clear indications of an interaction between ethics and action in the various Christian social movements, and so to posit a one-sided causal relationship without reference to the wider social context is inconsistent with evidence on the development of these movements and on their relationship with early union character itself.[30]

THE REVOLUTIONARY TRADITION

But the trade union and labour movement has also of course been a focal point for the Marxist perspective even though considering, as Banks has noted

> the many thousands of words he wrote about capitalism, it is surprising that Marx never undertook any detailed analysis of the place of trade unions in such a society or the part they would play in the 'transition to socialism'.[31]

Indeed, Marxist approaches to trade unions are many and diverse although, as Hyman has observed, they may be roughly classified into the so-called 'optimistic' tradition of Marx and Engels, in which a radical potential for unions was recognized, and the 'pessimistic' interpretations of Lenin, Michels, and Trotsky where no such eventualities were foreseen.[32] Equally, however, there remain essential divergencies in Marxist perspectives concerning the relative causal significance of structural variables (such as economic and technical movements) in shaping union development and of the role of consciousness in determining the economic, political and social action of trade union members themselves.[33] Finally, even though in all but the most fundamentalist structuralist models an appreciation of the conditioning effects of both subjective factors (such as attitudes and beliefs) and the distribution of power may be identified, there is still a tendency, in most Marxist positions, for the concept of values as an embodiment of the creative powers of social 'actors' and that of ideologies as referring to the political implications of ideas for the exigencies of struggle between the main social classes, to be conflated.

At a structural level, however, the germs of an explanatory theory can be readily isolated in Marxist scholarship itself. Indeed, as Banks observed, Marx recognized how large-scale industry effectively concentrated in one place people unknown to one another and how the maintenance of wages became a common interest against the employer, uniting workers together through combination. Moreover, unions were ultimately forced to pursue political policies as well since early attempts at combination were met by resistance by employers and by the hostile enactments of the legislature.[34] In addition, the Marxist system of ideas emphasized the uneven nature of technical and organizational developments in any given society and suggested that the 'vanguard' sections of the working class should emerge from large-scale enterprises with highly centralized systems of ownership and control.[35] Furthermore, in *Marxist Sociology in Action*, in respect of the British steel industry, Banks argued that the growth in the scale of enterprise and technical advance had indeed facilitated unionism (though not in the form of a single union covering the whole industry) and had encouraged the emergence of a 'revolutionary' class consciousness in the sense of a demand for nationalization of the industry. However, this reflected an organizational rather than political consciousness in which criticism centred 'on the *unfitness* of the capitalists to wield power and their *inability* to deal with the problems of large-scale production because of the divisive nature of the competitive system'.[36]

But the attention of Marxists has turned particularly to the radical or revolutionary potential of trade unionism. The so-called 'optimistic' tradition of Marx and Engels can be summarized as follows:[37]

> The evolution of industrial capitalism provides the preconditions of collective organisation by throwing workers together in large numbers, and creates the deprivations which spur them to combination. This unity, by transcending competition in the labour market, in itself threatens the stability of capitalism: it also develops workers' class consciousness and trains them in methods of struggle. The limited economic achievements of their unions lead workers to adopt political forms of action, and ultimately to challenge directly the whole structure of class domination.

However, it is clear that both Marx and Engels began to entertain doubts about the effectiveness of unions in this respect, partly because of the initial development of trade unionism only amongst the 'labour aristocracy' of skilled workers, but also on account of the character of the leadership and even of the 'embourgeoisement' of the working class associated, during the nineteenth century, with the hegemonic position of Britain in the world economy.[38] Indeed, in a famous passage in *Value, Price and Profit*, Marx observed that unions worked well only as 'centres of resistance against the encroachment of capital' but were not so effective as spearheads of a new economic and political system.[39]

These reservations were reinforced amongst writers of the 'pessimistic' school of which Lenin was the chief exponent: indeed as he noted in 'What is to be done?', Social-Democratic (i.e. revolutionary) consciousness could not occur amongst workers themselves and 'would have to be brought to them from without'.[40]

> The history of all countries shows that the working class, exclusively by its own effort, is able to develop only trade-union consciousness, i.e., the conviction that it is necessary to combine in unions, fight the employers, and strive to compel the government to pass necessary labour legislation, etc. The theory of socialism, however, grew out of the philosophic, historical, and economic theories elaborated by educated representatives of the propertied classes, by intellectuals.

Michels, too, suggested that in common with all other organizations, trade unions were not impervious to the iron law of oligarchy,[41] while Trotsky observed that unions could be 'incorporated' into the existing social order and turned into agents of capital.[42]

Moreover, in his assessment of the main variations in Marxist thought, Hyman has suggested that despite the persuasiveness of certain components of the 'pessimistic' interpretation, the 'optimistic' tradition cannot be rejected outright. After all even 'pure and simple' trade unionism can pose a major threat to 'capitalism' in certain circumstances, the iron law of oligarchy is subject to important constraints, and not all trade union leaders have been successfully incorporated into our current system of economic and political relationships.[43] But, at all events, in terms of explanations for union growth and development two major variables can be isolated here; first, growing scale of enterprise and technical advance which are in turn associated with general structural movements in the economy; and second, at a subjective level, the tendency for unionists left to their own devices to evolve a form of oppositional consciousness which for the most part falls well short of a desire for radical socialist transformation as such.

UNIONISM AS A 'PSYCHOLOGICAL' OR DEFENSIVE REACTION
TO THE EARLY CONDITIONS OF INDUSTRIALISM

Yet there have been many other attempts to discern the behaviour of trade unions and indeed some writers have concentrated particularly upon the formative environment of the early industrial revolution in shaping an essentially defensive or protective outlook amongst the membership. These commentators accept many of the arguments of the so-called 'pessimistic' school but draw very different conclusions by emphasizing what they regard as the deleterious effects of intellectuals upon the labour movement and the consequent necessity for 'organic labour' to struggle not just against employers but also against those members of the intelligentsia who seek to distort 'pure and simple' unionism from its 'essential' purposes. Some points of disagreement stem from the differences of degree or of political persuasion, although this third approach adds a further useful historical dimension to the debates and a valuable focus upon the components of trade union consciousness itself. However, it is correspondingly deficient at a structural level and the effects of any prolonged period of 'affluence' upon trade unionists' attitudes have not been satisfactorily assessed, partly because of the conditions of the period when many of the relevant theories were constructed.

It was Selig Perlman who, in *A Theory of the Labour Movement*, argued that three factors were dominant in explaining trade union and labour history; first, the resistance power of capitalism; second, the role of the intellectual who was always impressing upon the labour movement 'tenets characteristic of his own mentality', and third, and most vital, the labour movement itself.[44] Indeed,[45]

> Trade unionism, which is essentially pragmatic, struggles constantly, not only against the employers for an enlarged opportunity measured in income, security, and liberty in the shop and industry, but struggles also, whether consciously or unconsciously, actively or merely passively, against the intellectual who would frame its programs and shape its policies.

For Perlman, then, manual groups 'had their economic attitudes basically determined by a consciousness of scarcity of opportunity'.[46] Moreover, commencing with such consciousness of scarcity, the 'manualist' groups have been led to practise solidarity, to insist upon ownership of economic opportunities by the group as a whole, to ration these opportunities amongst members and to ensure some control by the group over its members.[47]

In brief, then, the homespun philosophy of labour was viewed as essentially one of communism of opportunity which is fundamentally different from socialism and communism; it existed in this form particularly in respect of unions enforcing job control through union working rules but did not, in Perlman's conception, extend to an ambition to control society as a whole.[48] Perlman thus proposed that the basic fallacy of all intellectuals was their conception of labour 'solely as an abstract mass and the concrete individual reduced to a mere mathematical point', as against the trade unionists' 'striving for job security for the individual and concrete freedom on the job'.[49]

Indeed, in this respect, Perlman took to task not just 'determinist-revolutionaries' but also 'ethical intellectuals' (the heirs of Robert Owen and Christian Socialists) and the Fabian 'efficiency intellectuals' since all these[50]

> reduced labor to a mere abstraction, although each has done so in his own way and has pictured 'labor' as an abstract mass in the grip of an abstract force, existing, however, only in his own intellectual imagination, and not in the emotional imagination of the manual worker himself.

Other scholars of the labour movement have also attended to the conditioning impact of the early industrial revolution on the perceptions of rank and file unionists. Hence Hoxie,[51] Parker[52] and Tannenbaum[53] all recognized the 'psychologically' defensive character of trade unions and the last mentioned, in common with Brentano[54] and Howell,[55] sought to establish parallels between trade unions and the medieval guilds. However, in Britain only craft unions really fit this interpretation at all closely, although in their opposition to skill reduction and to labour dilution and in their concern over demarcation and job rights they all reflect a particular form of consciousness of scarcity. Turner, too, in his classic study, *Trade Union Growth Structure and Policy*, noted the long-term consequences for the British labour movement of the early growth of unionism amongst the labour aristocracy of skilled craft workers particularly in respect of their concern over demarcation and 'job rights'.[56]

ECONOMIC FOUNDATIONS AND PURPOSES OF TRADE UNIONS

None the less, other explanations for union growth and character have revolved around economic conditions in terms either of their constituting an essential basis for unionism itself and then for determining subsequent fluctuations in overall membership, or of their informing the orientations of rank and file members. Both structural and subjective influences upon unionism have thus been embodied in this perspective but, particularly with regard to the objectives of union members, the overall focus is narrow and the salience of power in affecting the outcome of conflicts of interest have frequently been overlooked.

The foundations of the 'economic implications' school were systematically laid by the Webbs in their monumental study, *The History of Trade Unionism.*[57] The approach here was primarily structural since they argued forcefully that trade unions depended in the first instance upon a change in economic relationships which brought about a sharp cleavage of interests and function between employer and employee. Thus the Webbs observed how early organizations of working people had been impeded because of the substantial prospects for advancement enjoyed by the skilled handicraftsmen, the steps from apprenticeship to master or to procuring an independent business being relatively easy to traverse.[58] Moreover, they placed special weight on the salience of economic relationships rather than technology and factory size in shaping the character of modern trade unions and noted that in all cases in which trade unions arose

> the great bulk of workers had ceased to be independent producers, themselves controlling the processes, and owning the materials and the product of their labour, and had passed into the condition of life-long wage-earners, possessing neither the instruments of production nor the commodity in its finished state.[59]

More especially, too, they stressed that the growth of the factory system as such was not the primary cause of the origins of trade unions since 'the earliest durable combinations of wage-earners in England' preceded the factory system by a whole century.[60]

To be sure, the Webbs' account has been criticized by a number of scholars and the main points of disagreement will be the subject of later analysis but, in recent literature, not only has the role of economic conditions upon the labour movement been emphasized, but more especially, a series of specific indicators have been isolated as crucial determinants of fluctuations in so-called 'aggregate' unionism in any given society. The association between the business cycle and trade union density thus has captured the attention of various labour movement theorists such as Commons,[61] Davis,[62] Dunlop,[63] Bernstein,[64] and Shister,[65] who, while differing substantially in detail, all recognized the potency of general economic movements in affecting levels of unionization in given industrial societies over a period of time. Moreover, Bain and Elsheikh, in an impressive analysis, carefully measured the relative explanatory significance of such variables as changes in retail prices, money wages and unemployment levels for fluctuations in overall union density during the course of the present century.[66] Similarly, in a series of articles Bain and Price have concentrated upon recent economic changes in affecting the overall growth of unionism in Great Britain and have paid particularly close attention to the white collar sector in this regard.[67]

At a subjective level, too, other writers have turned to the economic objectives or purposes of trade unions: indeed, in the USA 'business' unionism has long been recognized as a dominant trait of the movement in question. Meanwhile, among British sociologists, while differences between the British and the American situation are almost invariably admitted, several writers (and notably of course Goldthorpe and his colleagues) have noted that, amongst affluent workers at least, commitment to trade unionism 'as a social movement or as an expression of class or occupational solidarity, is unlikely to be widespread'.[68] Indeed, on such assumptions, accompanying periods of unbroken affluence and major changes in the domestic and community circumstances of manual workers, 'aggressiveness in the field of cash-based bargaining' may prove to be typical at the expense of movements towards worker control.[69] And although the substance of this thesis has aroused controversy (not least because it is by no means wholly consistent with recent forays towards industrial democracy) what is important to note is the germ of a theory about union purposes in which economic issues are uppermost.

DEMOCRATIC AND POLITICAL ASPECTS OF UNIONS

Finally, other explanations for union growth and character have concentrated upon the effects of power in human relationships and have noted that unions have been formed largely as a means of extending workers' rights in both the place of work and in society as a whole. This perspective is an important corrective to cruder versions of structural and subjective determinism and it revolves largely around the critical issue of the power of unions in modern society. However, by the same token, it is often insensitive to the broader conditions of economic and technical change which facilitate the expansion of unions in the first place, and again the narrow compass of union objectives embraced here is far from satisfactory.

Several labour movement theorists and especially Chamberlain,[70] Commons,[71] Adams,[72] and Flanders[73] have thus focused upon the political objectives of unions in respect of extending workers' rights by means of industrial and political struggle. Chamberlain, for example, identified two main 'political' activities of trade unions: first in industrial government, and second in industrial management. Thus the 'sharing of industrial sovereignty' involved introducing the rule of law into management-worker relationships in order to obviate the worst elements of power struggle; the managerial focus, by contrast, rested on the principle of 'mutuality', which recognizes the right of all members of a concern to have a voice in decisions which affect them.[74] This belief in the extension of workers' rights through union activities was also developed by Commons who argued that 'bargaining between collective socio-economic groups tended to supercede individual political expression as the sovereign power in the democratic state'.[75] Moreover, for Adams, the genesis of trade unions and their ultimate rationale was dependent on the emergence of capitalism which had swept away all the feudal rights, laws and customs which had reduced competition between employees. It was therefore the main aim of trade unions and the primary aspiration of trade unionists to establish a new set of rights which were relevant to the new forms of society and of social relationships.[76]

In American literature produced immediately after the Second World War, a major and sharply drawn cleavage could be detected between political and economic interpretations of union policy. In particular, A. M. Ross, in criticizing Dunlop's economic view of wage determination, advanced a political theory of union wage policy 'based on the view that the union must be considered as essentially a political agency operating in an economic environment, but whose internal decision-making processes could only be understood in political terms'.[77] Moreover, he further asserted that the principal objective of the union leadership was to uphold the union itself as a viable institution and that it served ultimately to maintain the political position of the leadership within it.[78]

Among British theorists of the labour movement there has also almost invariably been a sensitivity to the political aspirations of trade unionism. This was once particularly evident in the work of G. D. H. Cole[79] but the leading advocate of this view was of course Allan Flanders who argued that the basic social purpose of trade unions was 'job regulation', not as an end in itself, but as a means for the free development of the individual worker during the course of working life *per se*.[80] The growth of workplace bargaining was thus viewed as a particularly obvious symptom of this concern, but this was not confined to the boundaries of an industry for it implied regulation at a national level as well in order to influence overall levels of employment, greater economic planning and so forth.[81] The recent interest in industrial democracy, founded upon the existing structure of the British trade union movement, has provided a cogent and interesting example of this development in unionism in the modern era.

CONCLUSION

The early theories of the labour movement have been analysed under the five main headings of: (1) moral and ethical approaches; (2) the revolutionary tradition; (3) unionism as a 'psychological' or defensive reaction to the early conditions of industrialism; (4) the economic foundations and purposes of trade unions; and (5) democratic and political aspects of unionism, in which the significance of power as a variable was emphasized. Moreover, we endeavoured to demonstrate how each perspective has an interesting lineage which may be traced back through several generations of scholars of the labour movement operating from within a British as well as an American context. None the less, there have been several fundamental analytical and theoretical advances since the origins of these main schools of thought and we now focus our attention on a critical survey of the main components of recent departures.

Indeed, with this objective in view, our analysis in the ensuing chapter will commence with a review of system models of labour relations. This will be followed (in chapters 3 and 4) by a detailed perusal of theoretical disputation surrounding the foremost British school of trade union theory which has been grounded in liberal-pluralist assumptions. Following and during our survey of 'radical' contributions in chapter 5, we shall demonstrate how the circuitous ascent to a modern theory of labour commences with due recognition of the vital significance of power to the phenomena under focus. But this, in turn, is only the preliminary for the mount towards a comprehensive explanatory framework in which the main levels of structural analysis (chapter 6), institutional and organizational constraints (chapter 7) and, ultimately, the highest order propositions of a 'culturalist' or 'subjectivist' model will be established (chapter 8).

2 System models of labour relations

Facts have outrun ideas. Integrating theory has lagged far behind
expanding experience. The many worlds of industrial relations have
been changing more rapidly than the ideas to interpret, to explain,
and to relate them.[1]

The emergence of contemporary theories of trade unionism may be directly
traced to the introduction of the systems approach to the study of industrial relations by John T. Dunlop.[2] Indeed, his momentous treatise, *Industrial Relations Systems*, has often been acclaimed as a watershed between
the earliest approaches which were surveyed in the foregoing chapter and
modern conceptions.[3] Yet the claim of a major 'paradigm shift' would
only be legitimate in terms of its analytical contribution since most of the
finer points of substantive detail were a monument to nineteenth- and
early twentieth-century scholarship. But if the first attempts at theorizing
had been concerned with 'understanding the nature and organization of
trade unions, and the purpose and functions of collective bargaining',
Dunlop substantially broadened the scope of the investigation by ground-
ing his model in analytical precepts bequeathed by the founding fathers of
social science and by placing trade unions in the broader nexus of relationships in the wider industrial relations system.[4] Moreover, his seminal exposition was produced at a time when empiricism was the dominant intellectual force and hence, whatever the specific defects of the approach itself,
by virtue of being so set apart from the dominant concerns of the era, his
ideas were inevitably to be acclaimed when attention ultimately quickened
in the theoretical analysis of the contours of trade union and labour
movements.

The novel elements of Dunlop's paradigm comprised mainly the comprehensive range of factors identified, the synthesis of propositions and
schemes of thought which had far earlier origins and the adaptation of
ideas of the principal analytical sociologist of the post-war period, Talcott
Parsons, to the study of industrial and labour relations. For the purposes
of this inquiry, therefore, it is apposite that we commence our account of
system models with a brief examination of the relevance of Parsonian
concepts for the study of trade unionism. This will be followed by a close
inspection of the substance of Dunlop's thesis since its principal components and theoretical status have resulted in considerable confusion and

20

misinterpretation in posterior literature. And finally, with special reference to British scholarship, the main criticisms and subsequent refinements of the systems analysis of trade unionism will be appraised.

TALCOTT PARSONS AND SYSTEMS THEORY

In so far as the study of trade union action and behaviour is concerned three relevant and fundamental postulates could be identified in Parsonian thought: the focus upon the problem of order, the definition of the subject matter of sociology as social action specifically as embodied in social systems, and the unique conception of the nature of social power.

The problem of order

By commencing his analysis of human society with the problem of order Parsons had of course grounded his general conceptual edifice in the precedents of such foremost moral philosophers as Hobbes, Locke and Mill.[5] All of these scholars — and this cannot be emphasized too strongly — were convinced that order was *not* a natural condition of human society. Hence, even though it was widely construed as the essential bulwark of civilization, its persistence and durability in any given social system could not be assumed: on the contrary, the Hobbesian 'war of all against all' was the perennial consternation. Indeed, this point has been emphasized in a trenchant passage in Mitchell:[6]

> The attainment of some degree of peace, or order, of more or less harmonious relationships . . . is in the Parsonian analysis a 'major contingency' and *not* an empirical fact. . . . Parsons emphatically does not believe that man is peaceful and societies inevitably orderly and harmonious: on the contrary, he thinks that conflict is ubiquitous. . . . Since conflict is inherent in the situation of action, how are we to account for whatever order is attained? . . . This is the reason Parsons deals more with the solution to disorder than he does to explicating conflict. He assumes conflict and analyses its handling and reduction.

Parsons thus shared with his distinguished predecessors a preoccupation with the problem of order but differed in the one crucial respect of identifying the rules of conduct, norms and values which guide the social actor in the course of action as being instrumental in producing this condition. Instead, therefore, of assuming order to be an accidental and spontaneous convergence of interests, the outcome of social contracts, or the result of men submitting to one authority, for Parsons the essential mechanism was 'common-value integration'.[7] But on the basis of such assumptions, it was essential to contain conflict and for Parsons this could be accomplished by a series of mechanisms within social systems and their subunits by means of the operation of four 'functional imperatives'.[8]

1 *Adaptation* — the complex of unit acts which serve to establish relations between the system and its environment.
2 *Goal attainment* — all actions serving to further the goals of the system and the mobilization and management of resources and effort to attain these goals.
3 *Integration* — unit acts to establish control, inhibit deviant tendencies, maintain co-ordination between the parts and to avert serious disturbances.
4 *Latency or pattern maintenance* — attempts to facilitate motivation via symbols, ideas, modes of expression and judgments. Prestige and 'a *capacity* to act in such a way as to implement the relevant system of institutionalised values'.[9]

Such central aspects of Parsonian thought were of course subsequently subscribed to by Dunlop for the more specific purpose of the study and systematic analysis of industrial relations. Indeed, not only did the latter concur with the belief that, when applied to an industrial society, these functional imperatives corresponded to the four specialized structures of (1) the economy (serving an adaptive function and having a specific output of production of income and wealth); (2) the polity (achieving the goals of society with a specialized output of power); (3) cultural value patterns and motivational structures (integration and solidarity); and (4) preserving the integrity of the values of the system (pattern maintenance and prestige);[10] but he also incorporated Parsons's general framework for social systems in order, 'to treat the industrial relations system . . . as an analytical subsystem of (industrial) society, to analyse an industrial relations system in terms of the four functional imperatives of any social system, and to identify the corresponding specialized structures or processes.'[11]

The analysis of social systems

In addressing ourselves to Parsons's second contribution to the conception of industrial relations and trade union action we shall focus upon the internal properties and mechanisms of social systems themselves. After all, Dunlop explicitly assimilated such a framework into his own model by observing that:[12]

The functional differentiation of an industrial-relations system and the corresponding specialized structures or processes may be defined as follows: (1) Adaptive — The regulatory processes or rule-making in which the specialized output is a complex of rules relating the actors to the technological and market environment and the frequent changes which pose problems of adaptation to the actors. (2) Goal Gratification — The polity or political functions in the subsystem are specialized toward the contribution of survival or stability of the industrial-relations system and to survival and stability of the hierarchies of the separate actors which is requisite for the attainment of goals by the actors. (3) Integration — The function of maintaining solidarity among the actors in the system is contributed by the shared understandings and common ideology of the system relating individual roles to the hierarchies and hierarchies to each other in turn. (4) Latent-pattern Maintenance and Tension Management — The function of preserving the values of the system against cultural and motivational pressures is provided by the role of the expert or professional in all three groups of actors in the system.

By the same token, too, the interrelationships between the principal differentiated functions were also explored by Dunlop and were perceived not only to contribute to each other but also to the unity of the industrial relations system as a whole. This, in turn, was envisaged as closely inter-linked with the 'larger society', since, for example, income and wealth generation was not only the goal of the adaptive function of society (the economy) but was also enhanced by the 'grid of rules' in the industrial relations system.[13] Again, in Dunlop's view, compatible power arrangements in the goal gratificational functions of society and of the industrial relations system were manifest for 'stability and survival' of the latter was perceived as being contingent upon the wider political structure and was in turn, of course, conducive to the endurance and persistence of the polity.[14] Furthermore, a high degree of solidarity and a 'large area of shared understandings' facilitated integration, while the pattern maintenance and tension management subsystems of society and industrial relations were conceived as ideally reinforcing, and indeed, where incongruent, could result in changes 'in one or both spheres'.[15]

Power and social systems

Parsonian structural-functionalism, which was embedded in a conception of society in terms of social systems, thus was very closely interwoven into Dunlop's specific conception of an industrial relations system. But before examining the principal components of the model it is worth commentating on Parsons's understanding of the nature of social power since this had close affinities with Dunlop's later usage of the term.

There are of course two fundamentally divergent conceptions of social power which correspond with the non zero-sum and zero-sum perspectives respectively.[16] Essentially non zero-sum theorists view power as a circulating medium similar to money in economic transactions which, when smoothly functioning, permits the coalescence of the disparate talents thrown up by the division of labour and, in turn, produces the so-called 'miracle of loaves and fishes' of modern industrial society, in which vast wealth may be generated by a small proportion of the population and the majority are guaranteed a standard of material civilization undreamed of by earlier populations.[17] Zero-sum theorists, by way of contrast, focus not upon the positive benefits of integration but rather visualize power as reflecting an incessant struggle over resources which are always scarce relative to wants, and where the gains of one party inescapably involve commensurate losses for another.[18] These twin conceptions also correspond with the disparate emphasis upon the problems of order and control in human societies and with the consensus and conflict models in industrial relations and industrial sociology respectively. Moreover, there can be no doubt that both phenomena may be identified in trade union affairs since industrial production and a range of procedures for the accommodation and resolution of disputes coexist alongside explosions of industrial militancy. Indeed, as Touraine has persuasively argued, in so far as labour movements are concerned there may well be a 'double requirement' of creation (facilitated under conditions of order) and control (occasioned only after power conflicts), that should both be analysed on a broader theoretical canvas.[19]

> The term social movement denotes all action that involves the historical subject — which is only an agent in so far as its actions are related to the double requirement of control and creation. One is justified in regarding trade union activity as an element in a system of industrial relations; one is no less justified in regarding it as a movement, oriented at the same time to economic development and social democracy. In neither case is it necessary at all to postulate any hypothesis concerning what workers 'really' want or concerning the general historical significance of trade union action. In both cases one has to go beyond concrete description and relate social phenomena to some kind of analytical matrix.

Talcott Parsons was of course the prime exponent of the non zero-sum conception and not surprisingly, therefore, defined power as 'the generalised capacity to get things done in the interests of system goals.'[20] In this respect, then, he clearly conceived power in *integral* terms (possessed by only one party or system) rather than in the *intercursive* sense of being shared, albeit unequally by different parties which possessed disparate authority sytems.[21] Hence, not only was one locus of power and authority envisaged in this definition but also, as Giddens has cogently argued, by interpreting power as an aspect of a system geared primarily to productive ends, Parsons was able to shift his analysis away from power as expressing a relationship *between* individuals or groups towards seeing it solely as a system property.[22] Indeed, Parsons even stressed that whether or not there is opposition in a system was of no significance on a theoretical count[23] and in this way avoided confronting the crucial issue of power *within* union-management relations altogether. While, in similar vein, Dunlop conceived of power as a variable *exogenous* to the industrial relations system rather than as a cardinal factor which helped to explain processes of interaction between the principal social actors themselves.[24]

DUNLOP'S MODEL OF AN INDUSTRIAL RELATIONS SYSTEM

The substantive elements of Dunlop's thesis will be examined only rather briefly since its main contours will be familiar to the reader, but on theoretical grounds the following salient points should be emphasized:

(a) The links with the Parsonian (and to some extent the Smelserian)[25] heritage were profound. Thus, in Dunlop's understanding of an industrial relations system, the problem of order was accommodated by rule-making, the conceptual apparatus of systems analysis was fully incorporated into the model, while the notion of power was again construed as an aspect of the 'larger society' rather than of the relationships between trade unions and management.

(b) Dunlop introduced his exposition of industrial relations systems by observing the sharply defined points of variance between industrial and agrarian-type societies and indeed commented that although 'industrial relations problems are not unique to modern industrial societies', nevertheless, *whatever their political form*, distinctive groups of managers and workers were created in all such societies.[26] Hence, for Dunlop the strategic break between the ancient and modern worlds was founded principally upon diverse modes of organization and administration rather than upon, say, types of property ownership in the societies concerned.[27] This perspective, too, affected the specification of the main actors in the industrial relations system for despite directly broaching the question of the ownership of the means of production, he disavowed the more traditional

Marxian and Webbsian versions of the structural origins of trade unions. And as a corollary, therefore, the main groups of actors to be identified consisted of the hierarchies, respectively, of managers and their representatives in supervision, of workers (non-managerial) and any spokesmen (these included, of course, trade union representatives) together with specialized governmental agencies (and specialized private agencies created by the first two actors) 'concerned with workers, enterprises and their relationships'.[28]

(c) In terms of the history of trade union thought, Dunlop's model was interesting in respect of the attempt to relate elements in ongoing disputation into a wider concept of an industrial relations system and, in all, six defining characteristics were identified: (1) it was perceived as an analytical subsystem of an industrial society on the same logical plane as an economic system; (2) it was not a subsidiary part of an economic system but rather a separate and distinctive subsystem of the society; (3) there were relationships and boundaries between a society and an industrial relations system; (4) it was logically an abstraction; (5) this conception of an industrial relations system, in turn, defined a distinctive analytical and theoretical subject matter; (6) three separate analytical problems were identified, the relationship of the industrial relations system to the society as a whole and to the economic subsystem and the inner structure and characteristics of the industrial relations system itself.[29]

(d) Although Dunlop's model was novel in its breadth and comprehensiveness, in other respects it comprised largely a synthesis of strands from within existing thought. Hence, on the one hand, in delineating the contexts of the industrial relations system he located a *series* of constraints upon action rather than fixing upon 'a single monocausal determinant', and these he adumbrated under now familiar headings: (1) the technological characteristics of the workplace and work community; (2) the market and budgetary factors which impinge on the actors; and (3) the locus and distribution of power in the 'larger society'.[30] Equally, on the other hand, his statement that an industrial relations system may be understood as comprising actors, contexts, an ideology which binds the system together and a body of rules created to govern the actors in the workplace and work community[31] is best appreciated as an eclectic synthesis of a number of strands from earlier approaches which had explicitly countenanced the role of structural variables exogenous to trade unions, such as market or economic conditions and technology (the revolutionary and economic traditions), of ideas and values (the ethical, revolutionary and economic schools), and of the functions of unions in terms of rule-making (the 'defensive' and political models).

(e) Nevertheless, Dunlop's conception of power and ideology was sharply at odds with that envisaged in these early traditions of labour theory: power was now interpreted as an ingredient of the wider social system and not in terms of endogenous relationships between unions and management themselves. To be sure, Dunlop conceded that power in the larger society tended 'to a degree to be reflected in the industrial-relations system' in the actor's 'prestige, position and access to the ultimates of authority', but equally, for him, the allocation of power in the wider social system was not a direct determinant of interaction between actors and should, therefore, be construed as 'a *context* which helps to structure the industrial relations system itself'.[32] Moreover, the interpretation of ideology 'or a set of ideas and beliefs commonly held'[33] has again stimulated considerable controversy in subsequent literature. After all, for Dunlop, ideologies in individual industrial relations systems were occasioned by varying properties of the different systems themselves. Indeed, in the case of Britain, Dunlop specifically referred to the dominant philosophy of voluntarism, which, when accepted by the three main parties, provided a harmonious foundation for establishing the rules in the first place.[34] But even though in Dunlop's paradigm there were a number of compatibilities between the ideology of the industrial relations system and of the wider society, these were construed as separate entities from an analytical point of view.[35] Of course, Dunlop acknowledged that over time one might expect a convergence between the ideologies prevailing in the two spheres and he even observed that hierarchies of managers and organized workers (i.e. trade unionists) tended to adopt 'intellectuals, specialists concerned with articulating systematically and making some form of order out of the discrete ideas of the principal actors'.[36] But while power was envisaged as a context constraining the actors, ideology was identified as an integral part of the industrial relations system itself.

(f) The notion of a social system formulated by Talcott Parsons also accommodated a series of interrelated functions and this was acknowledged in Dunlop's model by the recognition that the 'web of rules' constructed by the principal actors was, in turn, modified by external constraints.[37] Thus, while specific rules were seen to reflect technical and market or budgetary constraints, others were interpreted as a more direct consequence of the distinctive patterning of the distribution of power in the 'larger society'.[38] Furthermore, substantive rules were integral to the model of an industrial relations system deployed by Dunlop and whether these embodied rules governing compensation, the duties and performance expected from workers or the rules defining the rights and obligations of working people, they were all in principle the staple ingredients for a taxonomy and comparison of substantive points of variation in patterns of industrial relations in disparate nation states and historical systems.[39] Moreover, the internal cohesion of the industrial relations systems was also furthered by the special grouping of experts or professionals in rule-making who were in part created by the detailed and technical nature of the rules themselves. Hence, not only was the function of such actors conceived in terms of adding stability to the system and of binding the other participants in industrial relations closer together, but also the group as a whole was seen to be essential to interpret the highly complex nature of the *forms* of rules and of rule-making processes.[40]

(g) The principal focus in the corpus of Dunlop's volume, however, was upon 'actors' whose primary goal was construed as 'to establish rules at the work place and work community'; a viewpoint which echoed not only the Parsonian conception of the problem of order, but also that of earlier labour theorists particularly of the 'political implications' school such as Chamberlain[41] and Commons.[42] Furthermore, the distinction between procedural and substantive rules in Dunlop's commentary has featured prominently in subsequent literature in industrial relations and industrial sociology; the key aspects emerging here embodying: (a) procedures for establishing rules; (b) substantive rules; and (c) procedures for deciding their application to specific situations.[43] Similarly, Dunlop was fully cognizant of the wide range of possible procedures, the scope of which encompassed unilateral determination of rules by management, corporatism, workers' control, voluntarism, and a more eclectic combination of influence by management, workers and the state respectively.[44]

(h) Dunlop's overall thesis, then, consisted of a comprehensive delineation of attributes and determinants of trade union action and behaviour within a wider industrial relations network. Moreover, it was part of a concerted attempt to focus upon rule-making and administration rather than upon what he interpreted as the narrow concentration of traditional British scholars of industrial relations on patterns of collective bargaining. It was intended, too, as a means of exploring differences by the use of the method of *comparative statics*, and indeed, this was specifically envisaged as most fruitful 'when a specific system is examined in its historical context, and changes in the system are studied through time'.[45]

MODIFICATIONS, REFINEMENTS AND THE CRITIQUE OF SYSTEMS ANALYSIS

The impact of *Industrial Relations Systems* upon subsequent analytical thought on trade unions has no obvious parallel in posterior literature. Hence, despite deploying a different epistemological base, Flanders was specifically to adopt the emphasis upon rule-making in his interpretation of collective bargaining,[46] while Bain and Clegg have acknowledged the eminent contribution of both these scholars to the modern account of trade unions and of industrial relations.[47] Meanwhile, Walker has elaborated upon Dunlop's conception of a 'web of rules' and concluded that industrial relations processes are concerned essentially with procedural and substantive rule-making.[48] By the same token, Somers, while recognizing the utility of the notion of a 'web of rules', has attempted a fusion of the 'externalists' and 'internalists' in Dunlop's understanding of an industrial relations system via the theory and concepts of exchange.[49] Again, writers who have deployed system analyses in their subsequent empirical researches have included Anderson,[50] Blain[51] and Goodman and his colleagues.[52] For example, Anderson applied four conceptual categories from the industrial relations systems framework (the environment or context, the actors, the mechanisms for converting inputs into outputs or the procedures for establishing rules, and the outcomes of the industrial relations system),[53] while Blain's study of the airline pilots was based on a similar formulation[54] and Goodman *et al.* have envisaged industrial relations as a rule-making action system in their conceptual account of labour relations in the footwear industry.[55]

But the analysis of industrial and labour relations by means of social systems has been criticized on a number of counts and even those committed to focusing upon rules as the principal outcome of union-management relationships have almost invariably entertained a series of modifications and refinements to the original formulation. These subsequent advances may be examined under two distinctive but related headings: theoretical and substantive.

Theoretical

The structural-functionalist interpretation of social systems has of course been subjected to a series of logical and theoretical criticisms but the most far-reaching encapsulate the teleological nature of explanation (i.e., effects are treated as causes), the generation of untestable hypotheses, the demand for a level of scientific inquiry which has not yet emerged in the social sciences, and the problems entailed in the comparison of diverse institutional types.[56] These general objections to the thesis provide useful points of reference for a review of the principal theoretical objections to Dunlop's overall conceptual framework itself.

Teleological assumptions and the problem of explanation

In the first place, therefore, if trade union action and behaviour is interpreted in terms of social systems, there will always be a considerable barrier to formulating any genuinely explanatory model. Indeed, for Dunlop the ultimate goal of the industrial relations system was the survival and/or stability of the system itself,[57] which, as Wood *et al*. have indicated, further satisfied the 'need for order' in the production system.[58] But this generalization of course begged a series of questions about the origins of different modes of adaptation and, in any event, it remains open to debate whether it is even admissible to explain change other than by reference to its antecedent conditions.[59]

Modern formulations of system theory, however, rest upon the notion of open systems and upon the precise specification of input and output (i.e., independent and dependent) variables in the framework itself.[60] Somers, in particular, deployed sophisticated linkages between input and output variables in industrial relations systems,[61] while Craig[62] and Singh[63] have also introduced significant refinements which are worthy of mention. Hence, while retaining the basic assumption of an industrial relations system as a set of interrelated parts which operate in an environment, Craig applied 'open systems' terminology to stipulate a more complex analytical framework than that of the original Dunlop formulation. In Craig's interpretation, then, the overall framework of open systems consisted of: (1) *inputs* which included the concepts of goals, values and power and which were perceived as being conditioned by 'the flow of effects' from other environmental subsystems; (2) a series of procedures in the industrial relations systems to convert inputs into outputs; (3) the outputs themselves which embraced financial, social and psychological rewards to employees; and (4) 'a feedback loop through which the outputs flow back into the industrial relations system and whose effects flow also into the other environmental subsystems'.[64] Moreover, further refinements in Craig's model encompassed the distinction between structure and mechanism in the industrial relations system, the listing of several wider environmental systems (ecological, economic, political, legal and social) and an interrelated and multi-causal specification of the principal variables within a structural-functionalist framework (see Figure 2.1).[65]

In similar vein, too, Singh recognized that the earlier mechanized models of social systems should be replaced by modern conceptions from the natural sciences, cybernetics and engineering.[66] Moreover, in his view, of paramount importance was the discovery of mechanisms through which input is transformed into output.[67] To this end a dynamic open-system model was adopted to separate structure and process in the industrial relations system, to isolate the main environmental systems (social, political, economic and legal) and to incorporate a 'feedback loop' to accommodate multi-causal processes of change (see Figure 2.2).[68]

None the less, attempts to overcome the teleological bias of functionalism

Figure 2.1 *A framework for analysing industrial systems (a structural functional approach)*

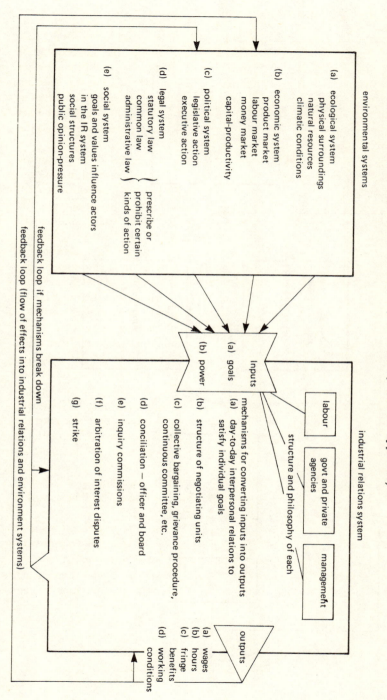

environmental systems

(a) ecological system
    physical surroundings
    natural resources
    climatic conditions

(b) economic system
    product market
    labour market
    money market
    capital-productivity

(c) political system
    legislative action
    executive action

(d) legal system
    statutory law
    common law   } prescribe or
    administrative law } prohibit certain
                          kinds of action

(e) social system
    goals and values influence actors
    in the IR system
    social structures
    public opinion-pressure

industrial relations system

Inputs
(b) power
(a) goals

structure and philosophy of each

| labour | govt and private agencies | management |

mechanisms for converting inputs into outputs
(a) day-to-day interpersonal relations to
    satisfy individual goals
(b) structure of negotiating units
(c) collective bargaining, grievance procedure,
    continuous committee, etc.
(d) conciliation — officer and board
(e) inquiry commissions
(f) arbitration of interest disputes
(g) strike

outputs
(a) wages
(b) hours
(c) fringe
    benefits
(d) working
    conditions

feedback loop if mechanisms break down

feedback loop (fflow of effects into industrial relations and environment systems)

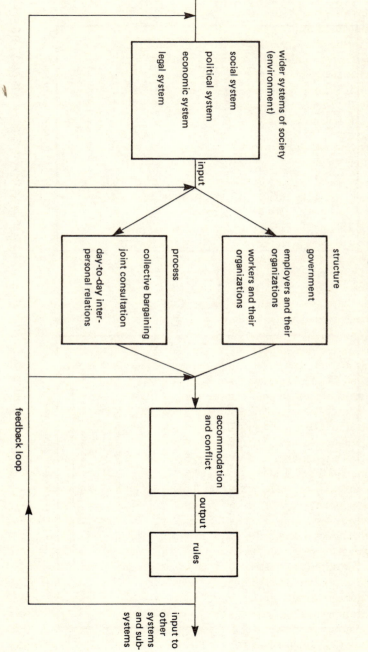

Figure 2.2 *Structure and process in union-management relations*

wider systems of society
(environment)

social system
political system
economic system
legal system

input

structure

government
employers and their
organizations
workers and their
organizations

process

collective bargaining
joint consultation
day-to-day inter-
personal relations

accommodation
and conflict

output

rules

input to
other
systems
and sub-
systems

feedback loop

by means of open-system models have invited the perennial charge of indiscriminate multi-causality.[69] Thus, to transcend objections such as these, a further qualification has been to identify *the rules of the industrial relations system* (including procedures for their establishment and administration) as the principal output to be explained theoretically in terms of the actors, technology, market factors, power and status, and ideology respectively.[70] Indeed, this was expressed in algebraic terms in the familiar model of Blain and Gennard.[71]

Dependent and independent variables in industrial and labour relations systems

$$r = f(a,t,e,s,i)$$

where
- r = the rules of the industrial relations system
- a = the actors
- t = the technical context of the workplace
- e = the market context or budgetary constraints
- s = the power context and the status of the parties
- i = the ideology of the system

But even with such modifications there are still fundamental problems occasioned by the analytical position of the industrial relations system in Dunlop's model. It will be recalled that Dunlop identified the industrial relations system as a subsystem of society on the same logical plane as the economic system; and, indeed, this was depicted by means of the diagram in Blain and Gennard's review (see Figure 2.3).[72]

Yet, as Wood and his colleagues have argued, since Dunlop accepted the definition of Parsons and Smelser that the social system comprised four (and only four) functional subsystems (the economic, political, integrative and pattern-maintenance), the industrial relations system could not therefore be conceived as on the same logical plane as the economic system, but should be construed rather as 'a sub-system of the economic sub-system of society, and thus on a *lower* logical plane than the economic system serving the functional need for "order" within the "production" system'.[73]

Moreover, the problem of levels of analysis constituted a special difficulty in the early Dunlop formulation. Indeed, this was especially true in the case of the conception of union action and behaviour in terms of social systems, for different models may be clearly applicable at national, district, local and workshop levels respectively. It was scarcely surprising, then, that Heneman in particular felt it fitting to isolate six main analytical levels encompassing: (1) society (e.g. national industrial relations systems); (2) associations (e.g. employers' associations, associations and federations of unions); (3) organizations (e.g. the firm, the union); (4) formal organization unit (e.g. department, shop); (5) informal group; and (6) individual.[74]

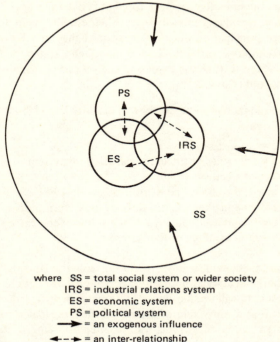

where SS = total social system or wider society
      IRS = industrial relations system
       ES = economic system
       PS = political system
        ➤ = an exogenous influence
     ◄– –➤ = an inter-relationship

Figure 2.3 *Relationship of the industrial relations system to the social system*

The generation of testable hypotheses

Turning, then, to an examination of the second notable theoretical objection to the system analysis of trade unionism involves the question of untestable hypotheses. For example, it may be reasonably asked, how can the need, say, for co-ordination be precisely formulated and tested in actual research into union behaviour itself?[75] Indeed, several writers have found Dunlop's framework wanting because of its difficulties in providing an integrated system of testable hypotheses and even Blain and Gennard accepted that the original framework did require modification to overcome such an impediment.[76] Hence, as these authors emphasized, adequate models depend upon the specification of input and output variables (or independent and dependent variables), the tracing of interrelationships between the relevant variables, the generation of testable hypotheses and a predictive capacity.[77] Although they contended that, with revision, system models were capable of satisfying 'some of these guidelines', there were still drawbacks in meeting the last two conditions.[78]

None the less, in a later study, Blain was to insist that 'a strong case can be made out in support of the view that the "systems theory" qualifies as an industrial relations model' in a strict sense; for, in his view, in the following equations the identified relationships could, in principle, be subjected to rigorous empirical tests.[79]

Testable hypotheses in labour relations

(1) $a = f(t, e, s)$
(2) $s = f(t, e)$

The first equation specified that actors will be influenced by the contextual variables in the system, while the second equation highlighted 'the role of technical and economic factors as determinants of status'.[80] Furthermore, in Blain's conception, research hypotheses of a more specific character may be generated by isolating given variables within the overall system model. Hence, the equations $r = f(t)$ and $r = f(e)$ 'require the testing of the hypotheses that technical and economic factors are determinants of the rules in a given industrial relations system' and this, in turn, suggests 'a crude predictive value' of the model itself.[81]

Levels and modes of theorizing

Yet even if the problem of untestable hypotheses may be satisfactorily counteracted there has been confusion over the ontological status of the system model and this relates to the issue of the level of theorizing in the social sciences themselves. Several writers, then, such as Gill,[82] Hill and Thurley,[83] Hyman,[84] Singh[85] and even up to a point Bain and Clegg[86] have commented that the model of an industrial relations system as deployed by Dunlop is essentially taxonomic. Indeed, Gill in particular relegated it to the status of an heuristic device or 'checklist for empirical investigation'.[87]

> the industrial relations system . . . is to be regarded as a model within which facts may be organised and must not be misunderstood as having predictive value in itself. It is rather a means of ordering a mass of facts relevant to the study of an industrial relations system.

None the less, following Parsons and Shils, Wood and his colleagues have persuasively argued that, although Dunlop is undeniably confused on a number of key issues, his concept of an industrial relations system may be fairly regarded as a 'categorical system' at a more advanced stage of theorizing than '*ad hoc* classificatory systems'.[88] As such, though, as all these authors again have noted, they fall short of propounding 'fully fledged laws' and are hence less sophisticated than 'theoretical systems' (which specify laws or empirical generalizations) or 'empirical theoretical systems' (which permit the formulation of highly precise empirical predictions).[89]

In general, therefore, it does seem best to regard Dunlop's model as 'a conceptual system or logical abstraction' rather than as a mere taxonomy,[90] and this would certainly echo the objectives of Goodman and his colleagues who have noted that if we define the industrial relations system 'as a rule-making action system in relation to behaviour in the production system',[91] it is then feasible to provide 'a central core for conceptual and empirical analysis, rather than simply an *ad hoc* and unconnected schema as with the taxonomic or heuristic device'.[92] Yet, whatever reformulations are introduced along these lines there will inevitably be substantial obstacles to evolving a fully-fledged 'empirical theoretical system' which would eventually enable a more precise prediction of trade union action and behaviour.[93]

Again, as Blain has argued in this respect, Parsons's method 'was to adopt the concept of a "system" in a scientific sense and subject it to the same type of theoretical analysis as had been used successfully in other sciences' and in so doing, 'the objective was to develop a conceptual scheme for the study of social systems of action'.[94] But of course in creating a special meaning for the concept of a system 'when applied specifically to trade union action' an ambiguity is introduced 'from the simultaneous use of the concept of "system" as a research tool in scientific method and as an empirical phenomenon requiring investigation and explanation'.[95]

Comparison

A final theoretical charge against models of social systems, then, rests upon the contention that adequate comparison of diverse trade union movements (either spatially or at particular points in time) is inhibited by the framework of analysis itself.[96] None the less, it is not easy to sustain this case against the Dunlop formulation or against the many refinements in which this problem has been specifically accommodated. Indeed, it is worth re-emphasizing that Dunlop professed that his paradigm was particularly well adapted to historical analysis and for the isolation of the principal distinguishing characteristics of contemporary industrial relations systems. But it was still reasonable for Somers to argue for a more dynamic theory of industrial relations than that offered by Dunlop,[97] and similarly Bain and Clegg have pointed to a need for more comparative and historically informed researches than those which, so far at least, have emanated from the studies based upon Dunlop's original formulations.[98]

It is worth mentioning, too, that the method used for contrasting types in the original model revolved around the principles of 'comparative statics'. Moreover, to accommodate processes of change, as Blain and Gennard have commented, the notion of an industrial relations system may be refined in an attempt to contrast different situations in specific labour movements at two or more points of equilibrium.[99]

Table 2.1   *Theoretical refinement to the 'system model': social change*

Equation	Time period	Output	Input
7	Situation 1	r_1	$= f(a_1, t_1, e_1, s_1, i_1)$
8	Situation 2	r_2	$= f(a_2, t_2, e_2, s_2, i_2)$
9	Change from situation 1	$r_2 - r_1$	$= f(a_2 - a_1, t_2 - t_1, e_2 - e_1, s_2 - s_1, i_2 - i_1)$
10	Process by which change from situation 1 is accomplished	p	$= f(r_1, a_1, t_1, e_1, s_1, i_1)$

By means of this method, then, critical changes may be located in, say, market or technical conditions at given points in time and implications for different processes of rule-making commensurately identified. But although the model of the industrial relations system would not appear to preclude comparative analysis, it is still deficient in that changes (occasioned by a dynamic force such as strike action or compulsory arbitration)[100] are taken as given and thus can never constitute the basis for an explanatory treatise on the *origins* of phenomena which are indispensable for trade union action and behaviour at all levels.

Substantive

Notwithstanding the widely acclaimed breadth of Dunlop's scheme, there have been several substantive objections to parts of the thesis and it is therefore on an examination of such points of contention that our attention now focuses. Indeed, as Walker has cogently argued, 'Dunlop's formulation and application of the concept of the industrial relations system has been criticised on various grounds'[101] and notably that: (a) 'it is static, not dynamic in time'; (b) it concentrates on structure and ignores processes; (c) it emphasizes the stability of industrial relations systems 'rather than the conflict and dissidence within them'; (d) it concentrates on formal rules and not informal rules and processes; (e) there is confusion over its use as an abstract entity and as a concrete or substantive formulation (e.g., 'the voluntarist' character of the British industrial relations system); (f) it does not entail an account of the ways in which inputs are converted into outputs; and (g) it is 'environmentally' biased and therefore 'provides no articulation between the "internal" plant-level system and the wider systems'.[102] For the purposes of our own review, however, the main factors which have been located in the literature so far will be analysed in terms of the following categories (i) the ownership of the means of production; (ii) the sub-institutional level of analysis (behavioural variables, personality, unstructured relationships); (iii) the main types of rule-making; (iv) processes in the industrial relations system itself; and (v) the problems of conflict, change, ideology, instability and power.

The ownership of the means of production

In Dunlop's interpretation of the actors within the industrial relations system one serious omission was that there was no place for owners and shareholders in the overall classification. Contrary to some impressions, however, Dunlop did, as we have seen, refer to the question of ownership in the relevant section on managers in the industrial relations system, but observed that when this was contained within an extended or narrow family (as in privately-owned, small-scale companies) its activities were to be explained not by reference to the wider nexus of, say, social class and interest group formation but in terms of *the family system of society*.[103] Moreover, state penetration into management was also examined and it was found that the 'hierarchy of managers need have no relationship to the ownership of the capital assets of the work place' at all, a situation which for Dunlop was especially germane under conditions where 'governments own varying amounts of shares of an enterprise and where special development program[me]s have been adopted'.[104]

But given the close association between density of unionization and the location of an enterprise in the public or private sectors respectively,[105] such a *desideratum* should be remedied. It must be confessed too, that it was scarcely surprising that Hyman[106] emphasized such a point or that Banks, in particular, thought it fitting to modify Dunlop's model in this crucial respect by incorporating the system of property ownership, which decides who is to direct operations, as well as the technical and social characteristics of the workplace, the market constraints on the enterprise and the power of the actors in the wider society.[107]

The sub-institutional level of analysis

There have been several writers, too, who have commented upon Dunlop's inadequate treatment of the sub-institutional level of analysis in relation to trade union action and behaviour.[108] Moreover, for the purposes of this study, such criticism and refinements of the overall model may be appropriately outlined under the three main headings of behavioural variables, personality and unstructured relationships respectively.

The principal case for adopting a behavioural science appraisal of industrial relations rather than one stemming from structural-functionalist premises was advocated by Margerison. Indeed, he proposed that a behavioural science approach should embrace not system goals but the *objectives* of company, management and operations (including production at a profit and survival, organization control and salary, work control and wages respectively), the *situation* of the enterprise which was somewhat at variance with the notion of contexts (organization social system, technology, work task and job content), the *interaction* amongst actors in the industrial relations system that was left unexplained in Dunlop's work (contact, organizational structure, group structures and relations, role and authority relations), the *type of contact* (distributive, structural and human relations), the potential *outcomes* of interaction and contact as well as diverse bases for the *resolution* of conflict itself.[109] Moreover, this specification of principal variables was obviously very different in emphasis from *Industrial Relations Systems* in which there were relatively few references to the disparate objectives of trade unions and management, to the patterns of interaction between the main actors and to organizational or group structures and relationships.

But in the last analysis, as Bain and Clegg have submitted, the weight to be attached to behavioural rather than structural variables is an empirical question which cannot therefore be resolved solely by *a priori* disputation.[110] Moreover, although they conceded that behavioural variables were not a major feature of Dunlop's framework, and equally that the system did not allow for a full analysis of the processes by which the rules of job regulation were determined, in their view, there was still room for compromise by incorporating behavioural variables into the overall conceptual system.[111]

> If these factors are formally introduced into the systems concept, then
> there is no reason why it should emphasize structural variables at the
> expense of behavioural variables, structured relationships at the expense
> of unstructured relationships, the institutions and rules of job
> regulation at the expense of the process of job regulation, or conflict
> resolution at the expense of conflict generation. In short, if these
> refinements are made to the Dunlop-Flanders approach, then the

subject of industrial relations may be defined as the study of all aspects of job regulation – the making and administering of the rules which regulate employment relationships – regardless of whether these are seen as being formal or informal, structured or unstructured.

The question of personality, too, has been a further issue to be raised in the general critique of the Dunlop model.[112] Shimmin and Singh, in particular, identified this problem and commented that 'personality, motivation, status and small group interaction have no place in the Dunlop system'.[113] But the task of remedying such a situation was accomplished by Blain and Gennard who confirmed that the processes by which rules were derived could be affected by personality variables in conjunction with wider economic, technological, power and status factors.[114] Indeed, in their view, personality could influence rules through its effects on the *processes* by which they are derived; a proposition which was expressed in algebraic form in the following equation:[115]

The effect of personality on processes in labour relations

$$p = f(r_1, e_1, t_1, a_1, s_1, i_1, x_1)$$
where x_1 = personality factors

But even if personality is formally incorporated into the model in this way, the lack of an adequate conceptual analysis of unstructured relationships remains a problem. Indeed, from rather different standpoints, Bain and Clegg,[116] Brown,[117] Flanders,[118] and Goodman and his colleagues[119] have all reiterated the same point. Moreover, the complication of whether or not unstructured relations may be legitimately incorporated into system conceptions of trade union behaviour[120] is compounded by Brown's observation that formalized plant agreements are often little more than the consolidation of agreements and rules established, in the first instance, under custom and practice *per se*.[121] Similarly, as Goodman and his colleagues have affirmed, norms at least may not only originate in custom and practice, but may also become 'reinstitutionalized' and organized on a more formal basis within the industrial relations system.[122] In trade union action and behaviour, then, not only are the divisions between formal and informal and structured or unstructured relationships problematical[123] but there is also the issue of whether or not it is *necessary* to *incorporate* custom and practice into the conception of an industrial relations system, if on any formulation (including Dunlop's) it appeared to be deeply embedded in rule-making processes themselves.[124]

Nevertheless, the ethnomethodological critique of systems theory has also concentrated attention upon the area of unregulated or unstructured behaviour[125] and upon the significance not only of custom and practice but also the *problematic* status of rules themselves in so far as these relate to the regulation of workplace conduct.[126] This approach, too, has entailed a critical examination of the mechanistic propositions which underpin structural-functionalist models and an examination of interpretative and reflexive procedures in interaction processes. But although it may be legitimate to indicate the ambiguous nature of rule application and of its linkage with behaviour,[127] the utility of this evaluation in turn depends largely upon the levels of analysis employed in the study of union action and behaviour, since its merit is obviously greater in the context of small-scale encounters in primary groups than, say, for the large-scale and comparative study of trade union growth, structure and policy. Moreover the theoretical and ontological assumptions of the system and ethno-methodological approaches are unbridgeable in any conventional industrial relations paradigm.

Rule-making and rule-interpretation

Although the primary merit of Dunlop's exposition has been understood in terms of drawing scholars of the labour movement away from merely descriptive researches, a number of further problems have still been occasioned by the specification of the rules themselves. And, although a range of such 'regulations of behaviour' were envisaged in the original treatise and these encompassed not only procedural and substantive issues but also methods 'for their establishment and administration',[128] subsequent writers have still endeavoured to produce a more precise taxonomy of the forms involved. One refinement in this respect has been by Goodman and his colleagues[129] who contrasted *customary* and *formal* and *interpretative* and *adjudicative* rule-making in order to countenance the problematic status of the application of specific regulations in given situations.[130] Similarly, in that study, power was considered critical to the question of the genesis of rules and their application and it was not, therefore, construed as part of the external context of the industrial relations system[131] but was rather central 'to establishment and defence of rules' and, in given empirical cases could be deployed quite independently of considerations of legitimacy.[132] By the same token, too, in given industrial contexts there may well be imperfect knowledge of the rules established, say, in formal processes of collective bargaining between trade unions and management, and in any event these are 'too general, imprecise or vague' or have entailed disputes over whether or not a particular rule is applicable in the first place.[133] Moreover, Wood *et al.* have commented on the value of taking into consideration not only the types of rule-making (formal, customary or adjudicative) and the form of each type at particular levels in the industrial relations system, but also the range of topics covered by each type, and the 'jointing' of principal modes of rule-making at the main levels.[134] Again, Anderson has distinguished between procedures for establishing rules and the rules themselves,[135] while Blain has emphasized the importance of differentiating between codified and uncodified rules.[136]

In short, then, although Dunlop envisaged a variety of forms of rule-making, subsequent scholars have introduced several valuable refinements which have particularly revolved around the distinction between *rule-making* and *rule-interpretation*. Moreover, in these later studies the role of power in the formulation and implementation of rules has been explicitly acknowledged rather than being lodged in the wider environmental context which serves to constrain the principal parties in union-management relations.

Processes in the industrial relations system

At a number of points in the analysis so far we have touched upon Dunlop's underestimation of the significance of process rather than structure in his own formulation of the rules. But, as Bain and Clegg have insisted:[137]

> The process by which the rules of job regulation are determined would seem to be just as important and intrinsically interesting as the rules themselves, and hence an adequate analytical framework must incorporate these processes and allow them to be analysed.

Moreover, as Blain has observed, the criticism levelled against the 'system model' in terms of processes is fundamental since these refer to the behavioural dynamics of the system rather than to its composition or structure. Indeed, the inadequate treatment of process in union-management relationships has been one of the traditional objections to the model of the industrial relations system; a problem which was not unconnected, of course, with the structural-functionalist basis of the original version of the thesis. Furthermore, the low theoretical status assigned to process in the overall model again reflected the preoccupation with conflict resolution rather than generation, the teleological status of function in the model and the concentration upon consequences rather than causes of social action. Hence, to overcome such sources of bias, in later versions of the conceptions of the industrial relations system, such as those of Bain and Clegg,[138] Blain and Gennard,[139] Somers,[140] and Wood *et al.*[141] these phenomena were explicitly countenanced. At the same time, however, as the last mentioned authors have explained, a distinction should be sharply drawn between *changes in rule-making process and movements in the other independent variables* (such as technology and market conditions).[142] After all, some rules will still be largely determined by structural exigencies and should not be viewed, therefore, solely as the consequence of complex processes of interaction between unions and management. Indeed, as the above authors further observed, this situation is indicated by the fact that rules may change over time even when processes of rule-making (such as collective bargaining) remain unaltered.[143] In sum, therefore, the specification of the process variable in the industrial relations system has been a valuable refinement of the original model, but should not signal an equally 'one-sided' examination in which the role of social structure in shaping the 'contexts' is omitted entirely.

Conflict, change, ideology, instability and power

Turning finally to the perennial complaint against system theory of the inadequate treatment of conflictual elements in union-management relations, it cannot be accepted that Dunlop's model, with its conceptual ancestry in structural-functionalism, disavowed the *significance* of conflict for union-management relations, but it is reasonable to underline its concentration on unifying elements in industrial relations systems. Moreover, although the genesis of stability and consensus within trade unions and in their relationships with management should be neither minimized nor assumed, but rather, as with conflict, should be the subject for rigorous examination, it was still the *continuation* of harmonious relationships which had problematic status in the Dunlopian and Parsonian formulations.

But in the limited theoretical treatment of the *origins* of conflict and change and also in terms of the deployment and understanding of such key concepts as power and ideology in the overall model itself, there were fundamental if by no means irredeemable weaknesses in the original conception. Hence, crucial from an analytical point of view was the placement of power in the context of the system and its exclusion from relationships between the main parties; for, as Wood *et al.* have noted, this made it 'an empty box in inter-industry comparative studies within a single country'.[144] Indeed, such a 'defocalisation of power' was later emphasized by Dunlop himself who observed that 'these exterior power relations or exterior political systems are given' and hence were *not to be explained* in terms of the other dimensions in the model itself.[145] Consequently, for Dunlop the intellectual task was 'to depict the industrial relations arrangements established by each political system and the character of the dynamic interaction between external political power and labour-management-government relations'.[146]

It must also be admitted that the concept of ideology as deployed in Dunlop's treatise entails similar sorts of problem. After all, not only is the term employed confusingly (as the philosophy, values and beliefs of the actors and as the integrative norms of the industrial relations system)[147] and treated as an *endogenous* variable, but its primary function is construed in terms of a capacity to 'bind the system together' (as with the commitment to voluntarism) rather than in any obvious way reflecting the varying orientations of the main parties in industrial relations itself. Of course, as Wood *et al.* have also noted 'the empirical existence of ideological congruence is to a greater or lesser extent contingent' in the Dunlop model; for after all, if ideologies always possessed such integrating qualities then the intellectuals and publicists 'concerned with articulating systematically and making some form of order out of the discrete ideas of the principal actors' would presumably have been superfluous.[148] But, at all events, it is manifest that a satisfactory conception of 'ideology' in so far as union-management relations are concerned must explicitly countenance its role as both the *reflection* and *harbinger* of change and be traced explicitly to the patterning of outlook and perception amongst actors in the 'larger society' as well as in the workplace itself.

Furthermore, although it is mistaken to assume that there is any underestimation of the *significance* of conflict and instability in Dunlop's formula, equally there is evidence that priority is given to explaining how conflict is handled in rule making to create and sustain order rather than to the question of conflict *generation*.[149] And this in turn supports the claims of *inter alia* Hyman,[150] Margerison,[151] and Laffer[152] that the nature of, and the forces shaping, conflict should have a more prominent role in industrial relations research and theorizing than is ever likely from the deployment of social system models.

This brings us to a further question, then, of whether these criticisms apply merely to structural-functionalist models of industrial relations or to all interpretations of trade union action in terms of social systems. After all, in some statements, such as that of Goodman *et al.*, the role of social action within the industrial relations system receives a measure of theoretical attention, while order has been redefined to constitute *regular patterned* behaviour rather than *peace*.[153] Again, at least in principle, there are no obvious objections either to transposing the concepts of power and ideology in the Dunlop model or to envisaging both as either external or internal to the industrial relations system itself. But at the same time, although such qualifications in the overall system enable some of the more specific pitfalls in Dunlop's thesis to be circumvented, the tendency for social systems to entail a focus upon points of equilibrium constitutes a substantial impediment which cannot be easily dismissed.

Moreover, even when it is absorbed into the system conception, the *structuralist* interpretation of ideology should be rejected. Indeed, as Wood has commented, 'ideology' should be understood not as a component of a social system but as a vital mechanism which helps to explain the 'creation, stability, development and instability' of different patterns of industrial relations.[154] And although this is in no way to introduce a one-sided 'idealist' bias into explanations for trade union action nor to dispute the saliency of wider structural conditions (such as technological or economic change) in *constraining* such action, it is to argue for a more 'subjectivist' and less 'structuralist' conception of this key term. Furthermore, this modification would in turn enable ethics to be counterpoised against ideologies as *theoretical* categories, and would further ensure a greater correspondence between the original concept of Parsonian formulation in terms of *values* rather than the otherwise narrow 'ideologies', which, after all, constitute only a part of the wider ensemble of subjective forces which have served to pattern trade union action and behaviour itself.

CONCLUSION

In this chapter, then, we have examined at some length the system model of industrial relations and its claims for theoretical status in the systematic study of trade union action and behaviour. Moreover, in this review we observed how the central analytical components entailed a conception of the nature of the function of trade unions in terms of actors in a social system constrained by a series of contexts in the wider environment and who, by processes of rule-making, endeavoured to secure the functional prerequisites for order within the industrial relations system. Of course, many of the substantive components of the model (the prominent role assigned to technology, economic conditions, values and ideologies, and power) had long been understood as fundamental explanatory variables by an earlier generation of scholars of the labour movement. But at the same time the approach was novel, especially with respect to its synthesis of disparate strands of thought and in its anchorage in the precepts and categories of structural-functionalism. Furthermore, its impact upon two subsequent decades or more of theoretical analysis in industrial relations, its stimulation of a series of refinements and modifications, and its significance for later theoretical critiques all bear testimony to the persuasiveness of the original formulation.

Ironically, though, its wide acceptance has at times served to deflect the attention of groups of theorists away from the study of trade unions as such, since instead of constituting the very essence of a particular field of inquiry, these organizations were now to be construed as only one part of a much wider industrial relations system. After all, it was Dunlop's specific objective to shift the industrial relations perspective from 'collective bargaining as it first developed in Great Britain . . . to the full spectrum of contemporary industrial relations'.[155] But unquestionably *Industrial Relations Systems* provided a major landmark in the development of theory and it served, more specifically, to introduce the concepts of rule and of rule-making into the general currency of industrial relations disputation.

3 The theoretical foundations of the 'Oxford school'

Notwithstanding affinities of analytical category, there are major divergences of epistemology, theoretical background, conception of accommodation of interests and empirical focus between the 'systems approaches' which have just been examined and the perspectives which will inform our review in this and in the subsequent chapter. Indeed, on the assumption that 'the dominant British school of industrial relations in recent years has been the liberal-pluralist or voluntaristic pluralist school',[1] then its principal characteristics have been: first, an initial pragmatism rather than enunciation of logico-deductive principle; second, the deployment of subsequent theoretical postulates grounded in a combination of Durkheimian analysis and a critically-informed interpretation of the Webbs' classic contributions to the analysis of British trade unionism; third, a conception of plural rather than unitary interests and perspectives of management and unions respectively; and fourth, a dominant focus upon institutions of collective bargaining rather than upon industrial relations systems *per se*.

Hence, despite the resistance by 'putative members',[2] the label 'Oxford school' has usually been deployed to pigeon-hole this essentially voluntaristic or liberal-pluralist conception of union-management relations.[3] To be sure, this is not a wholly accurate 'shorthand expression' for a highly complex theoretical position. Nevertheless, it serves a useful thematic purpose if it is used to designate the central premises of an approach based upon a focus on *job regulation*, a commitment to the *voluntary reform of industrial relations* and an association with the manifold varieties of *pluralism*. All these aspects are, however, ultimately linked by the common and overriding commitment to a circumscribed role of the state at least in so far as intervention into industrial relations and the affairs of trade unions is concerned.[4] Of course, although within this particular school of thought job regulation and pluralism have tended to be common points of focus, there is no obvious reason for this affinity. After all, to operate within a pluralist paradigm is entirely consistent, say, with emphasis on

47

control in union-management relations and, *pari passu*, to stress job regulation is in principle compatible with many varieties of political penetration in industrial relations (e.g., corporatist, socialist, and so on).

The main objective in the discussions which follow, therefore, will be to locate the foundations of the most significant theoretical assumptions of this predominant British school. Consistent with our practice we shall begin by focusing upon the main sociological premises which have informed this approach (which derived principally in this case, as we have mentioned, from Durkheim and the Webbs). Following our examination of these major tributaries of modern thought we shall then assess the contribution of Allan Flanders who was unquestionably the principal theoretical architect of the 'Oxford school' and whose initiatives are still evident in theoretical researches on trade unionism currently in progress at the University of Warwick.[5] An explicit account of recent contributions and a critical review of the assumptions and derivative propositions of the school will then be undertaken in chapter 4. Moreover, although for purposes of clarity we shall examine the approaches of the main founding fathers of the school consecutively, our objective throughout will be to identify common themes and points of comparison and contrast.

DURKHEIM'S INFLUENCE UPON THE MODERN THEORY
OF TRADE UNIONISM

The principal categories of Durkheimian sociology which have informed contemporary analyses of trade unionism and industrial relations include: (a) the significance of *ethics*, *values* and *social justice* (rather than of coercive modes of integration in rule making via *ideologies*); (b) *the division of labour* as a cardinal force shaping processes of societal evolution (this has the logical-theoretical status of a *deep structure*); (c) the problems occasioned by *anomie* and *the forced division of labour* for union-management attitudes and behaviour; and (d) the relationship between the individual, *'corporations'* and the state, which, though somewhat different in conception from the role of trade unions in the modern era, has obvious affinities with the underlying assumptions of pluralism.

Ethics, values and ideologies

In the previous chapter we saw that for Dunlop, the rules in the industrial relations system were viewed as being integrated ultimately by specific ideologies (such as voluntarism) which served to bind the principal social actors, and the overall system itself, into a common unity. For Durkheim, too, it should be emphasized, mechanisms of social integration were also at the forefront of attention but his interpretation was radically different since, on his testimony, social cohesion was seen to depend not upon ideologies but rather upon the pervasiveness of general moral values throughout any given society. To be sure, in Dunlop's formulation, ideologies would appear to correspond with a non-coercive envelopment of ideas and beliefs, but as was observed in chapter 1, this distinction has proved to be critical for trade union analysis and may be observed empirically, in terms of trade union structure, particularly among continental labour movements. More precisely, then, as Giner has indicated, the analytical difference between values and ideologies may be established as follows: [6]

> Values can be defined as principles of positive orientation towards a commonly felt good. They are about morality (such as honour), about aesthetics . . . and about truth (and, indirectly, about falsity). These three dimensions of value often appear intertwined, and show different degrees of prominence in each particular culture.

Values, then, refer to cultural and social predispositions which, in practical contexts, serve to fashion links between patterns of social action on the basis of ethical and moral criteria which, as such, fundamentally differ from the consequences of an ideology, the cohesive properties of which are accomplished through

> a conception of the social world explicitly and coercively maintained by a collectivity, which explains its existence through it, which derives from it a general plan of action and an identification of the sources of legitimate authority, and attempts the control of its social environment in a way consistent with this conception. [7]

For Durkheim, therefore, long-term social integration (and not least in the relationship between capital and labour) could be best achieved when the rules of actual conduct were infused by ethical standards and when general normative codes were widely upheld. [8] Moral considerations, then, coupled with the division of labour were viewed as fundamental in generating 'likeness of conscience' in organic social orders and were hence perceived as crucial in tempering the 'brutal action of the struggle for existence and selection' and in producing a fundamental bonding for effective collective life. [9]

Similarly, in Durkheim's estimation, moral and ethical forces were the essential foundations for liberty, which consisted not of *unregulated behaviour* but rather of the 'subordination of external forces to social forces' and of the consequent free development of all those *socially useful talents* which were critical for the long-term advancement of the division of labour.[10] But such ethical creeds could be detected not only in the constraint upon 'external conditions' in the struggle for interpersonal survival, but also in the furtherance of 'a work of justice', in which as close a match as possible between the distribution of natural talents and their deployment in the occupational structure (coupled with a principled basis for the allocation of economic and social rewards) were the most obvious accompaniments.[11]

Indeed, such interpretations have spanned the generations and have been emphasized frequently in the deliberations of labour movement theorists. Hence, the Webbs articulated such a concern throughout their voluminous writings and noted that even craft unionists almost invariably justified their development of 'the device of restriction of numbers' on the basis of ethical premises (which of course were viewed as being especially central to the device of the common rule).[12] Flanders, too, regarded the principal task of unions as that of establishing justice in industrial relationships, of securing common rights and of maintaining and enhancing the dignity of ordinary working people.[13] And, latterly, both Goldthorpe and Fox have insisted, above all, upon the significance of a just and principled distribution of economic, political and social rewards as an essential precondition for eradicating the consequences of the anomic division of labour.[14]

The structural significance of the division of labour

Yet an emphasis upon social justice in union purpose should in no way be taken to imply a one-sided 'culturalist' or 'subjectivist' conception of society and history. Rather, as will be familiar, Durkheim viewed the division of labour as 'the foundation of the moral order', since the capacity to produce an ever greater proliferation of occupations and modes of employment in turn facilitated the growth and interaction of modern populations (i.e. their density and volume) and provided a peaceful solution to the struggle for existence (its 'mellowed *dénouement*').[15] Hence, in its normal form, the division of labour in society has been associated with *solidarity* and *social order*, not only because individuals enter into a series of exchanges in the context of social life, but also because it would create 'among them an entire system of rights and duties', which would link them together 'in a durable way'.[16] Moreover, when coupled with ethics, restitutive law and 'the productive power and the ability of the workman', it could be construed not simply as the fountain of intellectual and material development in modern society, but also as the very 'source of civilisation'.[17]

But, viewed in this way, the theoretical status of the division of labour is clearly that of a *deep structure* which in many respects governs the disposition of higher level structures (such as the shape and direction of occupational change) as well as normative procedures. These points will be developed at greater length in chapter 6, but it is manifest that, for example, changes in the underlying division of labour have been associated with a proliferation and fragmentation of different occupations and this, in turn, has been consistent with the emergence and persistence of inter-union divisions, interests and policies rather than a cohesive movement based on the earlier bonding principles of 'mechanical solidarity'. And meanwhile, of course, the main trend occupational change has encouraged has been the rapid expansion of white-collar modes of employment; the *sine qua non* of the growth of white-collar unionism itself.

Abnormal forms of the division of labour

None the less, with the exception of Bain,[18] Banks,[19] and to some extent, Fox,[20] contemporary British scholars of the labour movement have focused rather less upon the *structural* significance of the division of labour than upon two, at least, of Durkheim's abnormal forms: anomie and the forced division of labour. In some respects this is scarcely surprising since Durkheim himself identified the relationship between capital and labour (together with industrial and commercial crises and the relationship among scientists) as a *locus classicus* of the breakdown of normative systems (i.e. anomie).[21] Moreover, accompanying the emergence of radical critiques of union function and union purpose in the late 1960s and 1970s, the analysis of the forced division of labour appeared to be reasonably consistent with the concern for equitable social orders.[22]

Furthermore, these twin concerns were, of course, to feature prominently in some of the most significant publications of the 'Oxford school'. Thus, the classical paper of Fox and Flanders ('The Reform of Collective Bargaining: From Donovan to Durkheim') seemed to accord well with those analyses in which the disintegration and breakdown of normative structures in British industrial relations had long been untuitively felt (whatever the justification appeared to be when examined against Britain's actual record of industrial conflict).[23] Moreover, in Fox's more radical account in *Beyond Contract*, the salience of conditions associated with forced division of labour was conceived of as paramount in explaining the underlying roots of Britain's industrial problems.[24]

None the less, as we have argued, some of the most interesting inferences from and parallels with Durkheim's account of abnormal forms have been less than fully explored in modern trade union theory and hence these are also worth a brief mention at this point. First of all, then, in his explanation of the emergence of anomic relations between capital and labour Durkheim's step-by-step model had remarkable affinities with the Webbsian formulation in *The History of Trade Unionism*.[25] Hence, for Durkheim, in the early small-scale establishments there was little overt conflict because worker and master performed similar tasks in 'shop' or 'establishment', they were members of the same 'corporation' and the ultimate possibility of promotion from apprenticeship to enterprise owner was by no means beyond the capability of a substantial proportion of artisans.[26] But, once the 'organization' became 'an exclusive possession of the masters' and, more especially, at a later phase when worker and employer were completely separated, conflict became ubiquitous; a state of affairs which applied particularly in the large-scale establishments where relations were judged to be 'in a sickly state'.[27]

In the second place, modern labour theorists have of course identified the crucial effects of size upon, *inter alia*, union density, the structure of shop stewards' committees, and the character and modes of interaction between union representatives and managerial personnel.[28] But it is less frequently appreciated that Durkheim attempted to explain this familiar empirical relationship by insisting that, 'since a body of rules is the definite form which spontaneously established relations between social functions take in their course of time, we can say, *a priori*, that the state of *anomy* is impossible wherever solidary organs are sufficiently in contact or sufficiently prolonged.'[29] But of course in large-scale establishments, such informal and regular interactions implied by the normal condition were easily vitiated by the irregular and unspontaneous nature of the contacts between management and worker; a situation which was clearly exacerbated by the proliferation of bureaucratic modes of administration governing social relationships in the enterprise.

Durkheim's conception of the forced division of labour has of course appeared prominently in recent accounts of trade union behaviour. Again, on the whole, it has been appreciated that Durkheim perceived this as emanating from a fundamental inequality in conditions of competition and conflict (i.e. in the *external conditions* of the division of labour such as the basis for allocation of people to different occupations).[30] And this implied, too, considerable frustration amongst those whose occupations were clearly ill-fitted to their physical or mental attributes and a general lack of co-ordination among the social functions themselves (a situation most obvious in rigidly stratified and non-meritocratic societies of a class or caste type).[31] But a third point worth emphasizing is that the crucial relationship between moral purposes (such as justice), the effective development of the division of labour and the contribution of both to long-term societal evolution has been less than fully understood. Yet for Durkheim not only was justice indispensable to the effective functioning of the division of labour, but also since this was conceived as the most basic force of societal evolution (and, above all, it enabled substantial urban populations to exist in the first place), then its pursuit, in turn, was by no means a pious objective of the Utopian but was to be regarded rather as in every way consistent with the principles of development which ultimately determined long-term change and transformation in the modern social orders themselves.[32]

Fourth, Durkheim also identified the general lack of co-ordination of functions as another abnormal form.[33] That is to say, anticipating the concerns of modern organization theorists, Durkheim observed that frustration could emanate from a situation in which each employee was not 'sufficiently occupied' and where movements were 'badly adjusted to one another'.[34] Although any association between such conditions and union action is by no means easy to demonstrate, it should logically be incorporated as a further hypothesis (together with anomie and the forced division of labour) for explaining contemporary labour relations problems by means of an examination of 'abnormal forms' of the division of labour itself.

Relations between individuals, corporations and the state

Perhaps the most crucial parallel to be drawn between Durkheim and the writings of the 'Oxford school' focuses not upon the rule-making processes and their problematic character, nor upon the salience of voluntary or spontaneous mechanisms for secondary association, but rather upon a shared emphasis on the 'desirability' of intermediary occupational and interest-groups 'intercalated' between the individual and the state.[35]

> Of course it remains true that the state itself has important functions to fulfill. It alone can oppose the sentiment of general utility and the need for organic equilibrium to the particularism of each corporation. But we know that its action can be useful only if a whole system of secondary organs exists to diversify action. It is, above all, these secondary organs that must be encouraged.

To be sure, there remain fundamental differences between Durkheim's conception of pluralism and that deployed by prominent members of the 'Oxford school'. After all, whereas Durkheim's most obvious contributions to trade union theory stemmed from his analysis of *The Division of Labour*[36] and from his discourse on ethics in *Sociology and Philosophy*,[37] it was actually in *Suicide* that he made his most explicit statement on the role of corporations. And it was scarcely surprising then, that Durkheim's concern for *pluralistic decentralization* was tempered by an 'organic' model of society from which he derived the view that individuals should be firmly located in the ongoing social activities of corporations (equivalent essentially to guilds). Indeed, Durkheim emphasized a three-fold 'advantage' in so far as integration was concerned: namely, the corporations' omnipresence, their ubiquitous character, and *their control over the greatest part of the life of the individual*.[38] Hence, such a conception was not an essentially oppositional one (as, indeed, Fox has emphasized)[39] and it also differed from Clegg's formulation[40] since, in the latter's interpretation, pluralism was to be understood essentially as a theory of *sovereignty* rather than social *differentiation*,[41] as 'pessimistic and traditional' in its distrust of power, and as viewing trade unions as the equivalent of an oppositional party to government (in providing checks and balances against the abuse of managerial power) rather than constituting harmonious units of the type which Durkheim had envisaged.[42]

Yet despite its consensual implications, Durkheim clearly provided a remarkably productive theoretical basis for modern trade union analysis. Durkheim's overall perspective, too, has manifest advantages over structural-functionalist models grounded in 'systems approaches'. After all, in his analysis he largely avoided excessively teleological notions of causation, he located the structures and functions of modern institutions in clearly recognizable processes of societal development and change and he identified the long-term evolutionary advantages of societies in which ethical rather than ideological premises infuse the highest levels of subjective conscience. Ironically, however, if by the term 'theory' we imply abstract generalizations about human action and behaviour, the central premises of which are in principle capable of refutation by rigorous empirical inquiries,[43] then, for the most part, probably the *least* theoretical of the Durkheim concepts have been deployed so far for the study of trade unionism. Indeed, stripped from the inner explanatory core in Durkheim's account (i.e. moral values and the division of labour), such concepts as anomie and the forced division of labour have tended to be used diagnostically and, therefore, not even as 'categorial systems'. Similarly, pluralism (like socialism, capitalism or communism) comprises less a theory of industrial relations as such than a *political philosophy* which incorporates an explicit creed and the prescription of 'ideal' modes of social formation and human conduct.

THE 'OXFORD SCHOOL' AND THE WEBBS

If Parsonian structural-functionalism provided the obvious theoretical foundation for system models of trade union action and behaviour while the analytical roots and preoccupations of the 'Oxford school' particularly reflect the influence of the Durkheimian heritage, it is still never an entirely satisfactory procedure to examine the epistemological assumptions of any major approach upon the basis of a single set of propositions however significant these have been to overall development. Moreover, given the major discrepancies in perspective amongst leading members of this school, whatever the affinities between the concerns of Durkheim (say, for justice, the breakdown of institutional machinery and pluralism) and of contemporary contributions there will of course be many other tributaries which have nourished specific suggestions and helped to shape orientations on trade union questions. While, therefore, from a sociological point of view it is entirely admissible to relate the principal contributions of the 'Oxford school' to Durkheimian postulates, such a procedure could still convey an entirely misleading impression of cohesive thematic and analytical unity, which has been far from typical of the 1970s at any rate.

Indeed, in terms of substantive theory (i.e., generalizations developed specifically in studies of trade unions) the classic British scholarship of the Webbs has been no less fundamental and, over the last decade or so, the theoretical attention directed towards their monumental contributions to the study of labour organizations has been a tribute to the durability of their impact upon contemporary thought.[44]

None the less, it should be emphasized that during the pragmatic phase of the 'Oxford school' (from the 1950s to at least the mid-1960s) only the Webbs' empirical and historiographical contributions received much attention and, at the time, amongst leading British theorists of trade unionism, only H.A. Turner showed any real appreciation of the perceptive character of their analytical work.[45] Hence, it was not until 1968 that Flanders produced his major theoretical analysis of collective bargaining which originated from his criticism of the classical conception of the Webbs, and in which he was to acknowledge 'the widespread influence which their views have had on subsequent thought throughout the world about the nature of trade unions and collective bargaining'.[46]

More specifically, it may be asked what were the contributions of the Webbs to labour theory and to the development of the 'Oxford school'? The parts of the Webbs' thesis which arouse the greatest theoretical interest undoubtedly revolve around the following major themes: (a) the salience of justice and the creation of social order embodied in rule-making processes; (b) the distinction between union structure and union function; (c) the methods of regulation employed in different unions; (d) the long-term consequences of the operation of the device of the common rule; (e) the strength of the democratic current; and (f) their prediction of the gradual replacement of collective bargaining by the method of legal enactment accompanying increasing collectivism in society as a whole.

(a) In the first chapter it was recognized that, in *The History of Trade Unionism*, the Webbs saw the creation of a class of wage-earners as the *sine qua non* for the emergence of trade unionism in Great Britain. Yet of course the bulk of their study of trade unionism consisted of reporting upon the fruits of six years of extensive empirical researches and it was less in *The History* than in the later sections of *Industrial Democracy* that a rigorous theory of trade union structure and policy could be identified, and even this was interspersed with substantial sections of narrative.[47]

But in *Industrial Democracy* the Webbs reinforced the Durkheimian view of the salience of justice in modern society and did so explicitly in the context of trade union action and behaviour. Indeed, for them, rather than the pursuit of rule-making and regulation being in any sense a conservative doctrine, it was premised on the determination by working people to secure a measure of *order* in employment relationships in the first place.[48] On this view, then, trade unionists eschewed 'the higgling of the market', and sought, as a *fundamental objective*, the *protection* afforded by a series of rules governing basic relations between employer and employee in order to ward off from the manual-working producers the 'evil effects' of industrial competition.[49] Moreover, in their support of this action trade unionists almost invariably marshalled the *ethical* and *moral* premises which were developing apace in the wider culture.[50]

(b) The familiar taxonomic distinctions of the Webbs between trade union *structure* (which encompassed primitive democracy, representative institutions, the units of government and relations between trade unions) and trade union *function* (covering the methods of mutual insurance, collective bargaining, arbitration and legal enactment)[51] ultimately rested on a deeper explanatory analysis which revealed many parallels with Durkheimian theory. And this in turn, therefore, combined an acknowledgment of the general structural development of a separation of interests between employer and wage-earner and the emphasis upon ethical and moral criteria which, in conjunction, produced among manual workers a determination to insist upon a measure of *order* in employment relationships by means of *regulation* by one or more of the methods listed above.

(c) The methods of regulation deployed by various associations of working people were to form the basis of the Webbs' classification of union type and union purpose and, hence, on such assumptions, 'the device of restriction of numbers' (founded on the doctrine of vested interests) was contrasted with 'the device of the common rule' of which the demand for 'a living wage' was the usual accompaniment.[52] The Webbs themselves expressed a clear preference for 'the device of the common rule' not least because of its appeal to higher ethical sentiments and values. Hence, even though the Webbs noted that 'the device of restriction of numbers' was almost invariably supported by *craft unionists* on the grounds that 'the protection of their means of livelihood from confiscation or encroachment appears as fundamental a basis of social order as it does to the owners of land',[53] they also emphasized the greater applicability of the appeal of regulations served by the common rule:[54]

> in the absence of any Common Rule, the conditions of employment are left to 'free competition', this always means, in practice, that they are arrived at by Individual Bargaining between contracting parties of very unequal economic strength. Such a settlement it is asserted, invariably tends, for the mass of the workers, towards the worst possible conditions of labour – ultimately, indeed, to the barest subsistence level – whilst even the exceptional few do not permanently gain as much as they otherwise could. We find accordingly that the Device of the Common Rule is a universal feature of Trade Unionism, and that the assumption on which it is based is held from one end of the Trade Union world to the other.

Moreover, although trade unionists almost invariably invoked the ethical validity of their methods, an evolutionary progression involving an increasing concern for equity and justice could be discerned in the Webbs' account of the development from the doctrine of vested interests, through supply and demand to a living wage; the last mentioned of course being principally associated with 'the device of the common rule'.[55]

(d) In the Webbs' conception, too, a general application of 'the device of the common rule' would bring in its train a series of major structural changes and, above all, a concentration of businesses in larger establishments (i.e. size and concentration were viewed as consequential upon regulation rather than upon technological change *per se*).[56] This was accounted for by the Webbs, first, in terms of the probable demise of the so-called 'parasitic trades'[57] (largely casual forms of employment); and second, because:[58]

> the regulated industries, by progressively raising the standard of mechanical ingenuity, organising capacity, and physical strength, will have added to the national capital in all its forms, their very superiority

makes continuously harder the struggle of the unregulated trades to maintain their position in the world's market.

(e) The subjective roots of such changes, too, were connected with what was termed the 'strength of the democratic current', founded upon an increase in scientific knowledge and in the growth of new habits of social cooperation.[59] Moreover, accompanying this movement was a further reinforcement of *regulation* in the form of general social planning in society as a whole.[60]

> There is a growing feeling, not confined to Trade Unionists, that the best interests of the community can only be attained by deliberate securing, to each section of the workers, those conditions which are necessary for the continuous and efficient fulfilment of its particular function in the social machine.

(f) In the final section of *Industrial Democracy*, the Webbs examined what they termed 'precept and prophecy' rather than empirically supported theory, but their predictions have still stimulated much detailed examination by successive trade union theorists and their conclusions have clear parallels with recent debates on 'corporatism' and the role of the state.[61] After all, in their view, the growth of the democratic current and resulting 'collectivism' would herald the abandonment of the doctrine of common interests; the modification of that of supply and demand and the extension of the notion of the living wage; the development of permanent functions of unions in the democratic state (involving Trade Union Officers in the 'cordial cooperation of the secretary of the Employers' Association and the Factory Inspector, in serving an exact obedience of the Common Rules prescribed for the trade'); the universal application of the common rule; and the 'vastness and complexity' of the democratic current which would imply the institutionalization of 'one regulation after another'.[62]

Durkheim and the Webbs

The Webbs' monumental contribution to the study of trade unionism consisted, therefore, of a number of distinctive but intertwined elements. The structural and ethical bases of the emergence of modern unions were both countenanced, the salience of rule-making processes as a *sine qua non* of union function was also emphasized, there were important taxonomic distinctions between union type, and the association of the common rule with modern unionism, large-scale industry, the democratic current and the movement towards collectivism was of major analytical interest.

Similarly, with progressive collectivization they envisaged a more 'scientific' process for the allocation of rewards in which collective bargaining would gradually be replaced by the method of legal enactment.[63]

Yet before turning to the influence of these postulates upon the work of Allan Flanders, whose ideas were to become pivotal in the genesis of the distinctive approach of the 'Oxford school',[64] it is worth drawing out the principal points of comparison and contrast between Durkheim and the Webbs; for there were several remarkable areas of affinity between the two conceptions. These embraced the significance of the separation of interests of employer and wage-earner for industrial relations, the salience of ethical and moral values in shaping social purposes, the focus upon rule-making in both accounts, and the ultimately integrative conceptions in which the state, intermediary associations and the individual would all be linked in an 'organic unity'. At the same time, however, there were several points of divergence which could be attributed particularly to the more direct focus upon actual trade unions and upon processes of collective bargaining in the Webbs' account. Hence, while for Durkheim the division of labour was the most decisive evolutionary force in modern industrial society, particularly in so far as trade unionism was concerned, the Webbs emphasized the 'democratic current'. Moreover, while both were cognizant of the significance of the scale of the enterprise, Durkheim's identification of the 'anomic' consequences and 'sickly state' of the relationships between employer and employee in such establishments contrasted sharply with the Webbs' more optimistic assessment of the potential for enhancing scientific capacity, industrial efficiency and the proliferation of rules and rule-making processes. On the whole too, the Webbs were inclined to view power conflicts in industry as necessary accompaniments of early struggles by trade unionists who were striving to overcome both anomic conditions and the exigencies of the forced division of labour; although, equally, they envisaged the gradual elimination of such problems during the steady progress towards a collectivist society. And finally, there were marked differences in interpretation and designation of intermediary associations in the two conceptions; for while Durkheim's essential notion was based around occupational associations ('corporations') for the Webbs the fusion of interests between trade unions, employers and the state would only be accomplished through representatives of all bodies being engaged in rule-making and administration (i.e. union officials, representatives of employers' associations and the factory inspectorate).

ALLAN FLANDERS AND THE EMERGENCE OF THE OXFORD SCHOOL

During the pragmatic phase of British studies on trade unionism in the 1950s and 1960s, Flanders stood out with Turner as the foremost theorist during a period which otherwise consisted principally of descriptive and evaluative researchers. But in some respects it is best to envisage Flanders's contribution as representing a crucial junction point or filter between, on the one hand, the Webbsian tradition of inductive generalization (based originally upon painstaking empirical research) the strategic and more deductive conceptual scheme of Durkheim and Dunlop, and the American contributions to labour theory of Chamberlain,[65] Derber,[66] and Ross;[67] and on the other, the systematic explanations for union growth and the nature of trade unionism under collective bargaining that were to be the notable analytical advances in the 1970s based on the premises of this school.

Precisely formulated models of trade union action and behaviour, however, seldom appeared in Flanders's theoretical writings although the germs of one may be readily pieced together from 'Collective Bargaining: A Theoretical Analysis'.[68] Indeed, Flanders clearly had in mind a multi-causal theory in which the principal explanatory dimensions could include organizational or *institutional* variables (the commitment of officialdom to the long-term survival of their associations and so on), the *internal political processes* within trade unions and the wider labour movement, a series of subjective or *'volitional'* factors which may be crucial in shaping objectives in actual bargaining encounters, the wider *economic environment* (including product as well as labour market conditions), *technology and production*, and at a broader level of subjectivity, the *accepted norms and cultural values* which obtain in given society at specific points in time (see Figure 3.1).[69]

Yet these are only indications of what Flanders had in view, since, as Clegg has informed us, he was primarily working upon a theory of union growth (which has been continued by G.S. Bain[70] – see chapter 6) 'as a first step to a general theory'.[71] What we have, then, from Flanders's published work is largely a set of explanatory dimensions which, while focusing on different levels of analysis, have no special weights attached to designate their relative significance.

None the less, despite being incomplete and clearly constituting something of a 'check-list', the analytical and theoretical advantages of such a formulation over the structural-functionalist conception of industrial relations systems are still considerable. Apart from its explicit focus upon union action and behaviour there is no artificial distinction between *endogenous* and *exogenous* variables in the 'system' as such and this avoids

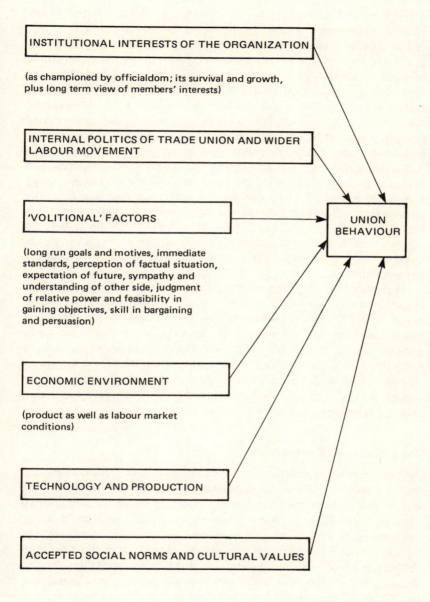

INSTITUTIONAL INTERESTS OF THE ORGANIZATION

(as championed by officialdom; its survival and growth, plus long term view of members' interests)

INTERNAL POLITICS OF TRADE UNION AND WIDER LABOUR MOVEMENT

'VOLITIONAL' FACTORS

(long run goals and motives, immediate standards, perception of factual situation, expectation of future, sympathy and understanding of other side, judgment of relative power and feasibility in gaining objectives, skill in bargaining and persuasion)

UNION BEHAVIOUR

ECONOMIC ENVIRONMENT

(product as well as labour market conditions)

TECHNOLOGY AND PRODUCTION

ACCEPTED SOCIAL NORMS AND CULTURAL VALUES

Figure 3.1 *Matrix of explanatory variables in Flanders's theory*

a series of problems over, say, the 'correct' placement of power and ideology in the overall framework. Thus, for example, power is conceived as operating at a number of levels (in the actual bargaining relationship, in trade unions and the wider labour movement, and in the socio-cultural environment); while again, subjective variables (far more broad in concept than ideology) encompass their specific effects in actual bargaining contexts, the commitments of union officers, and cultural norms and expectations. But structural constraints upon action are also incorporated (economy and technology) and hence in no way did the analysis entail an exclusively 'subjectivist' interpretation of union behaviour. Similarly, the problems identified by modern organization theorists of a commitment to the survival of associations and the somewhat different perceptions which may hence emerge of union officials and the membership are all readily countenanced. Stripped, too, of the unnecessary appendages of teleological prescription or of any notion of a 'binding of the system' by common 'ideological' predispositions, a series of the problems of system-based approaches examined in the previous chapter would thus appear not to be present at all.

Flanders's general theoretical concerns and his decisive significance in shaping the contours of the 'Oxford school' may be examined in greater depth, however, under the following principal headings: (a) the ethical and moral foundations of rule-making; (b) his debt to, as well as his major criticism of, the Webbs; (c) the explicit Durkheimianism in the account (with Fox) of the disintegration of normative structures; (d) the incorporation and major modification of Dunlop's work on the industrial relations system; (e) the focus upon institutions; and (f) the contribution to discussions on the voluntarist basis of pluralism.

The ethical basis of rule-making

We have already emphasized the extent to which both Durkheim and the Webbs traced the genesis of rule-making to ethical and moral purposes rather than to the salience of ideologies as integrative mechanisms in social systems. Wittingly or otherwise, Flanders was to echo such traditions by emphasizing that processes of rule-making had emerged historically not for any obviously conservative reason (except perhaps in the defence of skilled artisans of modes of unilateral regulation) but from the successful struggles by working men and women to obtain protection against the vagaries of an unplanned market in labour and against arbitrary or capricious actions by employers and their associations at the levels of industry and enterprise.[72] But Flanders went somewhat further than the Webbs in this respect by insisting on the centrality of 'the sword of justice' rather than of vested interest to union purpose itself, by emphasizing the function of unions in securing industrial order and by stressing their role in establishing rights which paralleled those in the political sphere.[73]

> Stated in the simplest possible terms these rules provide protection, a shield, for their members. And they protect not only their material standards of living, but equally their security, status and self-respect; in short their dignity as human beings.
>
> One can put the same point in another way. The effect of rules is to establish rights, with their corresponding obligations. The rules in collective agreements secure for employees the right to a certain rate of wages; the right not to work longer than a certain number of hours; the right not to be dismissed without consultation or compensation and so on. This surely is the most enduring social achievement of trade unionism, its creation of a social order in industry embodied in a code of industrial rights.

The significance of order and peace (secured through the permeation of rules throughout union-management relations) was also to be emphasized by Flanders, but unlike certain of his successors he was especially concerned with the considerable advantages for working people of such procedures. To be sure, he also recognized how structural exigencies (such as size of enterprise), functional rationality, the fragmentation of operations and the emergence of wider ideas (such as scientific management), had bestowed upon modern managers rather than the entrepreneur an interest in the formation of rules and of rule-making processes.[74] Moreover, in his critique of the Webbs (see next section) he was to argue explicitly that the idea 'that collective bargaining was something forced upon employers against their will' could not be accepted at face value since this left out the interest of employers and their associations in securing some form of order in the labour market.[75] But equally there was little doubt in Flanders's view that historically the prime beneficiaries of the modification, if not replacement, of market mechanisms by rules were trade union members themselves.[76]

The critique of the Webbs

Turning more specifically, then, to examine Flanders's debt to the Webbs, and there was clear evidence that this was considerable, he none the less took issue with several important aspects of their overall thesis. Above all, he considered that the economic analysis in which a substantial part of their account had been couched understated the political characteristics and social achievements of trade unions. More especially, he drew a sharp distinction between individual bargaining (which he regarded as an economic process) and collective bargaining (which entailed a process of rule-making and a power relationship between organizations).[77] And although Fox was to demur at any such rigid demarcation here he summarized Flanders's critique exceptionally well by noting how, on such assumptions, the Webbs had been led:[78]

> to set up a misleading model of the trade union; to misrepresent the relationship between collective negotiation and the individual contract of employment; to give rise to a mistaken view of the strike; to leave unexplored the transition from other methods of job regulation to collective negotiation; to treat collective negotiation as an exclusively economic process and thereby to overlook its non-economic aspects (which he sees as more important); and implicitly to set up a mistaken criterion for the social evaluation and justification of trade unionism.
> . . . they failed to register and explore other related themes such as the employer interest in collective negotiation and the historical part played by custom in regulating pay.

Basic to Flanders's critique, then, was the idea that individual bargaining was substantially different from collective bargaining and, hence, given this judgment, the term *job regulation* was considered to be markedly superior to the latter concept since it described more accurately the political and social aspects and purposes of modern industrial relations institutions.[79] Moreover, these crucial non-economic aspects included the social achievements of trade unions, the explanatory forces which shaped the actual conduct of negotiations, and the range and type of industrial conflict (encompassing managerial as well as market questions).[80] Again, although Flanders overstated his case in so far as union purpose was concerned (and this led him into an essentialist definition based on political and social objectives), and despite the fact that the Webbs, too, had particularly emphasized the ethical and moral concerns of trade unionism (in conjunction with economic aims), there is a valuable corrective here to the narrow perspectives of 'economism'.[81]

Although we shall consistently espouse the view that union purposes must be located in terms of the perspectives and motivation of social actors, there remains much force in Flanders's case; for, empirically, it does at least enable some realistic explanation of the growing concern in the 1960s and 1970s for democratic processes of control in the enterprise, for the erosion of managerial prerogatives, and for the extension of shop floor controls based upon the trade union channel.[82]

All these difficulties disappear once one goes out from an alternative assumption: that the value of a union to its members lies less in its economic achievements than its capacity to protect their dignity. Viewed from this angle, employees — white-collar no less than manual workers — have an interest in union organisation, however favourable their economic circumstances or the state of the labour market, for at least two reasons. They are interested in the regulation of labour markets and of labour management because such regulation defines their rights, and consequently their status and security, and so liberates them from dependence on chance and the arbitrary will of others. Equally they are interested in participating as directly as possible in the making and administration of these rules in order to have a voice in shaping their own destiny and the dimensions on which it most depends.

The relationship with Durkheim

The theme of political and social justice was seldom far below the surface of Flanders's most influential writings upon trade unionism. But until his classic paper with Fox ('The Reform of Collective Bargaining: From Donovan to Durkheim')[83] his direct references to Durkheim were sparse despite the obvious affinities and shared concern over the salience of moral and ethical forces as central aspects of modern societies. Moreover, when the ideas of Durkheim were ultimately incorporated in an integral fashion they were to centre not explicitly upon such questions at all, neither in any obvious way upon the evolutionary significance of the division of labour and its association with conditions for liberty, nor upon any direct reference to corporations, nor yet again upon the obstacles to justice occasioned by the forced division of labour, but, as is familiar, upon the contemporary significance of the breakdown of normative regulation.

It would of course be to labour the point to examine in any greater depth what is a well-known study in literature on trade unionism and collective bargaining and this is particularly so in view of its supersession by subsequent analyses upon which we shall focus at a later juncture.[84] Moreover, the substantive and evaluative concerns which also featured prominently in this paper are not, in themselves, of any great relevance in a theoretical text. But four main issues are worth emphasizing. The first is the preference for the wider concept of norm ('a rule, a standard, or a pattern for action') to that of regulation.[85] The second is that substantive and procedural rules seem to be used interchangeably with their norm equivalents.[86] Moreover, in the third place, anomie would appear to be principally deployed as a diagnostic concept to cover four main sources of disorder in union-management relations arising from the interaction between normative aspirations and prevailing norms: (1) where one group, against the resistance of another, acts to change the procedural norms and nature of the system; or (2) to change its substantive characteristics; (3) in the absence of regulation about certain issues on which one group at least has normative aspirations; and (4) when there is a progressive fragmentation and breakdown of existing regulative systems.[87] In the fourth place, there were nevertheless important explanatory variables identified, based largely upon changing 'structural' and 'subjective' conditions in modern British society; namely, inflation, industrial change and labour mobility, the escalation of technological and organizational change, the creation of new classes of work (and of workers) and the breakdown of traditional rules, and finally the 'rapid spread of union organization as labour scarcity brought power and awakened aspirations'.[88]

The influence of Dunlop

There were, then, certain major theoretical affinities between Allan Flanders's understanding of union purpose, the concept of anomie and Durkheimian analysis. But Flanders also drew heavily upon certain analytical concepts from the work of J.T. Dunlop in framing his overall theoretical position and hence the association between the contributions of these two analysts is clearly worthy of mention.

Flanders accepted that industrial relations were concerned with 'a system of rules', but he seldom adopted the structural-functionalist notion of causation and its links with system properties.[89] To be sure, his approach was in some respects even more restricted than Dunlop's since, as we noted in the previous chapter, he argued that only *regulated* or *institutionalized relationships* in industry could be legitimately incorporated within the analysis of industrial relations themselves.[90] None the less, Flanders also adopted from Dunlop the recognition that technological and market factors were crucial constraining influences upon union behaviour, but modified the account in three principal respects: (a) by substituting accepted social norms and cultural values for ideology, and placing these firmly in the wider context of union-management relations rather than in the industrial relations system itself; (b) by construing power not as an exogenous variable but as critical in the interaction between organizations (i.e. unions and management); and (c) by drawing the distinction between internal and external *processes* of job regulation.[91] This last mentioned dichotomy thus accommodated *managerial* as well as *market* questions and here Flanders introduced the idea that not only was there more than one centre of power but that the clash between unions and management could embody *values* (such as efficiency versus security in enterprise administration), as well as material *interests* in the market place.[92] Conflict was also incorporated into the model in this way and, indeed, Flanders explicitly criticized Chamberlain's theory of 'penetration into management' on the grounds that rule-making processes could not be perceived in terms of 'jointly conceived objectives' which resulted in 'functional integration', but argued, rather, that 'the need remains for both procedural and substantive rules to deal with conflict between the divergent interests of management and unions'.[93]

In sum, then, Flanders's account included certain central analytical concepts from the Dunlop model (such as rule-making, technology and market constraints) but avoided many of the theoretical difficulties which were highlighted in chapter 2. Hence, there is no obvious resort to teleological explanations, a series of levels of subjective analysis is identified, conflicting interests and values and the central role of power in relationships *between* organizations are well understood and even differences of goal and purpose between union officers and union members are fully countenanced. Moreover, in view of the obvious analytical and theoretical advantages of this approach over the original Dunlop formulation it is in turn scarcely surprising that in Britain this interpretation has been far more significant in influencing the dominant strand of industrial relations theorizing in the 'Oxford school' than structural-functionalism. Furthermore, even those theorists who have drawn upon Dunlop's notion of an industrial relations system have perforce introduced modifications very much along the lines intimated by Flanders himself.[94]

The focus on institutions

None the less, it must be admitted that Flanders's references to *institutions* of job regulation in his definition of the scope of the subject of industrial relations has been the source of a long-standing problem. After all, on such a conception, not only is reification a distinct possibility, but also essentially descriptive questions may be emphasized without, therefore, any proper reference either to the origins of institutions and to the factors which continue to sustain them, or to the processes of socialization that help to fashion the orientations and attitudes of the new recruit. To be sure, as we shall see in chapter 4, it is not necessary to deploy this concept in a restricted and descriptive fashion, but equally, given these obvious analytical difficulties, it came as no surprise that Clegg, in his recent statement on this question, sought to abandon the term 'institution' completely and make reference only to job regulation.[95] In brief, then, Flanders's conceptualization of institutions has proved to be controversial on three

main counts. First because it was inextricably bound up with union purpose and the role of tradition. Second, since in his interpretation, it was
crucial to understanding the focus on industrial over political *methods* in
the union movement. The third and final point of controversy arises from
his not infrequent reference to the reified notion of 'institutional needs'.

Hence, for Flanders effective trade unionism depended upon a satisfactory interrelationship between organization, vitality and social purpose.
Thus, as he insisted, 'trade unions need organisation for their power and
movement for their vitality but they need power and vitality to advance
their social purpose.'[96] But such vitality could easily be sapped by tradition, for, as he was fully aware, Britain's industrial relations institutions
were fixed at an earlier period and were clearly, in H.A. Turner's familiar
epithet, 'historical deposits and repositories of history'.[97] *Traditions*, then,
which were embodied in institutional customs and practices, expressed
'normative standards and therefore value judgements', they encompassed
routines, they were 'resistant to challenge of historical fact',[98] but were
still significant forces which helped to shape the actor's behaviour:[99]

> They derive their greatest strength from the fact that they embody for
> the group the lessons of its corporate, social experience. The normative
> and binding character which traditions acquire is due to their having
> proved their worth as patterns of behaviour which have consistently
> succeeded in advancing the group's goals and values. Indeed, its
> traditions become the sheet anchor of the group's goals and values
> which may never be separately articulated.

Expressed in this form the analytical basis of the argument carries much
conviction and, therefore, if the conditions obtaining at times of major
institutional growth or reform are properly accommodated, the approach
can be married with explanatory interpretations. But Flanders was to incur
opposition by arguing further that trade union institutions (anchored in
earlier struggles) were ill-adapted to the exigencies of structural change and
rising expectations in the 1960s and early 1970s.[100] Moreover, while he
envisaged a progressive penetration of unions into managerial functions
and an extension of controls at industry level (and notwithstanding his
acknowledgment that 'unions have to be involved in politics' in order to
defend such a strategy), equally, in his view, there was an 'upper limit' on
political involvement that was primarily the consequence of 'institutional
needs' themselves.[101] Hence, expressed in a somewhat less reified form,
Flanders recognized that the concern of leaders and bureaucrats for the
survival of their unions and for an active role in negotiations implied that
they would not readily subscribe to those forms of political system in
which union objectives were effectively determined by wider planning

agencies; and this was the case, in his estimation, 'regardless of their individual members' views on politics'.[102]

Viewed from this angle, then, such a perspective was by no means at variance with what Hyman has termed the 'pessimistic' tradition of Marxist thought in which the role of unions as agents of revolutionary change has been regarded as inevitably circumscribed.[103] But it should still be emphasized that, in our view, any such interpretation should be rooted in the categories of social action and social process, for, in this way, it is possible to attribute 'limitations' on political purpose not to 'institutional needs' as such but rather to the perceived interests of officials and members in maintaining independent associations and to those patterns of socialization which encourage the dissemination of particular orientations and outlook during processes of interaction amongst union members themselves.

Moreover, the term 'institutional need' was also deployed by Flanders to reflect the way in which, in trade unions, 'the social purposes of yesterday' became embodied in 'the social functions of today'.[104] That is to say, successful struggles by unionists in the past for extensions of shop floor controls become part of the day-to-day duties or functions of the modern representative and provide a basis in action for a further erosion of 'managerial prerogatives' in the future. But again the term 'institutional need' has no obvious relevance here because traditions may be embodied in the dimensions of social process and, in any event, they may be subject to major fluctuations, not because of changes in institutional structures, but as a result of wider environmental factors (such as labour market conditions), the shifts in values of managers and union representatives and their varying skill in the deployment of power resources in actual conflict situations.

Voluntarism and pluralism

Although it is no part of scientific discourse to debate the respective merits of one political creed against another it is none the less pertinent to identify in Flanders's work important implications for the deliberations of the voluntaristic or liberal-pluralist conception of industrial relations and of the role of trade unions in such a system. In explanatory vein, therefore, Flanders identified: (1) the saliency of accepted social norms and cultural values for voluntarism; (2) institutional developments which further the effective functioning of collective bargaining in a voluntarist system; and (3) the growing involvement of government and the legislature which pose a threat to 'the tradition of voluntarism'.

At the most general level, then, Flanders located the framework of

British industrial relations (based traditionally upon agreement and compromise rather than upon legislative fiat) in a dominant cultural predisposition for freedom:[105]

> the principles of any national system of industrial relations — and
> therefore their institutional consequences — are derived from the
> values by which the nation judges and legitimises the system's working
> and results. The main values supporting the principles of our traditional
> system have been those of economic freedom and industrial peace.

> The moral defense of the voluntary character of our system has always
> been conducted in the name of freedom.

But certain institutional arrangements and accepted social norms were also viewed as significant in producing an effective voluntary system and these included a sufficient degree of organization by the principal parties to collective bargaining, the entering 'into agreements with each other' upon the basis of a 'mutual recognition' of the interests of the other party, and the honouring, 'in good faith', of agreements established by processes for which there were no ultimate legal sanctions for default.[106]

Moreover, an effective 'voluntaristic-pluralist' system would be accompanied by the following main patterns of collective bargaining that appear in many respects to catalogue Flanders's principal concerns: the primacy of industrial over political methods, upper and lower levels of political involvement, 'institutional needs' for survival which could circumscribe the political aims of individual members and involve a concentration upon procedural questions, and the participation of unions as part of the democratic process.[107]

However, Flanders was keenly aware of the perceptible drift towards state intervention (the challenge from above), and the growth of workplace bargaining (the commensurate challenge from below) which were producing very serious strains upon traditional institutions.[108] Hence, although earlier he had censured the Webbs for suggesting that collectivism and 'the method of legal enactment' would gradually replace collective bargaining, there was clearly a recognition that structural changes, rising expectations and the public pressure for reform were beginning to produce a series of proposals, all of which were 'directed to achieving greater centralisation of control in the system to restore and advance economic planning'.[109] As such, therefore, his account in many respects anticipated the familiar pluralist versus corporatist debates which were to feature prominently in industrial relations and industrial sociological writings as the 1970s progressed.[110]

CONCLUSION

In this chapter, then, our main aim has been to examine the theoretical foundations for the development of Britain's dominant school of industrial relations and trade union analysis founded upon the assumptions of 'liberal-pluralism'. To this end, we have surveyed in some depth the works of Durkheim, the Webbs and Allan Flanders in order to delineate major points of comparison and contrast and to illuminate their heritage in the themes of modern theory. The purpose of our ensuing discussions will be to highlight recent contributions of this genre and to focus critically upon subsequent modifications and refinements which have surfaced in contemporary literature.

4 Pluralism and trade unionism

In the British context the modern extension of trade union theory has depended greatly upon the central precepts of 'the founding fathers' of the pluralist or Oxford school.[1] The focus on job regulation, on patterns of collective bargaining (conceived as principal determinants of trade union structure and of other manifestations of union behaviour), and on the characteristics of formal and informal institutions of industrial relations has all been derived from propositions clearly established in earlier discourses.[2] And yet to view contemporary theories as mere reflections of their origins and as in no way a revelation of novel deliberations would be far from accurate. Hence, in order to dispel such assumptions, our analysis of the advances and ongoing disputations in the theorizing of the Oxford school will now proceed by focusing upon: (1) the advances in pluralist thought; (2) job regulation, collective bargaining and the 'determinants' of union behaviour; and (3) the explanatory analysis of institutions.

THE ADVANCES OF PLURALIST THOUGHT

'Pluralism', as Richard Hyman has insisted, 'is in no way a homogeneous body of analysis and prescription; its development in philosophy, in sociology and in political theory reflects varied disciplinary roots, diverse conceptual and interpretative problems, and the impact of historically changing ideological forces.'[3] Moreover, as the same author went on to observe, there has been a particularly significant distinction between British and American versions here; since, while in the former case, pluralism emerged as part of a critique of theories of the dominant role of the state and tended to reflect Durkheim's emphasis upon the essential role of intermediary associations and of their functional independence, the American approach was a far more conservative doctrine, for it eschewed any association with radical versions such as anarcho-syndicalist, Guild Socialist and industrial unionist philosophies, and stressed rather the salience of inter-group competition.[4] Again, Hyman drew attention to the significant distinction between *societal pluralism* (in which the *autonomy* of industrial relations from state control is viewed as paramount) and pluralism *within* industrial relations in which, as British pluralists have usually emphasized, 'unions must be internally strong if they are to function effectively in their external relations as components of a pluralist industrial relations system'.[5]

Most of the major advances in British pluralism in the 1970s may be identified, however, by a detailed examination of the principal approaches of two of three main theorists of the Oxford school: Clegg and Fox. Yet, as we shall see, both accounts have certain disadvantages from an explanatory point of view since descriptive and prescriptive observations tend to predominate over the identification of those economic, political and social conditions which give rise to the main types of pluralism in the first place and which continue to have ramifications for the operation of particular patterns of industrial relations and trade union action and behaviour under pluralist political and social systems.

Clegg's thesis of pluralism

Clearly no account of Hugh Clegg's contribution to trade union theory could afford to ignore his influential defence of pluralism both as a diagnostic tool for the analysis of industrial relations and also as a prescription for the *modus operandi* of trade unions in the modern nation state and in their relationships with managements.[6] It was admittedly not until 1975 that Clegg's case for pluralism was set out in any detail, but certain of the critical assumptions had been deployed much earlier in his *New Approach to Industrial Democracy*, where, it will be recalled, he emphasized the significance of trade unions operating as oppositional institutions rather than being involved directly in participation in the overall planning or day-to-day management of the enterprise itself.[7]

What were the central propositions of pluralism in Clegg's general conception? These may be summarized as follows: first, that pluralism emerged as 'a criticism of the political doctrine of sovereignty'; second, that it was based on a process of concession and compromise; third, that it encompassed a body of rules (laws and customs) which ensure freedom of operation of interest-groups and a restraint on the abuse of power; fourth, that there was a *moral* imperative i.e. a duty to compromise in a way which 'necessarily overrides' a group's aims and interests; fifth, no *equality* of power between bargaining partners, however, was assumed; and sixth, pre-conditions for the successful operation of a pluralist industrial relations system included an adequate material base to enable all parties to accomplish some gains, and certain limitations at least on the powers of intervention by the state.[8]

In the light of our previous discussions, however, two further inferences are worth developing from Clegg's overall thesis of pluralism. First, it is clear that for Clegg, the critical ethical and moral underpinnings of pluralism — which sustain a semblance of social order and prevent irredeemable breakdown of the industrial relations system — comprise neither value-consensus nor normative integration but rather the willingness to make compromises and concessions.[9] In one sense, therefore, pluralism is about means rather than overall objectives although these means, in their turn, are viewed as conducive to liberty and a checkweight to the ubiquity of any 'monolithic and monotonous creed'.[10] Second, although Clegg was to emphasize the significance of ethics and morals (rather than ideologies) in his interpretation of pluralism and was to stress their significance in preventing the escalation of conflict towards a state of social disintegration and breakdown, by the same token, he insisted that pluralism was not a 'complete moral philosophy'.[11] After all, to make sense, its essential ethics required that 'men also respect other moral imperatives besides those of pluralism', such as those embraced by conservatism, socialism, liberalism, Christian democracy and so on.[12]

> This is the paradox of pluralism as a moral doctrine. Its aim is to combine social stability with adaptability and freedom; its means is compromise; but it can only give moral authority to the rules of compromise if it allows the validity of other moral values which may clash with these rules; and, if they do clash, social stability is at risk.

Interestingly enough, however, Clegg himself has recently recorded a number of doubts about the utility of pluralism for *explaining* trade union 'behaviour'. Hence, in *The Changing System of Industrial Relations in Great Britain* Clegg initially sketched out a number of affinities between pluralism and Marxism in so far as the analysis of industrial relations was concerned. In detail, these included the focus upon conflict *and* stability, upon the inevitability of conflict in industrial relations and hence the associated problem of explaining why modern societies have not been destroyed, and upon integration through the administration of agreements and the institutionalization of collective bargaining.[13] But although, like Marxism, pluralism operates on a high level of generality, advocates here claim only to be able to account for patterns of industrial relations operating in plural societies and this is a major source of analytical difference between the two approaches.[14] Yet, as Clegg has admitted, such general qualities in the theory also tend to invalidate its utility in explaining satisfactorily, say, why workplace bargaining has proved to be so important in the British context, and from there he went on to observe that students of industrial relations may well make 'more progress by concentrating on the relative cogency of various answers to questions in industrial relations than by trying to deduce Marxian or pluralist answers'.[15] As a corollary, as we shall observe, in so far as the explanation for trade union behaviour is concerned, *Trade Unionism Under Collective Bargaining*, rather than the theory of pluralism, must be classed as Clegg's most significant and enduring contribution to theorizing about trade unions.[16]

The radical pluralism of Fox

Clegg's conception of pluralism was ultimately based upon those political science assumptions in which democracy has been defined in terms of institutional opposition rather than of the participation of the majority in the principal organs of administration and government. As such, therefore, its analytical roots were different from Fox's version of 'radical pluralism', which reflected far more closely Durkheimian and Marxian assumptions (on the conditions of the forced division of labour and of class-based inequality respectively).[17] Indeed, Fox has recently clarified his position in his comments on the Wood-Elliott paper[18] by emphasizing the significance of pluralism in the cultural sense of providing an underpinning for individual liberty and for freedom of association and expression. Equally, he stressed his commitment to a 'root and branch' change in the underlying economic and social structure as indispensible for accomplishment of the substantive objectives of pluralism (i.e., justice) rather than merely of its procedural and institutional rituals.[19]

Fox's familiar distinction between 'unitary' and 'pluralist' conceptions of the industrial enterprise (the first admitting only one source of legitimate authority; the second accommodating the possibility of diverse interest-groups or 'stakeholders') that had appeared both in his Royal Commission paper[20] and in *A Sociology of Work in Industry*[21] may be originally traced to the thesis of Ross who argued that 'a theoretical approach to management which treats the firm as a plural society rather than as *the* organic unity' was an essential contribution to enlightenment on labour issues.[22] Yet following his successful 'popularization' of this distinction, in 'Industrial Relations: A Social Critique of the Pluralist Ideology',[23] *Beyond Contract*,[24] and *Man Mismanagement*,[25] a radical perspective of the business enterprise was counterpoised to pluralism and here, as Wood and Elliott have observed, 'the need for a restructuring of social relations and institutions *outside* as well as *inside* the factory' was fully countenanced.[26] To be sure, the radical approach had certain affinities with traditional versions of pluralism in that diverse interests continued to be identified but, as Fox insisted, 'unlike the pluralist, the radical does not see collective organisation of employees into trade unions as restoring a balance of power (or anything approaching it) between the propertied and the propertyless.'[27] Moreover, in Fox's view, such disparities in power were reflected in the kinds of issue focused upon in management-union conflict, 'socialization' via the propagation of 'values of wealth, position and status' in public communications, the recognition by subordinate groupings of major problems which could arise from the mobilization of oppositional power, the general cynicism and mistrust which abounds in industry, and a consequent lack of moral commitment to 'jointly agreed' negotiated settlements.[28]

This is all familiar enough but, in theoretical terms, the critical issues which arise here would appear to be embraced by the following central questions. First, what conditions were identified that encourage the development (in actual and in conceptual terms) of unitary or pluralist models of trade unionism and industrial relations? Second, in what circumstances do radical forms of social imagery emerge? And third, what are the grounds for assuming that radical solutions would actually produce higher levels of social integration in the long-term rather than other widely canvassed solutions to the problems of anomie (including the institutional approaches of *liberal*-pluralists)?

Yet these central theoretical concerns are by no means easy to settle on the bases of the discussions which have predominated so far in debates about pluralism. Indeed, as Fox has insisted 'pluralism is a complex concept and much work remains to be done with respect to its use in industrial relations practice and theory as indeed with respect to the "radical critique" and the relationship between the two.'[29] But, although the following distinctions in many ways reflect personal predilections, we have endeavoured to piece together an account of principal 'causative' influences which have appeared in Fox's work, by focusing upon the interrelationship between three principal sets of explanatory variables which encompass: (i) structural movements in modern industrial societies; (ii) 'subjective' predispositions and institutional factors; and (iii) the distribution of power.[30]

Structural movements in modern industrial societies

At a structural level of explanation, Fox has generally deployed Durkheimian and Marxian categories of analysis: first, to diagnose an 'immense asymmetry' in power relations between management and union;[31] and second, to identify certain underlying economic and technical changes which facilitate, say, union recognition and hence a gradual shift in managerial 'ideologies' from unitary to pluralistic forms.[32] In the first respect, then, Fox has frequently reaffirmed his interpretation of fundamental inequalities in British society which, in his view, are undergirded by contemporary social institutions (including collective bargaining).[33] But, in *Beyond Contract*, he went somewhat further by seeking to explain certain adaptations in conceptions of authority in the enterprise in economic movements (pointing, for example, to the likelihood of union recognition in keenly competitive markets where disputes could prove fatal to the organization).[34]

Subjective 'predispositions' and institutional factors

None the less, in his discussion of 'high trust roles and relationships', Fox also made it clear that economic and technical movements on their own could not effect such changes in the workplace; but rather insisted that 'a matching shift in institutions and ideology' was also a prerequisite.[35] Indeed, at several points in *Beyond Contract* Fox was to emphasize the saliency of social action categories for interpreting changes in orientations about work relationships. Moreover, these could also help to illuminate a wide range of possible outcomes and to explain, for example, why low discretionary roles did not always lead to low trust relations. After all, in Fox's view, a series of 'mediating frames of reference, ideologies and aspirations' were also critical elements in the overall equation.[36]

By the same token processes of institutionalization within trade unions could also be regarded as of fundamental significance in explaining why the membership did not always pass from a *pluralist* conception (presumably a necessary accompaniment of unionization in the first place) to more *radical* interpretations.[37] Certainly Fox was to emphasize the constraints of institutional pressures upon horizons by observing that new recruits into unions were frequently socialized into ideas of what to expect 'from their work and their life' and hence to eschew notions of 'a search for emancipation and alienation and for intrinsic meaning from work' and the desire for equality.[38] Of course, as they stand, these observations present a number of hypotheses which require more elaborate and rigorous empirical support if they are ultimately to be sustained as coterminous with trade union action and behaviour. But at least they provide certain tentative answers to the major explanatory questions raised about the conditions in which different perspectives are elaborated and begin to assume a measure of generality across different groups among the employed workforce.

In Fox's account, too, obstacles to the development of a radical perspective also included the point of Flanders about the interests which management and union officials developed in institutions of a pluralist character as a consequence of their own commitments to and participation in rule-making procedures and administration.[39] And yet, at the same time, there were powerful forces operating in favour of more radical solutions since, in Fox's view, such changes could well prove necessary as a means for stability, in the long-term, if the revolution of rising expectations and the problems of inflation and economic recession have no obvious solution under the aegis of existing pluralist institutions.[40] Yet even if Wood and Elliott have overstated their case in emphasizing that 'a more radical analysis of society . . . performs exactly the same legitimizing function of the pluralist ideology', there is force in their argument that an exacerbation of industrial conflict, on a quite substantial scale, could accompany genuine radical initiatives.[41] Hence, rather than producing a lasting solution to the problems of anomie, a very different and far from integrative outcome would appear to be more plausible.[42]

> a cursory survey of the current industrial scene suggests that the transition to a modified form of pluralism, where the range of bargaining is extended to wider issues of economic regulation, will be no smoother than the earlier transition (as yet still incomplete) from the limited form of pluralism which acknowledged collective bargaining over wages as legitimate but rejected bargaining on issues of what Flanders and others have called managerial regulation. Managerial resistance to extensions of pluralist bargaining to the area of corporate economic policy is reflected in the voiced hostility of so many managers and management bodies (not to mention City institutions) both to the concept of planning agreements and to the introduction of industrial democracy legislation providing for parity trade union representation on company boards.

The distribution of power

Turning more specifically, then, to the problems of power, Fox has of course acknowledged that its very imbalance constituted a major preventative of shifts in a radical direction. Hence, in his view, the very power of owners and controllers 'affords them facilities for creating and maintaining social attitudes and values favourable to that acceptance'.[43] Thus, although rising expectations, the denial of legitimacy to existing procedures, and increasing consciousness of material disprivilege (occasioned, in part, by a communications revolution which has widened reference groups) could all be construed as insistent pressures towards the furtherance of radical perspectives and the adoption of radical solutions to dislocation in society.[44] In practice these may well be held in check not just by 'structural' and 'subjective' exigencies but by the very disparities in bargaining power which obtain between the different social classes in the first place.

The crucial differences, then, in the versions of pluralism of Clegg and

Fox represent substantial variations in analytical perspective based on diverse conceptions of justice and liberty (the one couched in oppositional analogies and the other in social structural conditions), inconsistent evaluations of the working of pluralist institutions, dissimilar interpretations of the sources, locus and distribution of power, and divergent solutions to Britain's industrial relations problems. Yet on theoretical counts, both analyses so far have not come to grips sufficiently with the problem of identifying those conditions which give rise to different institutional structures, to the heterogeneous 'ideologies' in union-management relations, and to the likelihood or otherwise of particular programmes of action accomplishing their envisaged objectives. To be sure, given the high levels of generality involved here it is of course extremely difficult to formulate rigorous analytical models and to specify precisely the *potentially* relevant variables let alone to work out adequate procedures for testing hypothesized relationships. Hence, in view of these problems, it is not surprising that, from a theoretical standpoint, arguably the most satisfactory contributions from the Oxford school have been more specific in compass and have related not so much to pluralism as such as to job regulation and to the main dimensions of trade union 'behaviour' itself.

JOB REGULATION, COLLECTIVE BARGAINING AND THE 'DETERMINANTS' OF UNION BEHAVIOUR

In referring to Britain's predominant patterns of industrial relations Allan Flanders once observed that 'the first leading principle is one that our traditional system shares with many other national systems of advanced industrial countries which are pluralist societies. *A priority is accorded to collective bargaining over other methods of external job regulations.*'[45] Since that time, however, there have been a number of attempts to examine the precise meaning of job regulation and its relationship with collective bargaining and more explicitly to demonstrate the effects of the latter in 'determining' trade union 'behaviour'. In our review of principal developments and criticisms of the Oxford school, therefore, the arguments will continue in this section by focusing upon three main areas of concern: (a) the debates on the meaning of job regulation and its appropriateness in defining the scope of trade union purpose; (b) the relationship between job regulation and collective bargaining in which Fox's defence of the Webbs will be examined; and (c) the principal explanatory arguments in *Trade Unionism Under Collective Bargaining* which, as we have emphasized, comprise Clegg's most important single contribution to trade union theory.

Job regulation and union purpose

The focus upon job regulation as the primary objective of trade unionism and as defining the scope of industrial relations would appear to span a number of diverse contributions to labour theory. For Durkheim, rule-making processes were obvious manifestations of normative constraints upon action and were to be located ultimately not only in dominant ethical and moral premises in modern social orders, but also in their juxtaposition with ongoing evolutionary changes in the division of labour.[46] The Webbs, also, in their wide-ranging investigation of trade unionism sought to establish how the extension of the 'device of the common rule' was axiomatic to union purpose, to the advance of working people's interests and to the growth of the democratic current which they regarded as fundamental in advanced industrial societies.[47] Amongst recent writers, too, Bain and Clegg[48] have both supported the essential foundations of Flanders's position on the salience of regulation, while the parallel concentration upon rules in the industrial relations system amongst structural-functionalists developed in chapter 2 should also be mentioned.[49] Again, even amongst Marxist scholars who have sought to extend such a conception in order to encompass the broader question of control, there are still certain similarities in overall focus. Hyman, for example, has acknowledged that, despite his disagreement with Flanders's notion of institutions of job regulation, certain aspects of the overall approach are unassailable since 'rules of various kinds clearly do pervade the world of work and employment, and the institutions which devise and implement this network of rules are of critical importance for the study of industrial relations.'[50]

Naturally enough, the opponents of the focus upon 'job regulation' have concentrated upon several issues which were examined when the objections to the structural-functionalist position were explored in our second chapter. Yet in the context of the rather different theoretical premises of the Oxford school it is worth evaluating briefly the main points of contention and, in particular, stipulating the primary considerations deployed by Clegg in his recent defence of this approach.[51]

Hyman has summarized the principal objections to the definition of union purpose and of the subject of industrial relations in terms of job regulation as the concentration on stability and regularity, on conflict containment and not on processes through which conflict may be generated, on procedural issues which fail to accommodate questions of ownership and control, on the problem of order, on the self-correcting nature of conflict, and on an inadequate account of the structural basis of disagreements.[52] Yet, as was observed in the various modifications and refinements of the system approach in which similar criticisms had been considered, these objections may not refer so much to a focus upon rule-making as such as upon particular usages (or interpretations of these) in the available literature.

After all, there is no question that the pluralist frameworks in which rule-making processes have generally been conceived were originally founded precisely to accommodate conflicts of interest, and although it may be the case that only radical versions have really come to grips with wider questions of ownership and control, the assumption of self-correcting mechanisms by no means reflects the arguments of prominent pluralists. Indeed, as Clegg has observed, even though the definition of industrial relations in terms of the study of processes of control over work relations may be more general than job regulation (if less elegant and precise) there are still no obvious reasons why attention should be directed 'away from the structure of power and interests and the economic, technological and political dynamics of the broader society'.[53] Again, it should be reiterated that concern over problems of order reflects the assumption of the ubiquity of conflict and not of cohesion which, for the pluralist, can be accomplished only by a constant improvement and updating of existing institutions in the light of changing environmental circumstances and a willingness to persevere in making compromises and concessions.

Job regulation and collective bargaining

Allan Flanders, it will be recalled, preferred the term job regulation to collective bargaining on the grounds that, though he regarded bargaining relationships as basically economic in character, improvements in wages and working conditions, control over the work environment and so on were ultimately to be understood as means towards the accomplishment of the higher order political and social objectives of trade unionism.[54] Yet, in his major defence of the Webbs, Fox took issue with Flanders on this question, and hence, on account of its centrality to the concerns of the forerunners of the Oxford school, the main themes which were raised in this celebrated paper should be examined at this point.[55]

That the principal roots of the Oxford school are to be discerned far more readily in Durkheimian epistemology and in the classical scholarship of the Webbs rather than in Parsonian or Dunlopian models may be recognized particularly clearly in Fox's writings. Hence, although Fox was to accept Flanders's objections to the Webbs' analysis on three main counts (the inadequate treatment of the transition to collective bargaining from other modes of job regulation, the failure to accommodate the role of non-economic factors in actual bargaining processes and the omission of the 'whole question and nature of the employer interest in joint regulation'),[56] on all other issues he insisted that the Webbs' account could withstand Flanders's critique and, in so doing, he was further to under-score the contemporary significance of Britain's most eminent labour historians.[57]

None the less, it should be emphasized that on the most crucial point of his disagreement with Flanders, Fox in some respects carried the essential case of the latter to its logical conclusions by noting that *all* forms of bargaining are by no means exclusively economic but also entail a power relationship.[58] And, as a consequence, as Fox argued, collective bargaining *could* be reasonably construed as the collective equivalent of individual bargaining and that the precise difference lay not in a different emphasis on economic or political objectives respectively but was precisely 'what the Webbs said it was — a difference in the disparity of power'.[59]

Moreover, in Fox's view, a corollary of the similarity between indivi-dual and collective bargaining was that the differences between strike action and an individual refusing to work were more matters of 'contin-gency rather than of principle', while the two methods of bargaining could quite easily coexist with the former merely setting 'a minimum floor to terms and conditions of employment on which employers and employees, individuals or groups, are free to improve'.[60] By the same token, as Fox reasonably pointed out, the Webbs' conception of unions was far from that of a labour cartel (or selling agency), for, as we have seen, they clearly preferred the device of the common rule to restriction of numbers and this, in turn, 'embodied the Utilitarian thrust towards "clearing the markets" of all particularistic obstructions while at the same time protect-ing society, industry, and the worker from the destructive effects of *unregulated* competition.'[61]

To reinforce the view of the ramifications of the Webbs' influence upon modern trade union theory, Fox also emphasized the familiar point that the 'notion of regulation was central to the Webbs' conception of union functions'.[62] That is to say, rather than confining their notion of collective bargaining to economic purposes, the Webbs were also fully cognizant of its wider significance in securing a system of 'industrial jurisprudence' and in facilitating 'a fuller and richer concept of man'.[63] Finally, Fox was to argue that, although for Flanders trade unions were clearly not solely bargaining agents, the problems of essentialist definitions of union pur-poses (or what Fox termed a 'one factor theory') were clearly manifest here since insufficient account was taken of the role of the perceptions of members themselves in shaping the overall character of their associations:[64]

> Certainly the trade union is not *only* a bargaining agent. It offers its
> members a variety of services which fall outside that description, and

it plays a role in the political and social fabric which is also quite different in nature. . . . But . . . it is as a bargaining agent that the union finds its major justification in the eyes of its members and that issues relating to financial reward are still, whether for material or symbolic reasons or both, among its major bargaining preoccupations.

Trade unionism under collective bargaining

None the less, the dialogue between Flanders and Fox on the theoretical conceptions of the Webbs is of interest largely in terms of establishing the analytical background and assumptions of contemporary approaches to trade unionism rather than in illuminating the relationship between key phenomena in collective bargaining and union behaviour respectively. By far the most significant *explanatory* contribution has been Clegg's *Trade Unionism Under Collective Bargaining*, in which, while the substantial debt to Allan Flanders was acknowledged, there was at least to be a far more precise specification of the principal influences upon actual trade union 'behaviour'.[65] Moreover, for Clegg collective bargaining was identified as 'the "main", "major", "foremost" or "principal" determinant of union behaviour at least in those countries in which it was the predominant mode of job regulation'.[66]

For the nineteenth century, as Clegg observed, the Webbs and Turner developed adequate explanations by beginning with 'the general hypothesis that *the methods by which trade unions regulate* the terms of employment of their members were 'the foremost influences on other aspects of their behaviour'.[67] But with the demise particularly of unilateral regulation, this could no longer form the basis for an adequate contemporary theory which, in Clegg's view, should begin rather from an analysis of collective bargaining itself.[68]

But the variations in collective bargaining that were held to be the principal determinants of union behaviour were in turn interpreted in terms of complex changes in the dimensions of its overall *structure*.[69] The main relationships in Clegg's theory have been summarized in diagrammatic form in Figure 4.1 and these embraced the *extent of bargaining* (the proportion of employees covered by collective agreements), the *depth of bargaining* (the involvement or otherwise of union officers), *union security* (the support by employers and government), *level of bargaining* (plant, district, national and so on), the *degree of control over collective agreements* (obligatory standards and machinery for enforcement), the *scope of agreements* (the number of aspects of employment covered), and *union structure* (coverage by unions of industries and grades of

Figure 4.1   *Dimensions of collective bargaining structure, origins and union behaviour*

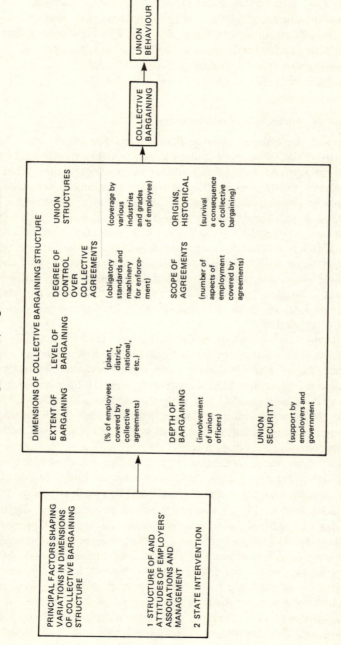

employee).[70] Furthermore, while in Clegg's assessment the origins of the dimensions of collective bargaining structure could only be determined by means of historical analysis, their persistence of course depended upon the effects of this mode of regulation itself.[71] And finally, the principal factors shaping variations in dimensions of collective bargaining structure were envisaged as: first, the structure and attitudes of employers' associations and management; and second, state intervention.[72]

But if this was the general model, then, of course, particular aspects of union behaviour could depend upon the operation of different combinations of the main dimensions in specific cases. Moreover, Clegg undertook a comparative review of patterns in six countries (Australia, France, Sweden, the UK, the USA and West Germany) in order to establish explanations for *union density, union structure, union government, workplace organization, strikes, industrial democracy* and *political action, employers* and the *state*.[73] In each instance under review the precise configuration of influences varied considerably but the method of Blain and Gennard[74] which was deployed in chapter 2 (of expressing in simple algebraic terms the central independent and dependent variables) may also be developed in this context to clarify the main relationships.

Taking first, then, trade union density, Clegg was able to demonstrate its critical dependence upon the interaction of the *extent* and *depth* of collective bargaining and upon the support, in given national contexts, for union *security*:[75]

A theory of trade union density

(1) $D = f(e, d, s)$

where D = trade union density
  e = the extent of bargaining
  d = the depth of bargaining
  s = union security.

Moreover, as may be observed in Figure 4.1, Clegg related the principal differences in the extent and depth of bargaining and of union security to three major additional influences: the attitudes of employers and managers to collective bargaining; the attitudes of trade unions to collective bargaining; and government pressure on employers to recognize trade unions.[76]

Other sets of forces were identified, however, in the outline of the theory of trade union structure. Indeed, an historical dimension was incorporated to accommodate *technology* and *industrial organization* (at the time of birth and growth of given unions), and *the methods of union regulation* employed in different epochs (collective bargaining, unilateral regulation and so on). But, in addition, union ideologies (e.g., in industrial-type unions), government pressure to secure recognition, the attitudes of unionists themselves (white-collar unionists perceive their interests as separate from those of manual workers and hence prefer their own occupational associations) were also delineated as major determinants of union structure:[77]

A theory of trade union structure

(2)   S   =   f (t, o, r, i, g, u)
where S   =   union structure
       t   =   technology (at time of birth and growth of a union)
       o   =   industrial organization (at time of birth and growth of a union)
       r   =   methods of union regulation
       i   =   ideologies
       g   =   government and employer pressure to recognize unions
       u   =   unionists' attitudes and relations with government.

The significance of *level of bargaining*, however, appeared of particular relevance for the theories of union government and workplace organization respectively. Above all, then, the level at which agreements are generally concluded would appear to be associated with the internal mode of distribution of *union power*. Thus, for example, in Great Britain, where this is typically decentralized, oppositional forms of union democracy are commensurately encouraged:[78]

Theories of union government and workplace organization

(3)   G   =   f (l)
(4)   W   =   f (l)
where G   =   union government
       W   =   workplace organization
       l   =   level of bargaining.

But the level of bargaining was also perceived as being in large measure a reflection of the *structure* of management and employers' associations; while subsidiary explanations for patterns of union government included *union constitutions* and *methods of administration* (especially formal organizational procedures).[79]

In Clegg's conception, strikes, too, were related to the level of bargaining, although procedures for handling disputes, economic variables and changing relations between unions and government were also of significance.[80] Similarly, industrial democracy was also seen to depend in part upon level of bargaining, although the existence of collective bargaining machinery itself tended to ensure that a single channel of representation would be the principal mode of employee representation.[81] Moreover, when collective bargaining institutions were firmly established then, *pari passu*, the role of the state and the legislature would be correspondingly circumscribed:[82]

Theories of strikes, industrial democracy and of political action, employers and the state

(5) $\quad$ St $\quad = \quad f(l, p, ec, u)$
(6) $\quad$ I $\quad = \quad f(l, c)$
(7) $\quad$ L $\quad = \quad f(c)$

where St $\quad = \quad$ strikes
$\quad$ I $\quad = \quad$ industrial democracy
$\quad$ L $\quad = \quad$ legislative influence on industrial relations
$\quad$ p $\quad = \quad$ procedures of handling disputes
$\quad$ ec $\quad = \quad$ economic variables
$\quad$ c $\quad = \quad$ collective bargaining.

Clegg's explanations for variations in union behaviour must be regarded, therefore, as an elaborate and in many respects original development of earlier work by Flanders and the Webbs rather than a minor modification or refinement of their central canons. After all, although the emphasis upon collective bargaining and job regulation remains paramount, the central propositions of an explanatory model have now been tested on an international basis, historical dimensions have been incorporated, and the extensive changes of the twentieth century (such as the implications of the growth of white-collar unionism for union structure) have also featured prominently. Moreover, as against Dunlop, there are no obvious handicaps of teleology, of comparative statics and of a level of generalization (in industrial relations systems) which would appear to militate against the identification of specific dimensions and against the attachment of appropriate weightings to each influence upon 'behaviour'.

Notwithstanding these major advantages of Clegg's explanatory approach, there remain however two important problems in so far as the genesis of a satisfactory model of trade unionism is concerned. The first and most crucial, as Warner has argued, is that bargaining structures and processes are in many respects best regarded as *intervening* variables between a series of wider influences (cultural, structural and so on) and trade union attitudes and behaviour.[83] That is to say, although in one sense the specific nature of Clegg's approach enables a penetrating analysis of the influence of different dimensions of collective bargaining structure, these are seldom placed against a broader theoretical canvas in which the operation of strategic movements in modern industrial societies are also fully acknowledged. Second, the term action is far preferable to behaviour here since this involves due recognition of the creative role of the main parties in industrial relations (union members, representatives and officials; employers and their organizations; and the state and the legislature) in shaping both collective bargaining institutions and actual behaviour within the constraints of a wider set of environmental exigencies.[84]

INSTITUTIONS: DESCRIPTION AND EXPLANATION

A focus upon *institutions* of job regulation was the unmistakable hallmark of the earliest studies of the Oxford school,[85] and of course such a *modus operandi* has frequently been the source of major dissension on the grounds that it tends to deflect the analyst's attention away from informal processes in union-management relations towards formal mechanisms and procedures and from explanatory studies towards primarily descriptive researches. Yet how far, it may be reasonably asked, are such criticisms of the Oxford school valid and to what extent does a concentration upon institutions lead inevitably to such consequences?

The first question has been addressed in some detail by Clegg in *The Changing System* where the argument was forcefully deployed that the notion of institutions need in no way signify *formal* to the neglect of *informal* organizations.[86] After all, Allan Flanders covered both such types in his *Fawley Productivity Agreements*.[87] Again, although it is apparent that *processes* as well as institutional *structures* should be examined in any comprehensive account of the workings of trade unions, equally the term 'institutions and processes of job regulation' embraces both these contingencies.[88] Indeed, as has been mentioned, a more radical solution was even entertained:[89]

> Job regulation cannot be studied in the abstract. It must be observed embodied in institutions and operating through processes. Consequently, the student of job regulation must study both institutions and processes. Nothing therefore is lost if Flanders' definition is reduced to two words — 'job regulation'; and any limitation implied by the word 'institutions' is thereby removed.

Clegg was of course to acknowledge that the causes of disagreement and conflict must be examined as well as the institutional processes through which these are handled to restore stability; but, in his view, any one-sided emphasis reflected a lack of 'comprehension' of the meaning of institutions rather than deriving in any obvious way from the essential rubric of the definition itself.[90]

In sum, therefore, it is clear that in whatever ways the concept of institutions was deployed in the early analyses of the Oxford school, the current emphasis is to encompass informal processes of union activity at workplace level as well as change and conflict. What is more, the importance of institutions as a source of *explanatory hypotheses* can be easily overlooked despite their significance in embodying *past* and *historical influences* which are crucial in transmitting basic *traditions* of handling disputes or approaching conflict situations, and through *processes* of socialization of the membership into defined roles, in ensuring that present practices in some measure reflect structures which were originally established at strategic phases of institution-building themselves. To be sure, the processes of institutionalization are also dynamic. Indeed, if we are referring here to important social phenomena which embrace value patterns and norms as well as distinctive structures, then, as Eisenstadt has also emphasized, institutionalization must be regarded as 'a process of continuous crystallization of different types of norms, organizations and frameworks' and 'the possibility of innovation and change . . . is given in the very nature of the processes of institutionalization and in the workings of institutional systems.'[91] This is not to deny, then, that once institutions become formal they tend to accommodate personnel with vested interests in the institution's survival or that established procedures and conditions for action tend to emerge, but if a term bearing any relationship whatsoever to the industrial context is to be employed, then it is clear that processes of change and conflict, as well as the possibility of institutions emanating from a variety of starting points, must all be encapsulated in the definition and in the subsequent use of these key concepts. Yet given these provisos, the complex patterns of tradition and change which are reflected in institutional structure and process may be deployed as significant explanatory dimensions of trade union attitudes and behaviour.

Furthermore, by means of historical analysis, it is possible to reconstruct the principal explanatory influences upon crucial periods of institutional growth and innovation and hence to observe the extent to which fundamental patterns shaped in the past continue to have an effect, say, upon current practice and procedure and the types of substantive issues which are raised in union-management bargaining. Indeed, a particularly fruitful approach along these lines has been that of Sorge who not only recognized the dynamic aspects of institutions and hence the considerable 'range of choice' (either for subjective reasons (the interpretation of actors) or more objectively (though changes in societal structures)) which obtains in institutional behaviour but also noted the importance of traditions which were established during the process of institutional construction.[92]

Observing, then, the inadequacies of structural-functionalist approaches in this regard on account of their failure to provide a realistic account 'of diversity and unity of institutions and functions', a non-tautological explanation of different patterns of institutional evolution, and a 'diversified but non-contradictory conception of rationality and functionality', Sorge suggested that the obvious solution to this dilemma was to develop a 'step-wise' historically informed mode of inquiry.[93] Moreover, in this conception, the development of institutions and of distinctive institutional patterns reflects the selection by social actors of a particular solution to emergent problems within 'the constraints on rationality' operating at the time when decisions were made. And, of course, since circumstances at such points of innovation and the perspectives of leading actors may vary historically and temporally, this in turn facilitates explanation of the variety of institutional types which ultimately emerge. Such historically-informed analyses of means-end relationships derived ultimately from Weberian scholarship, although, in Sorge's interpretation, rather than identifying the increasing dominance of *instrumental* rationality, he noted the possibility of a growing 'functional autonomy' of values and institutions in modern society, a view which has certain affinities with modern pluralist conceptions.[94] And certainly, this process of the increasing autonomy of intermediate organizations in modern society has provided for the creation of new values and the continuing *possibility* of value-rationality rather than instrumental-rationality in institutional structures and in the action of members.[95]

If the institutional approach, then, is refined to accommodate historically-informed analyses based upon action categories many of the problems of static descriptive accounts, and of reification through the use of terms such as 'institutional needs', would seem to be removed. Indeed, in this context, it is worth mentioning that even writers like Lester, whose work on the 'maturation' of union purposes through institutionalization has been the subject of much justified criticism, still focused largely not upon 'immanent' system properties or 'inevitable' processes of change in advanced industrial societies, but viewed such adaptations as consequential rather upon a decline in militancy, a concentration of power and control in the centre of unions, and the attitudes of union leaders.[96] Hence, although in the early writings of the Oxford school in particular, references to 'institutional needs' were not uncommon and an overly descriptive and excessively formal analysis of institutions was evident, refinements both by advocates of this approach to trade unionism and by subsequent theorists have now provided the basis for an explanatory account in which traditional forces (deriving initially from *actions* at strategic points in institutional building) coupled with those dynamic processes which are essential components of the structure of institutions may both be accommodated.

5 Social inequality and trade union behaviour

> There is no royal road to science, and only those who do not dread the fatiguing climb of its steep paths have a chance of gaining its luminous summits.[1]

The formulation of integrated models of trade unionism has been the product of painstaking upward ascent which is reflected in an undoubtedly sporadic pattern of overall progress. On the face of it, this would appear to run counter to that cumulative quality of research which typifies the acquisition of knowledge in the natural sciences, although, of course, even in these disciplines, fundamental 'paradigm shifts' have almost invariably punctuated the more mundane accomplishments which would seem symbolic of day-to-day advance. Thus, as Norbert Elias cogently argued, in[2]

> general terms, one might say it is characteristic of . . . scientific as distinct from non-scientific forms of solving problems that, in the acquisition of knowledge, questions emerge and are solved as a result of an uninterrupted two-way traffic between two layers of knowledge: that of general ideas, theories or models and that of observations and perceptions of specific events.

But, at times in the social sciences, an excessive striving after critical effect has often served merely to truncate a number of promising points of departure.

In this chapter, therefore, two main objectives will be uppermost. First, we shall proceed with our account of the genesis of modern trade union thought by considering the work of Weber and Marx and the contribution of each to the debates on the relationship between social inequality and trade unionism (once a *cause célèbre* between sociologists and industrial relations scholars). And second, with a view to establishing an essential pillar of modern trade union analysis we shall attempt to demonstrate that the *concept of power* may be deployed to integrate disparate departures which otherwise would appear to be based on irreconcilable maxims and premises.

The original traditions of labour theory were founded upon moral and ethical, revolutionary, defensive or conservative, economic and political premises and these served to cement transparent bonds and lines of filiation between classical and modern conceptions. For instance, the differing weights currently attached to 'organizational', 'external environmental' and 'subjective' variables closely parallel the deliberations in the nineteenth and early twentieth centuries between members of the 'administrative' or 'structuralist' school and their erstwhile colleagues with a commitment to more 'idealist' forms of interpretation. Yet conceptual rigour was not a noticeable strength of the first accounts (systems analysis and the contribution, in the 1970s, of liberal pluralists were thus markedly superior on this count). For it had clearly awaited the penetration of discipline-based assumptions (above all, from classical sociology) to attain the next transformations, which, by degrees, were gradually to alter the dominant propositions in general currency in theory and method themselves.

The concept of power featured prominently, of course, in the writings of the 'political school' and surfaced, from time to time, in the deliberations of 'conservative' and 'revolutionary' scholars, although in these latter cases the purposes of control over the job environment were viewed in sharply contrasting terms.[3] In sociological scholarship, too, power was axiomatic to the Weberian conception of social inequality (class, status and party were thus phenomena of the distribution of power),[4] while, particularly in modern Marxist accounts of trade unionism, an increasing accent upon processes of power and control over production relationships has been in evidence.[5] Contrary to certain impressions, power was also a prominent variable in sociological accounts of trade unionism (not least in the works of Goldthorpe[6] and Prandy[7]), while Goldthorpe and Lockwood viewed traditional proletarian forms of social imagery (in which union solidarism loomed large) as reflections of a 'power model' of society.[8] Meanwhile, in modern accounts by industrial sociologists problems of theory and measurement of power in management-union relationships have been a major concern (see e.g., Abell,[9] Bowen,[10] Edwards,[11] and Martin[12]). Similarly, despite the occasional hostility to industrial sociological approaches, as we saw in the previous chapter, power has been significant in the writings of modern industrial relations theorists, while of course, Fox's work straddles the two approaches.[13] Hyman has viewed the very definition of industrial relations in terms of processes of *control* over work relationships.[14] Finally, while rejecting the argument that social stratification has been of prime importance in shaping union growth and character (at least at the 'aggregative' level), Bain, Coates and Ellis were still to insist that 'if power is seen to stratify society into groups, then the way is open for a reconsideration of the relationship between social stratification and trade unionism.'[15]

Turning more specifically to examine the connection between power, social inequality and trade unionism involves abstraction from a broad ranging literature which presents many obstacles to lucid and coherent summary. But without too artificial a constriction on the subject, three main concerns may be isolated for examination: first, the general theoretical exposition of the concept of power and its links with 'class, status and party' and with trade unionism; second, the explanatory significance of power in bargaining; and third, 'resource' approaches to power and their reflection in harmonious and conflictual models of enterprise decision-making.

POWER AND TRADE UNIONISM: GENERAL THEMES AND APPROACHES

The main theme of this chapter will be that, *at least in so far as their relationship with trade unionism is concerned*, the various sources of social inequality in modern society may be most appropriately viewed as being occasioned by the distribution of power (at societal, institutional, work-place and workgroup levels). In order to establish this thesis, we shall focus on the following major points at issue: (a) Weber, Marx and social inequality; (b) inequality, social imagery and trade unionism; and (c) trade unionism, social inequality and 'the radical school'.

Weber, Marx and social inequality

On one view, to highlight the problem of control rather than order in union-management relationships is to operate quintessentially from the central maxims of Weberian rather than Marxian theory. Certainly the understanding that power is the substantive means by which society is stratified (and which, in turn, makes intelligible a wide range of workplace behaviour and action) is a direct reflection of the Weberian notion in which 'the distribution of power within a community' has decisive explanatory significance for 'class', 'status', and 'party' formation.[16] In conventional accounts, however, it has been the general opinion that Marx and Weber *both* defined social classes in terms of market situation,[17] although in actuality each acknowledged the importance of power for the phenomenon under review.[18] Indeed, while Weber argued that there were three underlying aspects of market situation (a common specific 'causal component' of life chances, represented in economic interests and *under conditions of commodity in labour markets*); equally, class situation was to be understood as being ultimately determined 'by the amount and kind of power, or lack of such, to dispose of goods and skills for the sake of income in a given economic order'.[19] Moreover, in Weber's conception, power itself did not necessarily derive from economic structures — on the contrary, 'the emergence of economic power may be the consequence of power existing on other grounds'.[20]

In recent Marxist expositions on industrial relations, the issues of control and power have also assumed a special prominence. Indeed, earlier assumptions within the Marxist tradition have been conceived as incomplete rather than as incorrect in concentrating less upon *control over the forces and relations of production* than upon such concerns as wealth and income distribution; educational, occupational and similar sources of social inequality; and the 'objective' and 'subjective' conditions under which transformations in 'consciousness' may be expected to develop.[21] Yet in the alternative accounts, the germs of which appeared in the various Marxist contributions to labour theory by Allen,[22] and which has been more thoroughly developed by Braverman,[23] Crompton,[24] and Crompton and Gubbay,[25] the argument has been advanced that the original aspects of the Marxist theory of class stemmed precisely from their anchorage in production relationships. That is to say, while Marx himself affirmed that while 'no credit is due to me for discovering the existence of classes in modern society, nor yet the struggle between them', equally the novel features of the thesis were seen as the relationship between social classes and 'particular phases in the development of production'.[26]

By extension, as Crompton and Gubbay have argued, class situations should be analysed in terms of 'flows of surplus product' and be understood as the ultimate derivative of changes in the workplace context in which the 'primary axis of differentiation' may be discerned in terms of the *controlling function of capital* versus *co-ordinated labour* (i.e. the collective workforce).[27] Notwithstanding certain structurally ambiguous class situations, therefore, the 'labour function' is entailed in the 'carrying out, under the control of capital, of tasks specified by capital'.[28] And this in turn echoed Marx's postulate that the 'labour-process, turned into the process by which the capitalist consumes labour-power', exhibits two principal characteristics: namely that 'the labourer works under the control of the capitalist to whom his labour belongs', and that the 'product is the property of the capitalist and not that of the labourer, its immediate producer.'[29] Hence, on such assumptions, it is labour-*power* and not the 'status' of labour as a commodity in the market that is ultimately decisive for class situation; a contention which receives further 'textual' support from Marx's brief commentary on class (at the very end of volume 3 of *Capital*) in which three 'great classes' of 'the capitalist mode of production' were identified (the owners of labour-*power*, capital and land, whose respective sources of income were wages, profits and ground rent).[30]

But from a sociological standpoint, it has been the Weberian conception of power that has proved to be especially focal in accounts of management-union relations, while earlier distinctions between 'class' and 'status' situation were very much the product of this branch of analytical scholarship.[31] To be sure, in order to apply to union action and behaviour a number of modifications in the Weberian conception are required to encapsulate the following major issues: (1) the problems imposed by a democratic as well as an administrative rationale when unions are studied as organizations; (2) the analytical difficulties which stem from the sharing of power and from the existence of more than one centre of authority in the enterprise; (3) the introduction of the concept of power resources (educational, material, organizational, technical as well as 'ideal'); and (4) the forging of appropriate theoretical and analytical linkages between the actors' motivations and orientations, and power and structural dimensions respectively.

Inequality, social imagery and trade unionism

None the less, it is one thing to propose that power, control and social class have a decisive role in precipitating patterns of social inequality in modern societies, but quite another to demonstrate any substantial link with union action and behaviour. The following fundamental issues deriving from sociological premises will therefore be addressed in this section: first, the impact of classical thought upon the study of inequality and trade unionism; second, the early sociological contributions to the debates; and third, contemporary expositions of the general relationship between social stratification and trade unionism itself.

Classical debates

Although Weber and Marx were concerned with the relationship between power, class and trade unionism, in neither case was this a prominent feature of their respective theories. If, for Weber, property (and lack of property) were unmistakable *symptoms* of class situation, equally 'mass action' depended largely upon 'general cultural conditions' (and especially those of an intellectual sort).[32] Yet in Weber's view societal or communal action need in no way emanate exclusively from a common class situation; but rather[33]

> the direction of interests may vary according to whether or not a *communal* action of a larger or smaller portion of those commonly affected by the 'class situation', or even an association among them, e.g. a 'trade union', has grown out of the class situation from which the individual may or may not expect promising results. . . . The rise of

societal or even of communal action from a common class situation is by no means a universal phenomenon.

Moreover, for Weber, the growth of class consciousness depended upon considerable transparency between causes and consequences of class situation,[34] but, for the most part, 'the determination of the price of labour' was the crucial manifestation of class struggle even though its thrust was primarily directed towards management (the most visible actors in the bargaining relationship) rather than towards other groups within 'capital', 'in spite of the fact that it is precisely the cash boxes of the rentier, share-holder and banker into which the more or less "unearned" gains flow, rather than into the pockets of the manufacturers or of the business executives.'[35]

In so far as social stratification and trade unions were concerned, Weber's understanding of status[36] ('every typical component of the life fate of men that is determined by a specific, positive or negative, social estimation of *honour*') also has been evident in later studies of trade unionism. Indeed, the reference to status (again as part of the distribution of power) serves to amplify four major concerns in this context: divisions amongst the working population reflected in trade union structure and policy, the significance of status groups for 'consumption', the relationship between occupation and status, and an identification of underlying structural conditions which lead to a varying emphasis upon 'class' and 'status' considerations respectively.

Weber, of course, had been concerned to show how status groups were stratified 'according to the principles of their consumption of goods', rather than, as in the case of class, according 'to their relations to the production and acquisition of goods', while occupational categories, too, may also be conceived in terms of status categories in union contexts.[37] But, above all, Weber argued that 'class' and 'status' forms of consciousness were variously encouraged by changes in underlying economic and technical conditions.[38]

When the bases of acquisition and distribution of goods are relatively stable, stratification by status is favoured. Every technological repercussion and economic transformation threatens stratification by status and pushes the class situation into the foreground. Epochs and countries in which the naked class situation is of predominant significance are regularly the periods of technical and economic transformations. Any slowing down of the shifting economic stratification tends, in due course, to the growth of status structures and makes for a resuscitation of the important role of social honour.

Yet even amongst Marxist scholars the view that trade unions *directly* reflect class divisions and class consciousness has been received with much circumspection. Marx himself was conscious that the growth of middle and intermediate strata could 'obliterate' primary lines of class distinction and observed that trade unions work well only as centres of resistance against the encroachment of capital,[39] while, as we noted in chapter 1, 'pessimists' in the revolutionary tradition have emphasized the incorporation of unions and the inherent limitations to trade union consciousness itself.

Early contributions to the debates on social inequality and trade unionism

Building upon the premises of Weberian and Marxian scholarship a series of contributions from industrial sociologists had of course focused upon the themes of social stratification, social imagery and trade unionism. Moreover, although the works of Lockwood, Blackburn and Prandy on the origins of white-collar unionization and of Goldthorpe and Lockwood on trade unionism and the class structure[40] are too familiar to warrant lengthy inspection, these studies were fundamental in linking classic and modern conceptions in the history of trade union thought. Hence, for illustrative purposes, we have selected three particularly interesting contributions from the formative literature: first, the general analysis by Max Scheler of social class position and social imagery; second, the Goldthorpe and Lockwood model of affluence and the British class structure; and third, the work of Popitz and his colleagues on social class, dichotomous social imagery and variations in outlook and perspective amongst trade union members themselves.

In *Die Wissenformen und die Gesellschaft*, Scheler noted that the proletarian lives from early youth under a contrasting system of social control from his upper class contemporary, and that this in turn is associated with the radically different ways of thinking employed by members of these two classes:

Scheler's categories of the relationship between class, control and world-views[41]

Lower class	Upper class
1 Tendency to look forward (prospectivism)	Tendency to look backward (retrospectivism)
2 Emphasis on becoming	Emphasis on being
3 Mechanistic conception of the world	Teleological conception of the world

Lower class	Upper class
4 Realism in philosophy; the world as 'resistance'	Idealism in philosophy; the world as a 'realm of ideas'
5 Materialism	Spiritualism
6 Induction, empiricism	*A priori* knowledge, rationalism
7 Pragmatism	Intellectualism
8 Optimism with regard to the future, the past as the 'bad old days'	Pessimism with regard to the future, the past as the 'good old days'
9 A dialectical mode of thinking; search for contradictions	Search for identities and harmonies
10 Emphasis on environmental influences	Emphasis on heredity and tradition

In general, therefore, we have the suggestion that there are major variations in basic values and perspectives of the world and that these are connected with the occupancy of structurally different social positions, on the one hand, and patterns of control in these classes, on the other. And of particular interest at this juncture is to note that teleological and idealistic world-views are more likely to be possessed by members of the upper class by contrast with those in subordinate positions for whom mechanistic and realistic perspectives are presumed to be more common.

In Britain, however, 'Affluence and the British Class Structure' has had a far greater impact upon subsequent analytical thought than any other single contribution of this type and, as will be recalled, the general interpretation by Goldthorpe and Lockwood rested initially upon drawing out from existing empirical researches five principal inferences on the social perspectives of the working and middle classes: (1) that the majority of people had a clearly defined image of society (i.e., they are aware of inequalities in 'the distribution of wealth, prestige and power'); (2) the 'power' or 'dichotomous' and the 'prestige' or 'hierarchical' models constituted elemental types; (3) these images roughly corresponded with the perspectives of wage-earning manual workers and salaried or independent non-manual workers respectively; (4) that when an image matched closely one or more of these basic types, it embraced a 'distinctive complex of social values and attitudes'; and (5) that this underlying distinction reflected collectivist and individualist modes of social consciousness. Nevertheless, as a consequence of economic, urban and technical change during a period of affluence, a gradual convergence of imagery might be anticipated revolving round *instrumental collectivism* which incorporated a dominant 'family centredness', the significance of modern communications and mass culture, the saliency of economic rather than status *goals* and an indeterminably political outcome of these various structural and cultural upheavals. Moreover, convergence towards instrumental collectivism was premised, of course, upon the unionization of a substantial proportion of non-manual workers as well as upon the rapid modification of the traditional cultures and communities of the urban working classes (see Figure 5.1).[42]

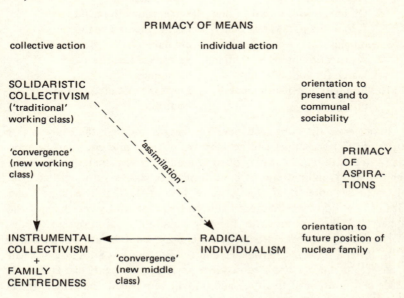

Figure 5.1   *The trend towards instrumental collectivism*
(Source: J.H. Goldthorpe and D. Lockwood, 'Affluence and the British Class Structure', *Sociological Review*, vol. 11, 1963, p. 153)

Yet, as Popitz and his colleagues demonstrated, even when workers develop a sharply class conscious and dichotomous view of the social structure, variations which have significant implications for the issues of power and control in trade union contexts may still emerge. Thus if we rework the principal categories developed by Popitz *et al.*[43] beginning with the view of the dichotomy as a static or ordered structure and following respectively with its perception as the collective fate of the working class, as a progressive order (whether individual or collective), as a reform of the social order, and as a class warfare, we can see certain very fundamental variations. These indeed reflect degrees of legitimacy accredited to the main control structures as may be seen in Table 5.1.

Table 5.1   *Values, class and control*

Values implying stability in control structures		Values implying change in control structures	
(a) Static order	(b) Collective fate	(c) Progressive order/ individual conflict	(d) Reform of the social order
		(e) Class warfare	
(a) Legitimacy of managerial domination	(b) Acceptance but no legitimation of managerial domination	(c) Slow progress predicted. Satisfaction with achievement so far gained by trade unions, or belief in possibilities of individual advancement	(d) Major changes perceived in the future via trade union and/or political party machinery
		(e) Major changes perceived in the future via revolutionary action	

Thus workers who viewed the dichotomy as an ordered structure not only assumed its inevitability but also legitimated the present structure of industrial control. By contrast, those who viewed it as the collective fate of the working class recognized but did not legitimate this situation. Such workers, however, consciously placed the issue of control at the centre of their particular social image. They felt that in human society 'there is an upper class and a lower class', which 'appear as rigid, inevitable and unchangeable'. 'We, the workers, belong to the lower class, and we cannot escape from it, *for the others are stronger*.'[44] But all other categories of workers considered that certain changes could be effected in class and control structures within society. Admittedly, certain workers perceived such alterations only in individual terms; that is to say, they considered it to be possible individually, but not collectively, to improve one's relative social position. However, among those workers who envisaged the dichotomy as a progressive order, there was *'a satisfaction with something attained, with the circumstances of a stage of development'*, and most importantly from our point of view, these workers felt themselves, almost without exception, bound to the union. In their judgment, and the italics are those of Popitz, *et al.*, *'the initiative must always lie with the labour movement'*,[45] but given this recognition, the power of the other side did not appear to be an insuperable obstacle. Finally, there were a minority of workers who had clearly developed noticeably context-independent perspectives and, through them, could envisage major structural upheavals whether brought about by reformist or by revolutionary means.

Contemporary formulations of the stratification thesis and the development of 'the radical school'

But while power, control, social class and status are clearly the decisive dimensions of social inequality in modern societies, it is not always easy to demonstrate an inseparable link with union action and behaviour. Moreover, although at a structural level we shall examine the relationship between politico-economic and occupational change and the implications of both these exigencies for modern unionism in chapter 6, it is worth commenting on the general relationship between stratification and trade unionism at this point. Of course work roles and position in the production process are a fundamental basis for stratification in modern societies in the first place. Consequently, changes in the former have commensurate implications for class and status 'structuration'; but a great deal of the literature on unionism has of course been concerned with tracing the relationship (if one exists at all) between the main dimensions of stratification and union attitudes and behaviour: Figure 5.2 sets out how Bain, Coates and Ellis designated the basic model (and the relevant independent, intervening and dependent variables).[46]

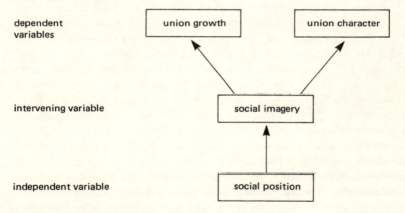

Figure 5.2   *Social stratification and trade unionism*

Yet Bain and his colleagues of course rejected the supposition that, at the 'aggregative' level, social stratification and trade unionism were related; *unless, that is, power was viewed as the main means by which groups were stratified.*[47] But ironically since Bain *et al.* also acknowledged that social stratification ultimately reflected Weberian categories of 'class' and 'status' (which, as we have seen, were viewed as derivative of the distribution of power), then, *pari passu*, the approaches deriving from this school of thought must ultimately have incorporated this very conception. Hence, these authors sought to establish that, contrary to the arguments of Lockwood,[48] Blackburn,[49] and Prandy,[50] social stratification was not a decisive variable in explaining union growth, while social imagery was only likely to be influential at the earliest phases of union development, since, at high levels of completeness, unionism was no longer a voluntary act but was rather 'to a greater or lesser extent, constrained by institutional norms'.[51] Similarly, in respect of *union character*, no straightforward association was apparent between social position and organizational membership, goals and behaviour; for, after all, social position would not appear to 'generate or sustain different organizational types'.[52] Furthermore, social imagery itself may, of course, be subject to manifold changes and fluctuations according to historical circumstance, social situation and the volition of actors.[53]

None the less, such a formulation does less than full justice to the 'social stratification school' not least because of the shift in recent radical accounts to the insistence on the primacy of power as an explanatory variable in union-management relations *per se*. Not all of these contributions have been Marxist in orientation of course: indeed, in the previous chapter, we observed how certain branches of radicalism (and notably that espoused by Fox) had grown out of a critique of liberal-pluralism and had rested principally upon Durkheimian postulates. This was a heritage shared by Goldthorpe who perceived social inequality as a cardinal factor which had occasioned a breakdown of social integration in the industrial sphere. Moreover, as he avowed, 'social inequality in all its manifestations can be thought of as involving differences in social power and advantage',[54] the two being closely intertwined. Similarly:[55]

> different forms of power and advantage tend in their very nature to be convertible: economic resources can be used to gain status or to establish authority; status can help to reinforce authority and to create economic opportunities; positions of authority usually confer status and command high economic rewards, and so on.

Notwithstanding, therefore, the possibility of status inconsistency, Goldthorpe emphasized both the consequences of social power for inequality and industrial conflict and also the role of political *action* (rather than technological advance and economic growth) as the only realistic basis for any principled amelioration of the situation.[56]

But the most important single attempt in modern times to construct a comprehensive theory of trade unionism from Marxian premises (in which, also, the transformations in trade union, management, and state relations have up to a point been acknowledged) has been that of Richard Hyman.[57] His explicit objective in *Industrial Relations* was to produce an introductory 'focus on theory' and to encapsulate a distinctively Marxist framework of analysis in which the themes of '*totality, change, contradiction* and *practice*' loom large.[58] Indeed, notwithstanding the heterogeneity and diversity of much of Marxist thought it is possible, as with much of our exposition, to identify within it 'structuralist', 'subjectivist' and 'power' dimensions. These, in turn, introduce a measure of clarity in enumerating the multiple references by Marxist scholars to the genesis and role of trade unionism itself. These are best summarized in the following form:[59]

Analytical elements in a Marxist explanation of trade unionism
1 Structuralist explanations

  (a) The dominant role of property as a distinguishing feature of class and the status of wage labour as a commodity in indicating basic lines of cleavage which encourage union formation.

  (b) The role of economic and technical change within the 'capitalist mode of production' in shaping, at least in part, the contours of modern unionism.

  (c) Patterns of union-management conflict occasioned by the extraction of surplus values (including over wages, hours, working conditions and so on).

2 Subjectivist explanations

  (a) Alienation as a factor generating private property in the first instance and 'in productive activity itself' in constituting a major source of dissatisfaction which may encourage union formation and explain certain types of union action.

  (b) 'Problems' of consciousness: 'pessimistic' versus 'optimistic' schools of labour theory. The radicalism (or otherwise) of trade union movements. The role of 'ruling ideas' and the modern impact of the mass media in this respect.

3 Dialectical approaches emphasizing the interrelationship between structural exigencies, consciousness, power, control, and trade unionism

  (a) Control and the concentrated power of capital at (i) a society level in affecting overall class relationships and (ii) an enterprise level in the determination to reduce the dependence of capital on the skills of the worker. Resistance by organized workers and consequent struggles particularly at 'the frontier of control'.

  (b) The relationship between trade unions, political parties and the state including (i) the role of political parties in extending 'trade union consciousness' and its conversion into 'class consciousness'

(ii) the state's impact on unions — normally viewed as the representative or 'executive arm' of the bourgeoisie.

(c) International political and economic conditions. The effects of multinational companies on unionism; the imperialist thesis and the effects of imperialism in depressing the radicalism of labour movements in advanced industrial countries.

Set against such a pattern of explanatory variables Hyman's own percepts would appear at times to be curiously heterodox. After all, little of his analysis is concerned with a direct specification of the main postulates of Marxism or with any real attempt to test the validity of varying propositions *within* Marxism, let alone alternative formulations and conceptions. Hence, although he would presumably wish to echo the view espoused *inter alia* by Bottomore that, as a body of ideas, Marxism has furthered the systematic analysis of modern society more than any other single set of postulates,[60] and to concur with Parsons that the 'Marxian view of the importance of class structure has in a broad way been vindicated',[61] there is little systematic anchorage in the account of trade unionism in the categories of Marxist social science *per se*.

Indeed, if we turn to his most rigorous passages, Hyman had apparently resolved to differentiate the Marxist perspective from liberal-pluralism by rejecting the focus on job regulation and by adopting the broader but cognate emphasis upon *'processes of control over work relations'*.[62] But, as Wood has commented, this may entail merely a *terminological* rather than *conceptual* change;[63] so much so, indeed, that Clegg has felt it fitting to observe that 'if students of industrial relations had to rub along with "processes of control over work relations" they would probably manage fairly well; and come to much the same conclusions at the end of the day.'[64]

In fairness, though, Hyman was to reaffirm his view of the strategic impact of the existing structure of *ownership* and control for union action and behaviour, and identified contradictory processes and forces in the industrial relations system which generate instability as well as the significance of the 'capitalist environment' (labour market exigencies and the commodity status of labour).[65] Moreover, although these were *not a direct derivative of the focus on control questions*, Hyman nevertheless recognized the primacy of 'the structures of power and interests, and the economic, technological, and political dynamics, of the broader society' for industrial relations and trade union action.[66]

Yet the most valuable sections of *Industrial Relations* would still appear to have little obvious affinity with Marxian *theoretical propositions*. Thus there are useful commentaries on power (being interpreted as 'the ability of an individual or group to control his (their) physical and social environment; and, as part of this process, the ability to influence the decisions which are and are not taken by others').[67] Despite resemblance to non zero-sum and zero-sum conceptions, a particularly valuable taxonomic contrast is drawn between power 'for' and power 'over': the first being non-exploitative and a resource used in the service of collective interests; but the second (which was viewed as characteristic of enterprise relations and also within unions in 'capitalist' society) normally involving relationships of conflict:[68]

> power is typically wielded by one individual or group *over* others. The power of management is founded, in effect, on the subjection of employees; and workers can assert their own control only *at the expense* of the employer. In capitalist society, because of the manifold conflicts of interest which exist, power relations are normally of this kind. Even when individuals band together to increase their collective power ('power for'), this is normally directed towards a conflict relationship with a third party ('power over'). Trade union organisation is an obvious example: workers develop their collective power precisely in order to counteract the even greater power of the employer.

Of course, Hyman identified a number of changes in power relationships in industry since Marx's time (notably, the contraction of 'the reserve army of unemployed'; the increase in unionization by more than a factor of ten; price inflation; and the 'historical' and 'moral' element which reflects 'relative deprivation' and helps to 'explain the differentials between the earnings of various occupational groups').[69] These, moreover, were seen to reinforce an analytical interpretation of the market in terms of power and control rather than 'narrowly economic processes of supply and demand'; an insight reflecting not only the premises of the 'political school' of labour theory but also the Weberian interpretation of market relationships,[70] the Webbs' understanding of collective bargaining,[71] and particularly Allan Flanders's reformulation to accentuate the significance of political and social factors in trade union action itself.[72]

MODERN THEORETICAL AND OPERATIONAL INTERPRETATIONS OF POWER

General propositions

The fundamental premise of recent contributions from the radical school has been based, therefore, on a conception of the saliency of power in the relationships within trade unions and in their interaction with employers and the agencies of the state and the legislature. Moreover, in conjunction with other formulations, this has contributed to the establishment of more advanced analytical and taxonomic models which will occupy our attention in the subsequent discussion. Specifically, too, contemporary interpretations of power are undoubtedly sharply at variance with the conventional systems paradigm in that the concept is now almost always construed as an *endogenous* variable rather than as part of the wider contexts in which action unfolds.

Yet certainly it has been widely held that, as the 1970s advanced, Britain's trade union and labour movement had assumed a responsibility for industrial and political policy to a degree previously unknown in peacetime. Moreover, such unparalleled involvement was perceived to be readily identifiable at both national and local levels and to be founded upon the twin bases of a steady augmentation of overall membership and a penetration of union organization into corners of the occupational structure where, until recently, the very principle of unionism has been abjured. Yet if such commonplace judgments (and the diverse formulations of the same 'problem') are ultimately to reflect other than supposition, a far greater analytical and conceptual rigour is required encompassing precisely established propositions which link theoretical and operational indices. Moreover, an indispensable preliminary would appear to be the development of a *consistently applied* terminology to juxtapose the concepts of power, control, authority, influence and so on.

Indeed, a useful illustration of what may be accomplished in such a context has been provided by Roderick Martin, who noted that the overall distribution of power in our society is[73]

> determined by its ecological and technological basis, its inheritance practices, the goals of its members and the distribution of control over desired resources, and by the means available to subordinates to escape from the dependences created by the distribution of this control.

Furthermore, on such counts, managements would still seem to be far more powerful than the workers whom they employ, and, like Goldthorpe,[74] Martin adjudged the distribution of *formal* decision-making authority still to be largely in managerial hands. It was thus the *distribution of influence* which was now roughly equal; a situation which would appear to have arisen because, while management has become increasingly dependent upon specific workers, employees have far fewer corresponding obligations to any given employer.[75] In short, for much of the period since the Second World War, transformations in the market situation (such as lower unemployment levels), different patterns of personal involvement in the enterprise and the questioning of traditional hierarchies have all weakened the *regulative* powers of management.[76]

> In the nineteenth century 'managerial prerogatives' extended over both market and labour utilization aspects of the work situation; in the mid-twentieth century the authority of management over market factors has been successfully challenged by workers collectively, through the development of trade unions, and its authority over labour utilization is now being questioned.

But why do patterns of power distribution fluctuate and what are the consequences for union action? Without wishing to pre-empt our later discussions much of the modern explanation rests on an awareness of structural movements together with substantial (and less predictable) alterations in 'subjective' predispositions (ethics, ideologies, values, orientations and so on). But in view of the reciprocal relationship between structures, values and control, an examination of the broad outline of this relationship would be relevant at this point, when we might usefully focus, for illustrative purposes, on the debates on the growth of white-collar unionization.

In the industrial relations literature, the most widely accepted documentation of the growth of white-collar trade unions has been by Bain, whose two-equation model was of course as follows:[77]

Bain's model of white-collar union growth

$$D = f(C, R) \qquad (1)$$
$$R = g(D, G) \qquad (2)$$

where D = the density of white-collar unionism;
C = the degree of employment concentration;
R = the degree to which employers are prepared to recognize unions representing white-collar employees; and
G = the extent of government action which promotes union recognition.

Similarly, bureaucratization was seen as a less direct determinant of white-collar union growth than concentration; the two, however, being viewed as 'a function of the techniques of production':[78]

Factors affecting concentration

$$C = h(D, T) \qquad (3)$$

where T = techniques of production

In the Bain model, therefore, processes of job regulation (furthered by the growth of white-collar unions) had to be understood ultimately in terms of a wider set of antecedent conditions which encompassed 'material' exigencies (concentration and techniques of production), the subjective criterion of recognition by existing power-holders, and wider governmental (i.e. political) action. Moreover, reciprocal processes of feedback were implicitly acknowledged in the various components of the model that implied, above all, that density of unionization was a power *resource* which could be converted into recognition, and in turn, come to augment density itself.

These complex multi-dimensional approaches (implying variously weighted but reciprocal exchanges between the variables in a model) were to some extent heralded in the earlier sociological expositions of Lockwood,[79] and Prandy.[80] The former conceived differences in the *degree* of 'blackcoated' unionization in terms of variations in the *work situation* while attributing *character* to *market* relationships, with the main conceptual distinctions being defined as follows:[81]

Market situation: economic position 'narrowly conceived'; including
  'source and size of income, degree of job security,
  and opportunity for upward occupational mobility'.
Work situation: 'the set of social relationships in which the individual
  is involved at work by virtue of his position in the
  division of labour'.
Status situation: 'position of the individual in the hierarchy of prestige
  in society at large'.

Moreover, Prandy identified the relevance of 'class' and 'status' consciousness for union and professional associations respectively, but related these to the varying circumstances of those in subordinate groupings (mechanization, routinization and physical concentration) together with factors which facilitate or constrain organization (concentration, and 'technical', political and social conditions).[82]

Our understanding has been consolidated in recent years by an analysis of the factors which produce white-collar employment and the varying structural locations of white-collar workers at the outset. Crompton, for one, has attempted to account for the growing proportion of 'middle-class' employees in terms of structural changes in the 'capitalist mode of production' (occasioned largely by the replacement of smaller enterprises outside this framework); pressures to accumulate (forcing employers to concentrate upon relative rather than absolute methods of extraction of surplus values); an increasing number of employees required to develop and administer the new techniques; and finally, the extension of occupations which serve to ensure a stable environment for accumulation.[83]

Moreover, the propensity among the diverse white-collar groups to unionize was interpreted in terms of the degree of structural ambiguity prevalent among these groups. Hence, in Crompton's view, while certain occupations (especially higher managerial) will be unambiguously tied up with the 'capital function' and others will be unmistakably 'labour', others again will be more ambiguous (because of their role within the production process, the specificity of particular services (e.g. accountancy, advertising, finance and so on) to a given mode of production, the existence of 'oppression' but not 'exploitation' of 'unproductive' labour, and variations in the 'capitalist mode of production' which result in different interests).[84] Such structural heterogeneity amongst white-collar workers was perceived as germane for the explanation of rates of unionization amongst salaried employees and for the variations in 'strategy and behaviour' between 'middle-class' collectivities themselves.[85] Hence, although there are many difficulties in this argument (e.g. changes in organization, state participation and the expansion of local and national government services which are manifestly not *specific* reflections of the 'capitalist mode of production'),[86] the saliency of deeper structural movements has been underscored yet again.

Theory and measurement

Turning more specifically, then, to the actual measurement of power and the problems of the relationship between theory and method themselves, the techniques deployed in modern analysis are undoubtedly the reflections of underlying premises. Hence, the subjects upon which Dubin has focused in his functionalist account of power in union-management relationships (control over functions and hierarchy of functions)[87] contrast with those isolated by liberal-pluralists (e.g. range of bargaining)[88] and radicals (the significance of strategic decision-making over investment, plant location and so on).[89]

Indeed, a recognition of this problem began with Carter Goodrich's classic work, *The Frontier of Control*, in which he identified basic disparities which reflected the 'conservative' and 'revolutionary' (or in this instance, radical) traditions of labour theory.[90] Hence, there was a sharp contrast between dependent and independent control, negative and positive control, and old craft or customary and conscious or contagious control respectively (see Table 5.2).[91]

Table 5.2   *Variations in types of shop floor control*

'Conservative'	'Radical'
(1) Dependent control Presented by management to the workforce (otherwise termed *agreeable* control).	(1) Independent control Control seized by the union ('Real control of industry cannot be presented like a Christmas box'; otherwise termed *enforced* control).
(2) Negative control An 'Opposition that never becomes a Government.' Control over hiring, apprenticeships, demarcation and so on.	(2) Positive control Involving initiatives. For example, the determination not *under what conditions* machinery *might* be introduced but actually *where it should* be introduced.
(3) Old craft or customary control Conservative existence. Resistance of encroachment by management. Small groups of skilled workers. Survival from earlier technology.	(3) Conscious or contagious control Not to resist encroachments but to make them. Industrial unions. Demands arising under new industrial techniques.

Such theoretical problems involved in measurement were also well understood by Herding who noted that various approaches to the analysis of job control not only reflected definitional issues but also theoretical positions ('system', 'liberal-pluralist', 'Marxist' and so on).[92] Thus, for instance, the primary interpretations of job control have been based on such conceptions as individual rights and enlightened management, functional differentiation in corporate government, the industrial accommodation process, managerial self-restraint under bureaucratization and job control as a means of 'capitalist' integration of the working class.[93] Moreover, as we shall now discover, the focus on particular *conceptions* of power also has considerable implications for measurement technique.

The exercise of power

The work of Abell has thus been outstanding for the measurement of *outcomes* in actual bargaining encounters (the exercise of power) but later modifications in his approach have been deliberately designed to accommodate theoretical advances in the literature on power itself.[94] Hence, in this conception, job regulation and job control were ultimately construed as the consequence of outcomes in bargaining contexts, the zones of which were subject to periodic negotiated adjustments. Moreover, as Abell has insisted, there is an insufficiency of 'models which reflect actual social process', and which at the same time generate reasonably general explanations of social phenomena.[95]

Indeed, as Abell has further recorded, 'the seemingly intractable problems of locating operational definitions which capture the concepts in anything like their full complexity, have not been solved'[96] and this of course is especially true if, following Lukes, distinctions are formulated between: (1) the decision-making approach to power; (2) the focus on non-decision making; and (3) latent interests.[97] Of course, Abell's own researches on union-management bargaining have so far converged on the first set of questions, and he has drawn the well-known distinction between *revealed preferences* and *outcomes* as elemental components in the structure and explanation from power.[98] More specifically then, while *influence*, *manipulation* and *power* were all contrasted *conceptually* in the *decision-making content* (e.g. in bargaining relationships) three main assumptions have been evident:[99]

    (i)   that both A and B have clearly articulated preferences;
   (ii)   that they are more or less successful in getting these preferences embodied in outcomes;
  (iii)   that the outcomes constrain A's and B's subsequent behaviour.

Recently, however, Abell has turned his attention to measures of power which reflect non-decision making and latent interests. In the first place, therefore, in the non-decision making approach, manipulative relationships would appear to be uppermost and *'we have a situation where A "affects" B's behaviour without B's overt opposition'*.[100] Moreover, in so far as the question of latent interests is concerned, as Abell has proposed, teleological as well as causal determinism may ultimately prove to be inevitable if we are to appreciate fully the relationships concerned (after all, latent *interests* are by their very nature almost incalculable by reference to *efficient causes* of *observable* phenomena).[101]

Resource approaches to the study of power

Nevertheless, to identify underlying power *resources* in union-management relations has a number of analytical advantages over the approach in terms of the exercise of the power. Indeed, it is precisely when operational measures are linked with *latent processes*, such as non-decision making (manipulation), interests, the tendency for decisions to be taken in full cognizance of perceptions of *underlying* strength of an oppositional group ('the rule of anticipated reactions'), the marshalling of *resources* prior to conflict situations, and indeed, the very control over such resources themselves, that a further appreciation of the wider ramifications of power in trade union action and behaviour may be accomplished.

    In the literature on power resources, however, distinctions may be drawn between consensual (based principally on structural-functionalist and system assumptions) and conflictual models ('pluralist', Marxist and other radical perspectives). In so far as management-union relationships are implicated, then, the basic models are enumerated in the following list:

Resource approaches to power in union-management relationships

1 *Integrative*

  A Bases of power
- (i) exclusiveness and essentiality of functional processes;
- (ii) knowledge and expertise; organization and information resources.

  B Values
- (i) harmonious, 'commonly-held' values;
- (ii) meritocratic values in the deployment of individuals to given functional positions.

2 *Conflictual*

  A Bases of power
- (i) numbers — completeness of unionization;
- (ii) organization — e.g. particular structures of shop steward organization; mobilizational opportunities;
- (iii) resources — e.g. educational skills, technology, material resources, etc.

  B Values
- (i) 'unionateness': oppositional challenges to managerial decision-making responsibilities;
- (ii) the degree of militancy considered to be appropriate in trade union action (role expectations).

Integrative models of the resource approach to power are thus founded ultimately upon structural-functionalist conceptions coupled with the solutions proposed by Durkheim to anomie and the forced division of labour. Robert Dubin thus once noted that the functions performed in social systems have two characteristics: (1) they are interdependent and (2) there is a hierarchy of functions of varying importance to the maintenance of the system; distinctions which in turn permitted two associated indices of power: exclusiveness and essentiality.[102] Hence, if actors have unilateral control over functions and perform them exclusively they may be said to have greater power than where several share control over a particular function.[103] Moreover, since on structural-functionalist premises (not least in the context of stratification), some functions are more fundamental to the maintenance of the system than others, then control over essential functions implies greater power than when only less essential functions are controlled.[104] Yet, of course, on Durkheimian assumptions, harmonious social systems require meritocratic processes of selection of personnel into essential and non-essential functions in the first place. Similarly, knowledge and expertise, organization and information are strategic resources of power in an integrative social system. Finally, for the maintenance of such a system, 'commonly held' values are also of course decisive.

In the British context, however, most resource models of power in management-union relations have been conflict-based. Hence, on these assumptions the power of trade unions has been typically expressed in terms of three principal measures: numbers, organization and resources.[105] Up to a point of course, the overall size of a given trade union may be suggestive of numbers and this is especially so in the case of the British trade union movement on account of the system of block voting which effectively ensures that any given trade union has a voice in the Trades Union Congress in accordance with its overall membership. However, at workplace level, completeness or density of unionization is a more worthwhile measure which expresses the proportion of trade unionists in a given constituency in relation to potential membership[106] in the following way:

$$\text{Density or completeness of unionization} = \frac{\text{Actual membership}}{\text{Potential membership}} \times 100$$

Yet, in conflict conceptions, the power of trade unions is also conditional upon the effectiveness or otherwise of their organizations. A rough guide is provided by the ratio of officials (and especially shop stewards) to the membership[107] but a knowledge of the *type* of organization, together with its degree of bureaucracy or democracy, is also pertinent. This is especially relevant at workplace level where multi-unionism can lead to the fragmentation of even a highly unionized workforce, and therefore, in this regard, any evidence of the existence of joint organizations is apposite since these serve to reduce substantially any potential inter-union hostility.[108]

But the 'resources' of a trade union may be multifarious and, indeed, this category has historically included 'money, property, prestige, knowledge, competence, deceit, fraud, secrecy' and so on.[109] None the less, in terms of the underlying power of any individual trade union, education, technological and material resources have usually been regarded as vital.

The nurturing of an effective power base is, however, no guarantee that the intrinsic power of any given trade union will eventually be employed in decision-making contexts: indeed, militancy or passivity is an indispensable part of the equation. Moreover, in the literature to date, two main measures of militancy have proved to be particularly salient: first, 'unionateness' and second, role expectations.

'Unionateness' was a term coined by Blackburn and Prandy in their work on white-collar trade unions,[110] and this provides succinct expression of the degree to which any given association approximates to specified central trade union aims. The composition of the concept thus requires consideration of:[111]

1 Whether a given body declares itself a trade union;
2 Whether it is registered as a trade union;
3 Whether it is affiliated to the TUC;
4 Whether it is affiliated to the Labour Party;
5 Whether it is independent of employers for purposes of negotiation;
6 Whether it regards collective bargaining and the protection of the interests of members, as employees, as a major function;
7 Whether it is prepared to be militant, using all forms of industrial action which may be effective.

More latterly, too, Prandy, Blackburn and Stewart have split the concept of unionateness into two divisions covering: (1) *enterprise unionateness* (aspects of behaviour of an organization which are concerned with the pursuit of interests of its members as employees through collective action); and (2) *society unionateness* (aspects which cover relationships of the organization with other similar organizations and its behaviour in the wider society).[112]

On classical sociological assumptions, however, the distribution of power and of patterns of social control were of course construed as intervening variables between deeper explanatory levels and dependent relationships. Indeed, the recognition of underlying and logically anterior phenomena which contribute to patterns of control in human organization was one of the most important of the various 'paradigm shifts' ushered in by the founding fathers of modern sociology. Hence, without wider reference to the kinds of 'structural' and 'subjective' movements acknowledged in the foregoing, the power approach is undeniably limited. Once, however, it is examined in conjunction with such wider dimensions (which involve drawing upon but refining aspects of the main analytical models of trade unionism outlined so far) the basis of a comprehensive modern theory of unionism begins to take shape. It is, therefore, towards the enumeration and evaluation of the components of such a model that our attention turns in the chapters which follow.

6 Modern structuralist approaches

Liberated as we are from the antiquated notion that all cultural
phenomena can be *deduced* as a product or function of the
constellation of 'material' interests, we believe nevertheless that the
analysis of social and cultural phenomena with special reference to
their economic conditioning and ramifications was a scientific
principle of creative fruitfulness and with careful application
and freedom from dogmatic restrictions, will remain such for a very
long time to come.[1]

In our theoretical review of the main contributions to labour theory a
progressive maturity in the formulation of central concepts has been
apparent. At the outset, in the earliest empirically based traditions, the
disciplinary foundations of the various approaches were seldom distin-
guishable but, by degrees, as the input from classic sociological scholarship
and modern operational technique has been magnified, more rigorous
models have been established. Moving, then, towards the higher points of
modern theorizing our discourse will now proceed by drawing upon but
extending a number of earlier threads and by delineating the effect of
structural 'forces' in shaping union action and behaviour. Such a survey
will form the basis for a subsequent evaluation of organizational and
institutional variables and of culture, values and perception in the overall
explanatory equation.

This chapter, therefore, is devoted to setting out in some detail the
major elements of contemporary structuralist models. Since, as has been
indicated, these derive much of their analytical force and substantive
content from their origins in the classical assumptions of sociology and
labour theory, for purposes of clarification it will accordingly be of value
to trace the primary assumptions and points of divergence prior to
embarking upon a structural analysis of trade unionism itself.

STRUCTURAL EXPLANATIONS FOR TRADE UNION BEHAVIOUR

In view of its dominance in (and in some formulations against) sociology,
it is scarcely surprising that as Robert K. Merton once observed, 'the
evolving notion of "social structure" is polyphyletic and polymorphous'
and hence reveals 'more than one ancestral line of sociological thought'.[2]
Yet there can be little doubt that Durkheimian and Marxian versions have
constituted the main traditions contributing to the general notion of
structure as 'the external constraints social conditions impose upon the

116

choices and behaviour of human beings'.[3] Indeed, although approximation of terminology and of semantic content can never be guaranteed, there is common ground in the idea of economic, political and social movements having an effect upon trade unionism largely irrespective of the beliefs and perceptions of actual members. Indeed, some structuralists even regard the proper object of social science as 'social structures and not individuals' and knowledge as 'the product of theoretical activity and not a series of abstractions derived from empirical study'.[4] Social structures are thus understood as possessing a reality independent of human action, while individual 'actors' (such as trade union members) are conceived of as mere 'agents' who occupy a position in a structure which ultimately conditions their conduct and behaviour. Similarly, on such premises, not only are the actions of a trade union officer or of a shop steward perceived as the mirror of structurally-determined role requirements rather than of their ethical, political, or social outlook but also, by the same token, major variations in international labour movements are traced not to diverse cultural or institutional contingencies but to differential temporality entailed in 'unevenness of development', 'survivals', 'backwardness' or 'under-development'.

But there are a number of structuralist models and theoretical pre-suppositions in general currency. This state of affairs was affirmed at the 69th meeting of the American Sociological Association, where, although the common ground was that, whatever 'the specific orientation, the structural approach is designed to explain, not the behavior of individuals, but the structure of relations among groups and individuals that finds expression in this behavior', equally:[5]

Many different approaches have developed to improve our understanding of social structures and their dynamics. They centre attention on a great variety of subjects, including the class structure and its significance for historical developments; the evolutionary process of increasing differentiation in social structures; the dialectical process of structural change; the division of labour with its consequences for interdependence and conflict; the forms of associations that structure social relations; the structural functional analysis of institutional subsystems; the status-sets and role-sets that help clarify the dynamics of social structures; the structural roots of deviance and rebellion; the interrelations between environment, population and social structure; the microstructures emerging in face-to-face interaction; the constitution of social reality; the structural analysis of kinship and myths.

Yet there are at least four main issues in the widespread disputation *within* structuralist accounts of relevance to the theme of trade union action and behaviour and these properly merit our attention at this point.[6] These involve first, the difference between social structures as enduring and persistent elements in social behaviour and as dynamic forces respectively; second, the contrast between structural and historical explanations; third, the analysis of levels of structure; and finally, the controversy over structural differentiation and structural complexity.[7]

The first major point of contention, then, hinges upon whether social structures are defined as having a reality independent of human action or a power independent of the producer;[8] or whether they are rather better conceived of as 'a living network of relations amongst men', in which people constantly renew structures which thereby exist in a state of 'precarious equilibrium'.[9] These differences are important since they have radically influenced the ways in which industrial sociologists and industrial relations scholars have understood British trade unionism. Thus those for whom structures are forces which encourage stability and the long-term persistance of social patterns point to evidence of increasing trade union maturity, of the institutionalization of conflict within the British industrial relations system, and of the emergence of tripartite processes of decision-making between trade unions, employers and government.[10] But by contrast, those who favour a more dynamic conception of social structure, regard developments of this nature (which are after all only a part of reality) as depending upon a precarious equilibrium forged by the interaction of the leading parties to industrial relations.[11] Moreover, on these latter assumptions, in the absence of struggles by powerful trade unionists, the reality of industrial relations would also change, taking either a more radical direction in the event of rank-and-file pressures from within the labour movement gaining ascendency, or a markedly different course if employers or government could achieve specified disparate ends without the opposition of organized labour.

The second well-known disputation amongst structuralist thinkers refers to the contrast which is frequently drawn between historical and structural approaches.[12] Advocates of the first position focus only upon 'the distinctive constellation of historical conditions in a society',[13] while those of the second view societies as reflecting the unfolding of a series of underlying structural determinants (for example, of economic or technical forces) and human history as thus largely their by-product.[14]

This argument may be most aptly illustrated by reference to the contributions of Marxist structuralists (such as Althusser,[15] Balibar,[16] and Godelier[17]) who have aspired to the construction of a 'scientific' analysis of modes of production to render intelligible concrete social formations.

For Althusser, then, 'all knowledge is the product of definite theoretical practices taking place inside thought itself'.[18] Moreover, it is the outcome of theoretical work on raw materials 'constituted by existing theoretic material';[19] therefore, as Turner has observed:[20]

> New knowledge results not from discovery of hitherto unknown facts nor by observation and experimentation. Similarly, knowledge is not cumulative, but involves epistemological breaks or ruptures with existing theories. Consequently, any epistemology which claims to describe the acquisition of knowledge in terms of abstractions from observable, concrete facts is false. Any such epistemology is located within an 'empiricist problematic', but the term 'empiricism' for Althusser also covers the activities of philosophers, historians or sociologists who have been conventionally regarded as 'idealist'.

For the Althusserians, then, a crucial epistemological break in Marxism occurs between the 1844 manuscripts (particularly in the writings on alienation, in which an essential humanism can be detected) and subsequent work culminating in *Capital* in which 'a theory of history based on the radically new concepts of social formation, modes of production and superstructure' appears to be formulated. On such assumptions, the 'proper' reading of *Capital* is to view not human beings but 'social structures, their determination and articulation' as the relevant objects of social science.[21]

Determination by structure, then, is the overriding epistemological conception of Althusser. Whereas classical theories of causality admitted two models, *linear causality* (the effects of one element on another; the conventional paradigm of structural explanation) and *expressive* (or teleological) *causality* (the parts being determined by the whole, the structural-*functionalist* position), structural *determinism* is envisaged as a more sophisticated process in which the 'totality of the structure in dominance is a structure of effects with present-absent causes', the appreciation of which can be grasped only by *knowledge of the complex organization of a given mode of production*.[22] Such a formulation, too, is radically opposed to conventional historical forms of Marxism by being a determinist theory in which men manifestly do not make their own history (albeit in circumstances not of their own choosing) but rather are epiphenomena of the mechanisms which *produce* economic, political, ideological and knowledge *effects*.[23]

Indeed, Althusserian structuralist formulations 'exist' in a further irreconcilable relationship with so-called 'vulgar' Marxist notions of economic determinism and with the consequent conception of ideas being superstructural reflections of deeper economic *causal* processes, for, in

Althusserian terms, the two are inseparably linked by the *structure in dominance* which is defined by the totality of a given mode of production. In Godelier's view, too, an economic system is 'a determined combination of specific modes of production, circulation, distribution and consumption of material goods'[24] with the mode of production playing the 'dominant role' (the mode of production, in turn, being composed of productive forces and relations of production).[25]

On such premises, however, trade union action and behaviour cannot be explained in terms of *antecedent* structural movements in say economic conditions (viewed as efficient causes) since these are in turn determined by and to be understood in relation to the wider ensemble of political, economic and ideological practice in a given mode of production.[26] But the aversion to historical modes of explanation ('abstractions from an essential complexity of historical/empirical processes') and the substitution of a determinist model for multi-causal explanations of complex processes has invited sharp criticisms, notably from Bottomore[27] and E.P. Thompson.[28]

Bottomore has proposed that Althusserian structuralist theory has served to narrow the range of Marxist scholarship and has himself preferred to persist with historically informed accounts of structural change in which conceptual categories and empirical circumstances are inexorably fused.[29] This line of inquiry, in his view, was warranted not least by the realization that in the twentieth century class relations have become more complex as a result of the growth of the bureaucratic state, the rise of the technical expert and manifold cultural change; indeed, he quoted Bernstein approvingly to the effect that:[30]

> the polarisation of classes anticipated by Marx was not occurring; the
> concentration of capital in large enterprises was accompanied by a
> development of new small- and medium-sized businesses; property
> ownership was becoming more widespread; the general level of living
> was rising; the middle class was increasing rather than diminishing in
> number; the structure of capitalist society was not being simplified,
> but was becoming more complex and differentiated.

Moreover, in so far as trade union action and behaviour is concerned, it is to the deployment of empirically informed structural categories that historical modes of analysis of this type have been typically directed.

Yet the notion of *levels* of analysis is of theoretical utility and this, therefore, brings us to the third main area of discourse in structuralist explanations. There are two main variants to the idea of levels. The first incorporates the familiar 'macro' and 'micro' distinction,[31] while the latter refers to what have been variously described as primary and secondary structural determinants, deep and surface structures, and, in some formulations, base and superstructure.[32] Both are useful distinctions which on the whole clarify rather than confuse the principal questions involved. The protagonists of 'macro' forms of approach adopt the 'holistic' position of examining total societies and then infer trade union activities from these general characteristics, whereas those who have a preference for 'micro' investigations tend to focus on group and individual problems in the first instance and then make judgments (about, for example, the characteristics of trade union activists) from these initial observations.[33] Indeed, since there is no necessary cleavage between these perspectives, it is the distinction between primary and secondary structural determinants which merits greater attention; for, on this view, some elements of social structure are accepted as analytically more basic and hence more theoretically significant than others. To take an obvious example, there have been important changes in the occupational *structure* which have provided a fertile terrain for the growth in white-collar unionism.[34] But these very alterations in occupational distribution may themselves be traced to certain changes, say, in the technology employed in particular enterprises, that ultimately caused the shift in the occupational structure in the first place.

Finally, a further interpretation of social structure which is compatible with a number of structuralist models is to view evolutionary processes as encouraging a progressively greater differentiation and complexity of structural-type. This, according to writers like Lenski, works against polarization and may in the long run be expected to affect all human societies and perhaps may be best recognized in the complexity of the division of labour in industry itself.[35] Hence, in the twentieth century, rather than progressive homogeneity of productive tasks becoming evident, fragmentation has been the norm and is reflected, in trade unionism, not only in the existence of multi-unionism, but in the numerous occupations and skills which are embraced under the aegis of any large-scale national association of labour.

STRUCTURAL FACTORS AND THE ANALYSIS OF TRADE UNIONISM

So far, then, we have observed that controversy about the nature of social structure has had far-reaching implications for the ways in which developments of trade unionism have been understood. But for the purposes of our own analysis, a number of clear implications emerge from the foregoing discussions; first, that, despite its obvious merits, a structural approach is on its own an insufficiently comprehensive framework of explanation; second, that there is a potential disjunction between historical and structural researches; third, that the idea of levels of structure is a valuable one; and fourth, that several divergent elements have been identified in a long-term process of structural differentiation. These salient considerations have been accommodated in the construction of the accompanying structural model of trade unionism:

Structural components of a modern analysis of trade unionism

1 Basic or primary structural elements
   (a) the politico-economic structure
        (i)   the materialist conception of history
        (ii)   public ownership of the enterprise
        (iii) corporatism
        (iv)   cyclical economic movements
   (b) technological structures (and evolutionary movements therein);
   (c) the division of labour.
2 Derivative or secondary structural elements
   (a) the class and occupational structure;
   (b) the size of the enterprise;
   (c) the community structure;
   (d) micro-structural elements.

In brief, therefore, we have endeavoured to develop an original theoretical framework in which structure is viewed as an external constraint on trade union action and behaviour but in no way reflects any determinist assumptions in the Althusserian mould. Indeed, in the general explanatory conceptual system to be advanced in this and the following chapters it will become clear that both institutional and organizational variables, coupled with the prevailing cultural values and perceptions of social factors, are in integral component of any comprehensive analysis. Of course, this is in no way to dispute the saliency of structural modes of explanation, however, and this applies especially in studies in which general patterns of historical change are examined; but it is to highlight their partial character in accounting for the main aspects of the phenomenon under review.

Yet, as we have mentioned, the notion of levels of structural explanation is of utility and hence, to accommodate such an advance in theoretical thought, we have not only incorporated the familiar macro-micro distinction, but also, more especially, we have isolated the deeper or primary structures in terms of politico-economic movements, technology and the division of labour, and in abstract terms, the higher order dependent formations such as the class and occupational structure, the size of the enterprise, the community structure, and micro-structural elements involved in the patterning of workgroups and in union-management interaction.

BASIC OR PRIMARY STRUCTURAL INFLUENCES UPON TRADE UNIONISM

Our outline of structural constraints upon trade union action and behaviour is thus launched by an examination of deep or underlying structural movements which have been significant in shaping many of the broadest outlines of overall union development itself. These effects are to some extent mediated through both the distribution of power in given industrial relations contexts and also through higher level and largely dependent social formations (e.g. occupational changes) though there are reciprocal (or feedback) relationships of importance in this respect as well. For example, the growth of corporatism and state intervention in the economy which, on one view, constituted part of the deeper structural patterning of political and economic forces, on another has been encouraged by the growth of independent labour organizations and by the ensuing problems of 'system integration' which this has occasioned. But for our purposes here, the three basic or primary structural elements which would appear to have substantial repercussions for the British labour movement are: first, the politico-economic structure; second, technology; and third, the division of labour. Moreover, these interrelated movements may be seen as typical of the majority of advanced industrial societies and up to a point may be occasioned by a protracted process of societal evolution.

The politico-economic structure

If we turn first, then, to the politico-economic structure which, on certain formulations, has widely been held to be a supreme 'determinant' of trade unionism, four recurring themes have dominated research to date: (i) the materialist conception of history; (ii) public ownership of the enterprise; (iii) corporatism; and (iv) cyclical economic movements.

The materialist conception of history

Proponents of the materialist conception of history of course have identified economic and technical forces as the decisive foundations of structure, and for some writers, these are seen to operate in large measure quite distinctly from human purpose, volition, or will. Indeed, in extreme versions of this thesis, human history itself is understood as being moulded wholly through processes of contradiction in these primary structures without any intervention by human consciousness or political organization whatsoever.

On these assumptions, too, the trade union movement ultimately reflects the 'contours of capitalism' and a series of structural economic (and politico-economic) transformations in the underlying material base.

Moreover, since the fabric of the British economy – and hence the milieu in which trade unionists find themselves – has undoubtedly undergone modification since the nineteenth century, then this in turn should be expected (albeit indirectly) to be evident in changes in unionism itself. Furthermore, in this respect, three particularly profound changes have been apparent: first, the growing scale of enterprise and the tendency for monopolistic and oligopolistic forms of private enterprise to become dominant; second, the emergence of publicly-owned industries and corporations; and third, the increasingly pervasive role of the state in the planning of the so-called macro-economic order.

Structural evolution of the first type is easily illustrated. Estimates of the concentration of British industry vary, but at present approximately 200 firms control half of all UK industries and services, 100 firms control half the assets in manufacturing industry, and 75 firms are responsible for half the overseas trade. But such a milieu has proved favourable to an escalation in trade unionism: indeed, there is unquestionably a strong correlation between enterprise size (brought about by industrial concentration) and the propensity of workers to join trade unions.

The growing scale of industry is associated with another phenomenon, namely a rise in the 'organic composition' of capital and the consequent tendency for a decline in the rate as opposed to the level of profit to occur in manufacturing industry. Major economies of scale and more efficient production are of course usually correlated with the establishment of modern productive units: indeed, these provide the main stimuli for the introduction of highly expensive machinery, buildings, capital equipment and so on in the first place. Nevertheless, since on Marxist suppositions productive workers rather than capital machinery ultimately create value, the rate of profit is likely to be depressed in direct relation to the increase in investment in capital goods. In short the ratio of constant capital (plant, machinery and so on) to variable capital (i.e. labour) alters to cause a rise in the organic composition of capital and to reduce the rate of profit.[36] Moreover, the vast outlay of initial resources upon capital equipment involved in any major investment programme has to be recouped in the actual labour process itself.

A rise in the organic composition of capital has two principal effects in so far as trade unionism is concerned. In the first place, pressure is clearly placed upon management to ensure the full utilization of valuable equipment and machinery. This is achieved either by prolonging the working day (by means of overtime and shift working) or by the intensification of work activities (by the speed-up of manufacturing processes, the implementation of productivity agreements and the use of time and motion study, measured day work and so on), or again of course, by a combination of these various techniques. However, such arrangements have in turn facilitated an extension of the range of bargaining between management and union and have further enhanced potential sources of antagonism, conflict and dispute between employers on the one hand and the workforce on the other. But in the second place, paradoxically, the very cost of modern machinery and the complexity of highly sophisticated techniques of manufacture, on the whole, have reinforced the bargaining strength of workers and their trade union representatives, because management has a clear interest in ensuring that machinery is not left idle, as is the case, of course, if disputes are not rapidly resolved.

Public ownership

But the growth of the public sector constitutes the most important manifestation of the changes which have taken place in the British economy since the birth of the trade union movement during the nineteenth century. Moreover, this phenomenon has been widely acknowledged to have produced an enhanced political dimension to labour disputes and the gradual abandonment of so-called 'liberal collectivism'. Certainly Crouch has noted that 'to continue to pursue free collective bargaining alone is to pursue a strategy which will lead to increasing conflict with the state without being prepared for it' and that 'to treat increasingly with the state, but to trust it less; to extend and politicize the area of bargaining, but to make firmer wider agreements which bind the membership' may be the increasing product of 'bargained corporatism'[37] and the harbinger of the future role of the union movement.

None the less, the relationship between trade unions and state intervention has been conventionally analysed under two main heads. In the first place, there has been a series of studies in which the connection between public ownership and union density has been charted; and in the second, there are the more recent formulations, with which we shall be concerned in the next section, in which the debates on corporatism (i.e. the intervention of the state in the private sector) have added a new dimension to a long-standing theme.

There is undoubtedly, then, a strong correlation between public ownership and union density. Moreover, although, in the case of manual workers, many of the industries which have become publicly owned had in fact a high density (or completeness) of unionization prior to nationalization, equally, amongst white-collar and managerial employees public ownership has undoubtedly spurred recognition of unionism and of bargaining functions and hence fostered a growth in membership itself.[38]

For purposes of illustration such a relationship may be appreciated by an examination of the expansion of managerial unionism which well highlights the close intertwining of structural change, transformation of control and the subjective issue of recognition. Gospel listed the principal factors responsible for the growth of managerial unionism as 'the ambivalent position of managers in the workplace; decreasing wage differentials between managers and other workers; increasing bureaucratization; and the supportive (or non-supportive) stance assumed by government and top management'.[39]

However, Gospel also observed 'United Kingdom public sector managers have a long history of union membership',[40] and this can be attributed in part to growing 'bureaucratization and standardization of managerial terms and conditions of employment, which treat managers in egalitarian rather than individual terms'; which has the further consequence of leading 'many to reciprocate by acting collectively'.[41] The attitudes of top management and government to managerial unionism are also significant in this respect:[42]

> It has become a commonplace of industrial relations theory that the attitudes of government and employers toward trade union recognition are important in explaining union growth. Employer recognition and government support, or at least neutrality, not only make trade union membership more socially acceptable and legitimate, but also provide the union, as an organization, with the means to establish its position and provide positive benefits for members via collective bargaining.

Managerial unionism in both its 'aggregative' and 'disaggregative' forms has been highly sensitive both to general political intervention occasioned by public ownership and also, at a more specific level, by the changing dispositions of governmental and senior managerial personnel on the question of recognition itself. Certainly in his pioneering work on managerial unionism in the coal industry, McCormick noted that not only was public ownership an indispensable foundation for unionization amongst these grades of employee, but also commented that 'employer recognition appears to depend upon the type of employer — public or private. Centralization and bureaucratization have a part to play . . . but they appear to be supplementary factors.'[43] Indeed, these arguments were further pursued in *Industrial Relations in the Coal Industry* where as the same author insisted:[44]

> Before nationalization unionism among officials was weak. Colliery managers strongly identified themselves with their employers and this tie was particularly strong when there were kinship bonds. . . .
>
> What nationalization did was to alter the employment relationship for managers; instead of many employers there was now one.

Nationalization brought about a change in ownership and a centralization of authority. These distinct, although interrelated, changes had a profound effect on colliery staffs.

Indeed, of signal importance in this respect were the changing patterns of *control* consequential upon structural changes of ownership. For, certainly, local managers would appear to have suffered a diminution in decision-making authority and discretion as a result of increasing bureaucratization and regulation and from the arrogation of powers over strategic issues of policy by the members of regional and central boards.

Corporatist debates and implications for trade unionism

On one view the escalation of intervention of the state by way of actual public ownership has been paralleled by a restructuring of the private sector as part of a wider proliferation of corporatist political and economic forms. Theoretically, however, there have been a number of strands in the corporatist thesis all of which have radically different implications in terms of their analytical placement in an overall model of trade union action and behaviour. Hence, if we leave aside for the moment the contributions of Pahll and Winckler on the grounds that these constitute an interpretation of corporatism as a distinctive *ideology* by means of which, in a comprehensive economic system, 'the state intensively channels predominantly privately-owned business towards four goals, which have become increasingly explicit during the current economic crisis: Order, Unity, Nationalism and "Success",'[45] two points of divergence remain between the interpretations of Schmitter and of the Marxist writers such as Panitch[46] and Jessop.[47]

In Schmitter's conception, corporatism was a form of post-liberal interest intermediation which informed his fundamental distinction between state and societal corporatism.[48] For after all, societal rights and the influence of intermediate organizations (such as trade unions) were, on this conception, demanded by the membership (or their leaders), rather than being viewed as a concomitant of the 'post-liberal, advanced capitalist, organized democratic welfare state'. To be sure, the 'imperative necessity' was identified[49]

for a stable, bourgeois-dominant regime, due to processes of concentration of ownership, competition between national economies, expansion of the role of public policy and rationalization of decision making within the state to associate or incorporate subordinate classes and status groups more closely within the political process.

But, equally, in Schmitter's judgment, changes in the mode of 'interest representation' could not be attributed primarily to 'independent changes in economic or political processes'.[50] In short, the growing power and aspirations of labour movements could themselves bring about corporatist modes of political and economic governance. Although this may be of little empirical consequence, it is theoretically relevant since it sharply separates Schmitter's account from rival formulations in which the changing role of unions in the moden era is seen as following rather than as occasioning these fundamental transformations.

In Panitch's thesis, briefly, corporatist tendencies were to be located in the change in the balance of class forces although a *structural* inequality in the terms of the labour contract was still manifest.[51] Moreover, Jessop has extended this notion in terms of Althusserian categories. Thus, envisaging corporatism as the highest form of social democracy, he has further analysed its development in terms of an institutionalized political form within the 'capitalist mode of production'. Hence, by defining social formation in terms of an amalgam of overlapping modes of production (which produce a complex and specific class structure and also the uneven development of economic, political and ideological practice), the state may in turn be construed as a factor of cohesion in the social formation.[52]

The analytical placement of the state in the overall explanation of modern trade union practice has thus been a source of dispute amongst leading writers on corporatism. But in so far as its more detailed effects upon union-management relations are concerned the rather different works of Offe[53] and Crouch[54] again are also worthy of mention. For Offe, the increasing intervention of the state may be disrupting the character of union-management bargaining by its steady erosion of the achievement principle.[55] Hence, at a macro economic level, a number of structural changes would appear to have been destroying the basis for rewarding members of the enterprise on the grounds of criteria such as effort, responsibility and skill. After all, the 'technical politicization of society' occasioned by state power in the 'reproduction process' (e.g. in the provision of investment capital) has served to reduce the significance of 'material incentives' as a control mechanism because *administrative* rather than *market* criteria have progressively governed interaction between the state and the organization's members.[56] On these assumptions, not only have the principles of the achievement society been commensurately eroded but there has also been a steady displacement of the 'initiative functions' to anonymous decision making centres, the replacement of market-guiding mechanisms by the administrative application of state power and the loss by growing sections of the labour force of their immediate link with the sphere of production with the consequence that patterns of distribution are increasingly *independent* of industrial performance.[57] By extension, such a process encourages collectivist rather than individual strategies, and a focus on 'task-discontinuous status organizations' in which institutional loyalties and additional normative orientations take precedence over technical and economic modes of control and distribution of rewards.[58]

The relationship between advances in corporatism and *trade union* action and behaviour has also been considered in the work of Crouch who has referred to '*bargained corporatism*' rather than to societal corporatism to designate the typical industrial relations pattern which, in so far as trade union, management and state relations in Britain are concerned, has been prevalent in recent years.[59] This being so, then, the state, which has become implicated in economic policy and investment, is obliged in turn to have a detailed policy on industrial relations. But:[60]

> The strategy of bargained corporatism represents a subordinate response to dominant corporatist strategies in the same way that a certain form of liberal collectivism constituted the subordinate response to dominant strategies in the era of low unemployment and mass prosperity. It involves the acceptance by unions of several strategies which, compared with liberal collectivism, constitute a set-back for subordinate interests. But it also holds out the chance of advances. Unions are tempted — and frightened — by corporatist developments to sacrifice some of their entrenched but narrow and unambitious achievements in exchange for the possibility of greater political influence and more and broader power for their members in the workplace, but at the same time to accept more restraint, a more obvious role for unions in restraining their members, more state interference and fuller acceptance of the existing industrial order and its priorities.

Economic variables and long-term economic movements

Yet the modern politico-economic school of labour theory has also involved attempts to relate changes in trade unionism to cyclical movements rather than to evolutionary trends in the nature of state and industrial relations. As a result, the analysis of variables underpinning the growth of unionism has become more sophisticated in terms both of the quality of industrial relations scholarship and of the level of operational expertise (especially in the use of econometric models). This assessment applies particularly to the study of Bain and Elsheikh, *Union Growth and the Business Cycle*, in which the effects of a limited number of economic variables upon union growth have been extensively documented.[61] The authors have thus related their model both to data for the UK from 1893 to 1970 and to material from the USA, Australia and Sweden and sought to determine the effects of four main explanatory variables; namely, the rate of change in retail prices, the rate of change of money wages, the level and/or rate of change of unemployment, and the proportion of all workers legally entitled to unionize who are in fact members.[62] Thus the general form of the model was: $\Delta T = f (\Delta P, \Delta W, U, D, \epsilon)$. This suggests 'that the determinants of the proportional rate of change of union membership are the proportional rate of change in retail prices, the proportional rate of changes of wages, the level and/or the proportional rate of change of unemployment, and the level of union density' (with ϵ being a random disturbance term).[63]

Many early contributions about the determinants of union growth had of course related major fluctuations in membership to the business cycle and especially to the key components such as the cost of living, unemployment and wages. Davis, in particular, drew a relevant distinction between rising prices and improvements in business conditions and argued that the former provided the main stimulus for an advance in union membership.[64] Moreover, Bain and Elsheikh employed complex econometric methods to demonstrate that rising prices undoubtedly encourage union growth because of the major 'threat effect' upon living standards. Similarly, as this study also recognized, there is a corresponding 'credit effect', in terms of wages, on the part of unions which have secured rises for the membership in such exigencies. Equally, increases in unemployment which are consequential upon reduced economic circumstances will tend to depress the bargaining power of unions and eventually overall membership totals, while at high levels of union density the general effect of these fluctuations of course will be only moderate.[65]

Again, in the analysis by Bain and Price of recent changes in union growth (particularly in the white-collar sector), the significance of economic variables and particularly of the respective 'threat' and 'credit' effects in a period of rising inflation have been emphasized.[66] And, although if the varying rates of growth in different unions are analysed for the 1970s, it would seem clear that the spectacular rises in membership in public sector, managerial and white-collar unions were also consequential upon the expansion of state activities and the shift in the pattern of occupations from the market sector to public administration and services,[67] equally there is little doubt that inflationary forces were critical as well.

In the debate between Richardson[68] and Bain and Elsheikh[69] on the determinants of union growth, however, some interesting points were raised on the effect of economic variables which are worth a brief mention. Richardson contrasted what he suggested were the fresh and perceptive insights of the pioneers of labour theory with contemporary mechanical models and commented that, as it stood, the Bain and Elsheikh formula lacked analytical penetration, a claim which he tried to justify in terms of an account of the hypothesized relationships (such as the effects of price inflation, union recognition and unemployment on union growth). However, his more serious and interesting criticisms centred on the direction of the causal link between the main variables (e.g. he considered that union growth itself could be a cause as well as a consequence of inflation) and on the explicitly aggregative character of the overall model.[70] In their reply, Elsheikh and Bain defended the model and restated the view that changes in union membership were conditional upon the *propensity* and *opportunity* to unionize.[71] Moreover, the disaggregated variables, which, on the face of it, appeared to yield inconsistent results were the subject of a later paper.[72] Hence, in their *inter-industry* analysis of unionization in Britain, Bain and Elsheikh noted that determinants of unionization had usually been examined under three main heads: the business cycle, the composition of the labour force (age, sex, proportion of part-time workers, degree of labour turnover, region, occupation) and establishment size and market structure.[73] Since we are considering here the question of *levels* of structural analysis it is of interest that they also documented the structural underpinnings of union growth and the change in the impact of given variables (e.g. skill level) over time. Moreover, the significance of the institutionalization of unions in British society and of the links between this and the individual characteristics of firms and industries were explored:[74]

> The insignificance of the manual skill, white-collar status, and part-time employment variables, as well as the declining significance of sex and, to some extent, the age variables, over the period 1951-1971 points to the increasing institutionalization of unions in British society. . . . In short, as unions are increasingly accepted as part of the structure of British society and union membership becomes increasingly widespread, it becomes less dependent upon the self-selection of individuals with similar personal characteristics and attitudes and more dependent upon the characteristics of the firms and industries in which individuals work.

In short, not only should a number of levels of structural analysis be incorporated into the explanatory model, but the institutional and organizational properties of unions examined historically would also seem to be an important element in the overall equation.

Technological structures

But political-economic factors are not the only structural variables to have moulded the character of British trade unionism, for associated developments in technology have been crucial too, as, indeed, proponents of the so-called 'technical implications' school have persuasively argued. Thus, drawing upon the writings of Blauner,[75] Sayles,[76] and Woodward[77] especially, the case has been advocated that technology substantially affects a number of key components of workplace industrial relations such as alienation, the structure of workgroups, the patterns of managerial organizations, and, of course, the ultimate character of trade unionism itself.

Thus the general movement in the technical base of manufacturing industry typically involves a gradual withering away of early craft forms of production and their steady replacement by intermediary forms of technology (and notably machine-tending and assembly line processes of manufacture) together with fully automated factories, as in the petrochemical industries.[78] A transition of this kind almost certainly bears upon technical alienation and the nature of productive tasks in the enterprise, both of which, in turn, have an impact upon the patterns of union formation and the social attitudes and aspirations of the membership. To be sure, as Braverman[79] and more recently Nichols and Beynon[80] have observed, the work environment of technically-sophisticated plants can still provide only limited opportunities for satisfaction, but there remains a grain of truth in Blauner's view that technical sources of alienation follow the patterns of an inverted 'u' shaped curve.[81] In other words, at both extremes of the technical scale (craft production and full automation) work tasks may be *relatively* satisfying, at least by way of contrast with intermediary forms of technology where highly repetitive, fragmented, and meaningless work tasks are commonplace. In consequence, in workplaces in which intermediary ranges of technology are a dominant feature, the greatest hostility in the relationships between management and worker is usually evident and the highest incidence of militant action by trade unionists in support of any claim is most to be expected. Moreover, the perennial outcrop of disputes in motor manufacturing industries are usually explained at least in part upon the basis of such assumptions.

The effects of technology on workplace alienation are exacerbated in two further respects: first, by management structures; and second, by the different levels of skill demanded in various enterprises. Indeed, as Woodward has demonstrated, authoritarian and bureaucratized management systems are most commonly found in intermediary-range technical environments, and these thereby compound the already considerable asperities which arise from the spread of repetitive and insignificant work tasks.[82] Moreover, as the technical scale is ascended, the ratio of clerical and administrative staff to manual workers almost invariably rises, an inclination which obviously facilitates a growth in trade unionism amongst white-collar and even managerial employees. But, by way of contrast, the extremes of the technical scale tend to produce similar proportions of skilled to semi- or unskilled workers, a situation which potentially induces cyclical patterns in the growth of unionization amongst shop floor workers.[83] Furthermore, recurrent alterations in technology reflect instabilities which in turn imply that customary procedures for handling disputes, established arrangements between particular unions and so on may be in continual need of redefinition and reformulation.[84]

But the relationship between technology and union structure and character cannot be reasonably held to be determinist. This is evident not only in the diverse prognoses of 'technical implications' theorists themselves but also in view of the major inter-industry and international variations in unionism in situations in which roughly equivalent technological systems have been installed.[85] Thus, for example, Mallet perceived bureaucratic union structures as in part a reflection of mass production technologies but was confident that radical reconstruction of the union movement and a major shift in union goals would be a consequence of automated forms of production.[86]

Blauner took the opposite view suggesting that the very same process of evolution would lead to an integration of the worker into the enterprise and even to a disavowal of the legitimacy of oppositional modes of organization themselves.[87]

The division of labour

Yet movements in the politico-economic and technical bases of modern society are associated with a third primary structural influence upon the character of its constituent trade unions. This is the intricate division of labour which obtains in all indigenous industries and which is indeed a characteristic shared by all societies of the industrial type. The recognition of the social ramifications of the division of labour can be attributed, of course, to both Durkheim[88] and Marx,[89] although each offered a unique appraisal of the phenomena involved. For Marx, the division of labour was associated with the progressive alienation of mankind and hence its transcendence in future socialist societies was a cardinal goal, whereas for Durkheim, as Giddens has suggested[90]

> the growth of the division of labour, is portrayed in terms of the integrating consequences of specialization rather than in terms of the formation of class systems. Consequently, Durkheim treats class conflict, not as providing a basis for the revolutionary restructuring of society, but as symptomatic of deficiencies in the moral

co-ordination of different occupational groups within the division of labour. . . . According to Durkheim's standpoint, the criteria underlying Marx's hopes for the elimination of technological alienation represent a reversion to moral principles which are no longer appropriate to the modern form of society.

In short, on these assumptions, the division of labour is an essential foundation of all industrial-type societies and its unfolding can only be reversed by the deliberate destruction of the very roots of modern communities with a consequent return to more primitive economic and technological forms. To be sure, in the long-term, the full automation of industry could permit the flowering of post-industrial cultures and facilitate the growth of harmonious social communities at a higher evolutionary stage, but, until such time, the division of labour will continue as a permanent constituent of the underlying social framework itself.

But the division of labour has unquestionably affected trade unionism on two main counts. First, it serves to fragment the interests of working people, to produce major variations in income, skill levels, and working conditions, and to reduce the propensity for an augmentation of explicitly class forms of consciousness. Second, the multifarious tasks associated with the division of labour require co-ordination, a state of affairs which facilitates a spread of administrative, bureaucratic, and managerial staff and the formation of a cleavage between those who exercise decision-making power and those over whom this power is exercised. Hence, the general process of social differentiation accompanying the progressive advance of the division of labour has major consequences for union structure. After all, by comparison with large general unions (which have been formed around discrete industries and services), the small occupationally specific crafts and even the industrial unions are by no means well adapted to long-term survival. Of course, while the Marxian idea of the progressive elimination of the division of labour would seem inconsistent with advanced economic systems, equally, Durkheim's notion of the *integrative* consequences of this deep structural condition have not been fulfilled.[91] On the contrary, it is clear that a wide range of dissatisfying and alienative work environments, in which the creative capacities of working people have been stunted and constrained, have evolved during the course of the development of the twentieth century.[92] But this in no way invalidates the *significance* of the division of labour for union structure, for the genesis of work tasks which would seem to generate hostilities which find expression in union action, and for the requirements of bureaucratic (rather than spontaneous) modes of integration which create a cleavage of interests along the control dimension itself.

DERIVATIVE OR SECONDARY STRUCTURAL 'DETERMINANTS'

It has been our intention in this chapter so far to indicate the extent to which three primary structures (the politico-economic framework, technology, and the division of labour) have shaped the contours of modern trade unionism. In this section, therefore, it is appropriate to modify the focus of our attention in order to illustrate the effects of certain derivative or secondary structures. These, as we have seen, consist of social structures which, while undoubtedly affecting developments in trade unionism, are themselves explicable in terms of movements in the primary structures which we examined in the foregoing pages. There are many potentially relevant secondary structures, but four main clusters are especially salient: first, the class and occupational structure; second, the size of the enterprise; third, the enterprise environment; and fourth, micro-structural factors.

The class and occupational structure

We have dealt at some length with the relationship between social class, occupation and the distribution of power in the previous chapter and any lengthy recapitulation of themes would be superfluous at this point. It should not be forgotten, however, that a number of theorists of trade unionism have attempted to link structural levels in a way which encompasses these key distinctions.

From a Marxist standpoint, the works of Crompton[93] and Crompton and Gubbay[94] have been the most sophisticated here. Crompton, in particular, has argued that the 'structuration' of class (and of working-class organizations) is functionally integrated into the market structure of capitalism. Moreover, although in the early phases of development a fusion of ownership and control could be detected, gradually the many and varied tasks and operations in the capitalist function have been absorbed by specialist agencies and this has produced a more complex class composition in which certain white-collar workers, especially, perform both capital and labour functions.[95] But changes in the formation of classes (in terms of both numbers and 'objective' interests) can potentially be predicted from a knowledge of underlying movements in 'the capitalist mode of production' and these, in this sense, mediate between these primary movements and the concrete organization and development of trade unions themselves.

Meanwhile, non-Marxists have also perceived such changes in occupational structure to be crucial for the long-term evolution of trade unionism and have predicted the gradual enlargement and even the eventual dominance of the white-collar sector in future years.[96] Occupational changes, though, are to be explained on these rather different assumptions in terms of movements in technology (the eradication of certain types of jobs and the creation of others), increased material well-being, accompanying economic advance (which facilitates the expansion of the service sector), and the progressive differentiation of occupations which has been further encouraged by the division of labour.[97]

Size of enterprise

Trade unions, then, have patently been transformed by a distinctive pattern of occupational variation, but, looking at other derivative structures, enterprise size is also of decisive significance. However, the composition of capital and of the labour force in productive operations is, in turn, of course, in part a product of other undercurrents in the politico-economic and technical structures, notably a build-up in the organic composition of capital, an extension of publicly owned industries and services, and the emergence of complex technical and organizational 'systems'.

The association between enterprise size and density of unionization has by now been well documented[98] and although the precise factors involved in this relationship are open to dispute, the following are the most noteworthy. To begin with, when large numbers of working people are congregated together they are apt to perceive common interests vis-à-vis their employers and this stimulates joint action via trade unionism. Equally, the quality of work experience is not the same in large- as opposed to small-scale companies. Thus as Ingham has pointed out, work tasks in the small firm are usually more varied and allow for greater autonomy than is possible in the very large enterprise.[99] Third, the levels of non-economic rewards are closely and inversely related to the size of firm, a factor which is obviously conducive to trade unionism in the larger enterprise because dissatisfactions at work are correspondingly more intense. Fourth, the large scale company is also likely to be administered on bureaucratic lines, and as we have already seen this encourages trade unionism. Finally, trade union officers will probably concentrate their recruitment campaigns on the large-scale companies because potential gains are optimal under these conditions. These factors, in combination, undoubtedly help to produce a very strong association between enterprise size and density of trade unionism, a connection which is especially noticeable amongst white-collar, salaried employees.[100]

Size of enterprise has also been related to variations in union *character*. In addition to Ingham's work, the Bolton Committee of Inquiry,[101] E.F. Schumacher,[102] and Batstone[103] have all propounded the view that vertical social relationships will be more rewarding in the small firms 'because they promote direct and close associations with owners and managers in ways which are virtually impossible in the large firm' and, by extension, they thereby reduce the propensity for indirect forms of industrial action.[104] None the less, Curran and Stanworth have suggested that an appreciation of deeper modes of structural patterning is necessary to an understanding of such relationships, noting more specifically, that:[105]

> Workers in small firms do not escape the deprivations of the capitalistically organized enterprise . . . it has also been argued that the industrial subculture, that is, the technology and other meanings, definitions and institutionalized social practices peculiar to an industry are also sociologically more important than the alleged 'size effect' in discussing social relations in the small firm.

Hence, although the connection between size of enterprise and union militancy remains a plausible hypothesis, it should be examined in the context of a wider nexus of relationships and structural patterns at a number of different explanatory levels.

Community structures

Yet no productive enterprise is an entirely closed system: on the contrary, the community structure in which it operates places limits on the nature of its operations and, by extension, the character of trade unionism at workplace level. Moreover, in the sociological literature, the pervasive role of such locally based communities in affecting relationships in the firm *and* union has been frequently illustrated.

The salience of local communities in the context of trade unionism is potentially twofold: in the first place, the fabric of communities affects the extent of individual commitment to trade unionism itself; and in the second, it influences the degree of solidarity which can be anticipated during the course of any industrial dispute. The most general statements upon the repercussions of community environments for these patterns have been developed by Salaman,[106] and of course, by Kerr and Siegel,[107] who traced variations in inter-industry propensity to strike very largely to the structure of various occupational communities. To be sure, in the light of later analysis on the Kerr-Siegel thesis it may be that a thorough reappraisal of the validity of this influential argument is required,[108] although on *a priori* grounds a single industry community, with little occupational differentiation and geographical or social isolation would appear conducive to solidary trade union action even if its effects on strike patterns has been greatly exaggerated. Moreover, from recent researches it would certainly appear that occupational communities play a role 'in directing dissatisfaction towards a *structural* target' (e.g., employers); a phenomenon which is in turn associated with industrial militancy and organized forms of conflict themselves.[109]

Nevertheless, it is worth emphasizing that the social composition of local communities is profoundly affected by underlying movements in economic and technical structures. Thus, with technical advance, the number of workers employed in mining, shipbuilding, textiles and so on (and hence in their attendant communities) has been severely curtailed. Moreover, any acceleration in the pace of technical change has profound consequences for the propensity of workers to develop stable communities based around distinctive and traditional occupations. Again, enhanced economic opportunities have served to promote processes of urban renewal and, by degrees, to impinge upon family and community relations in urban locales. Hence, variations in these two primary structures have decidedly reduced the opportunities for building lasting and sustained community ties during the post-Second World War period, a departure which may offer some explanation for the emergence of strong instrumental goals amongst disparate sections of the working population.[110]

Micro-structural elements

Nevertheless, factors associated with enterprise environment by no means exhaust all the structural influences upon the character of the British trade union movement. Indeed, the focus of our analysis so far has been confined almost entirely to macro-structural factors: in order to redress this balance, therefore, it is appropriate at this juncture to turn our attention to the so-called 'micro-level'.

Aspects of the day-to-day operation of trade unionism at plant level are thus in many ways contingent upon micro-structural factors as is evidenced by the volume of research in industrial sociology which has focused upon the composition and dynamics of workgroups, and the ways in which these may condition commitment to trade unionism.[111] Hence, an essential distinction between occupational categories, task groups and sociable groupings in industry has evolved[112] and these elements in turn reflect the division of labour, technology and community influences respectively. Secondly, with respect to trade unionism, an early statement of the effects of workgroups upon its character was made by Sayles,[113] who posited a typology which included apathetic, erratic, strategic and conservative workgroups: the lowest levels of participation in union affairs obtaining, as one would anticipate, amongst the apathetic and conservative workgroups.[114]

In Britain, too, a strong association has been identified between levels of skill demanded of workgroups and the propensity of members to join and to take an active part in union affairs.[115] Indeed, even in the affluent worker studies, where Goldthorpe and his colleagues judged the role of workgroups to be limited, a caveat was none the less introduced to exempt craftsmen and, to a lesser extent, setters, from this overall assessment.[116] Earlier research by Lupton[117] and Cunnison[118] also revealed the diversity which exists in the attitudes and conduct of different groups of workers and both drew attention to wider community as well as technical and organizational factors to explain these variations.

The recent industrial relations and industrial sociology literature have also reflected an interest in the role of workgroups in conditioning the outlook and behaviour of shop stewards and other plant-based trade union representatives.[119] Hence the relationship between stewards and the 'member network' has been highlighted in a number of studies and the evidence suggests that, although stewards enjoy a substantial measure of autonomy in terms of the initiation of issues, in the long run they have no power without the support of workgroup members.[120] The configuration of workgroups and the role of opinion leaders would thus seem to have a bearing upon shop steward actions and behaviour even though stewards are not merely workgroup leaders and, indeed, may derive much information and formulate their overall social and political perspectives from steward rather than member networks.[121]

Moreover, the relationship between *structure* and *process* may be identified particularly clearly at the micro-level as, indeed, the analyses of Levinson[122] and Walton and McKersie have indicated.[123] In these studies, the strategy and features of the bargaining process were examined as well as 'the role of the economic, political and other environmental forces that determine the more basic power relationship of the parties'.[124] Walton and McKersie identified four systems of activity 'each with its own function for the interacting parties, its own internal logic, and its own identifiable set of instrumental acts or tactics'.[125] More specifically, these corresponded to four subprocesses: *distributive bargaining* (to restore conflicts of interest); *integrative bargaining* (to find common or complementary interests); *attitudinal structuring* (to influence the attitudes of the participants towards each other); and *intraorganizational bargaining* (to achieve consensus within each of the interacting groups).[126]

SUMMARY

The objective of this chapter has been to highlight modern *structural* approaches to the analysis of trade unions, focusing on a number of different explanatory levels in which the developing arguments have been conducted. In addition to the power of the constituent groups and 'subjective' aspects associated with culture, values and perception, a number of fundamental institutional and organizational theories of labour have been formulated and it is to our enumeration of these that our attention now turns.

7 Organizations, institutions and their environments

The concept of social structure as interpreted in our argument so far has been paralleled in literature in which organizational *structures* have been viewed both as external to the individual and capable of exercising constraint upon action and behaviour. Of course, modern versions of organizational analysis have been sensitive to strictures against interpreting social action as being conditioned entirely by the properties of social systems,[1] but an appreciation of union behaviour in terms of the structure of bargaining systems and of the properties of formal union organization at national and local levels has become increasingly widespread.[2]

In this chapter, then, after a brief recapitulation of the salience of the *structure of collective bargaining* for trade union action and behaviour, we shall focus on the major approaches to the study of trade unions as organizations. From an analytical point of view, organizational and institutional structures have usually been understood as *intervening* variables which, while having demonstrable effects upon internal decision-making processes within unions, have in turn been shaped by a variety of wider conditions. These have been conventionally classified as environmental variables.

Hence, if these relationships are expressed diagrammatically we have Model A in which 'structural', 'subjective' and power factors are all incorporated in the usual formulation, and the principal variation, Model B, in which the significance of institutional and organizational variables are countenanced. Bearing in mind that, in the literature on organizations, the focus has tended to be on union government rather than union structure, growth or character, in terms of modern theories of unionism, the analytical placement of the main sets of variables would appear to be as set out in Figure 7.1.

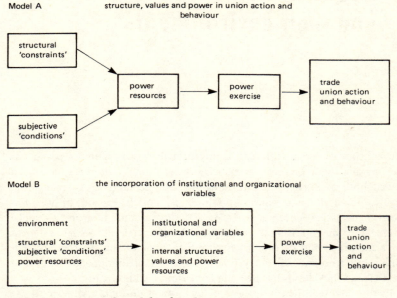

Figure 7.1   *General models of trade unionism*

THE STRUCTURE OF COLLECTIVE BARGAINING:
THE FOCUS ON INSTITUTIONS

We highlighted in chapter 4 the theory of union behaviour under collective bargaining associated with Clegg's contribution to trade union analysis in which variations in union behaviour were explained by collective bargaining.[3] More specifically, structural variations in the institutions of collective bargaining were identified as significant determinants of international differences in overall density of union membership, in union structure and government, in workplace organization, in strike propensity and in industrial democracy.[4] While bargaining structures should be construed as *intervening variables* between broader structural pressures, or cultural or subjective contingencies, or again the power of participants to collective bargaining, this explanatory interpretation was itself the culmination of a series of earlier contributions of the 'institutionalist' tradition associated with the founding members of the liberal-pluralist or Oxford school.

MODERN ORGANIZATIONAL APPROACHES

Issues and problems

The emergence of organizational 'theory' as a dominant perspective in the history of sociological thought was originally closely associated with the rise of structural-functionalism during the 1950s and early 1960s.[5] At that time, there was a prevalent fashion for establishing middle-range propositions about human behaviour, following a growing disenchantment with highly abstract and general sociological theories and a widespread view that researches based solely on an individual or group level of analysis were of only limited sociological import. Moreover, in direct contrast with the inter-war period and with the later 1960s and 1970s there seemed to be far greater and more widely shared prosperity, economic growth of an apparently lasting character, and a reduction in the pervasiveness of social class antagonism.[6] In consequence, in this milieu, the emphasis in these middle-range inquiries was at the time focused one-sidedly upon notions of order, stability and value consensus (as successful solutions to ubiquitous conflict) and this could be one explanation for the manifest limitations of the early varieties of organizational sociology.[7]

Yet these criticisms of organization theory are now hardly valid since there have been many recent modifications, theoretical and empirical, with the result that, at present, no serious analyst of organizations would deliberately underestimate the significance of conflict and power in processes of decision-making.[8] Beyond this, a sophisticated theoretical debate has been conducted between advocates of the 'constraint' and 'choice' perspectives, which, as Sorge and Warner have recognized, is an indication of the range of methodological and theoretical assumptions which undergird the study of organizations.[9] Similarly, in modern organizational analysis an attempt 'to marry up "micro" and "macro" perspectives' as well as environmental constraints and internal functioning has been evident. Indeed, as these same authors have insisted:[10]

> Instead of getting caught between the opposing notions of unilinear constraints and free choice, and the attached monopolistic claims of methodological legitimacy, we propose a way of studying organizational functional equivalents as parts of the wide context of society.

At the same time, the input of action variables has in substantial measure overcome the familiar problem of reification which arises when organizations, which, after all, are ultimately sociological abstractions, are envisaged as exhibiting the properties of active human beings, as indeed Silverman has noted:[11]

By treating the 'goals' and 'needs' of organizations as givens, it seems to us that we are attributing apparently human motivations to inanimate objects: in other words, we are reifying the organization. Instead of attempting to establish empirically the conceptions of ends and needs held by its members, we begin with *a priori* notions of an organization's 'needs' and then examine the processes through which it secures them. This can only divert attention away from 'why' questions and towards 'how' questions; away from causes and towards consequences.

Yet, the action frame of reference and, by extension, the interpretation of organizations as *artifacts* would seem to allow most of the aforementioned problems to be resolved satisfactorily.[12] Conflict, change and power, for example, are all central themes of this analysis, while reification is simply dealt with by defining goals as the attributes of individuals or groups within the organization. Indeed, such a perspective entails identifying the primary objectives of the membership (especially those of the most active) and where conflict exists, gauging the distribution of power amongst organized groups within the union itself.[13] But it should also imply a recognition of various structural constraints (both within and external to the organization) which shape the terrain of social action.

The most successful models of unions as organizations would thus appear to involve an integration of *environmental constraints* with *formal organizational* (including social action) *variables*. Traditionally, however, adherents of the first perspective have sought to explain variations in different unions by reference to (a) *general societal movements*; (b) the *evolution of union forms*; or (c) factors in the *context* in which unions are located. By way of contrast, those who favour organizational approaches have examined the operation of forces *within* trade unions and emphasize the significance of different (a) *functions*; (b) *modes of regulation*; and (c) *internal structural procedures* and the *actions of members*.

ENVIRONMENTAL APPROACHES

General societal movements

The first branch of environmental theory involves the delineation of fundamental economic, political and social forces which are deemed to constrain the growth of certain types of union government while encouraging other forms to flourish. Implicit in this approach is the recognition of an association between the degree of centralization in trade unions and the proliferation of oligarchic and bureaucratic modes of organization.[14] Indeed, on these assumptions, centralization in trade unions is enhanced by three primary structural elements: the supremacy of the state in economic planning; the concentration of economic resources in private and public sectors; and the pervasiveness of Britain's largest unions.

None the less, the environmental theory of trade union 'administration' is by no means confined to the examination of a number of strategic structural variables, for writers of this genre have also generally recognized the conditioning effects of ethical and normative codes. Indeed, these *subjective* forces are believed to influence the government and internal structure of unions in three main respects. First, a commitment to democratic values is a source of inspiration for those who wish to challenge any regression to bureaucratic and oligarchic practices. Second, acceptance of a variety of interpretations of the democratic ideal (these being understood by reference to broader political philosophies) has doubtless been reflected in institutional procedures. Third, the prevalence of bureaucratic arrangements may be traced, at least in part, to the spread of rationalism and of 'mass' democratic and egalitarian creeds. But until Max Weber demonstrated the connection, it was not fully appreciated that bureaucratic and democratic currents typically advance in parallel. Indeed, for Weber bureaucracy was the principal institutional manifestation of western rationalism:[15]

> The bureaucratic structure is everywhere a late product of historical development. The further back we trace our steps, the more typical is the absence of bureaucracy and of officialdom in general. Since bureaucracy has a 'rational' character, with rules, means-end calculus, and matter-of-factness predominating, its rise and expansion has everywhere had 'revolutionary' results, in a special sense still to be discussed as had the advance of *rationalism* in general. The march of bureaucracy accordingly destroyed structures of domination which were not rational in this sense of the term.

But its progress was at the same time enhanced by two other phenomena, namely socialism and 'mass' democracy. For in Weber's words bureaucratic organization 'has usually come into power on the basis of a leveling of economic and social differences'.[16] And again: 'The democratization of society in its totality, and in the *modern* sense of the term, whether actual or perhaps merely formal, is an especially favourable basis of bureaucratization.'[17] To take the example of a large-scale union, the policy, say, to accord all members equal treatment and identical benefits at times of ill-health, sickness and so on, engenders in turn standard procedures and rules governing a whole series of contingencies. In short, therefore, it acts as a spur to bureaucratic administrative practices.

Moreover, the prevalence of bureaucratic procedures may well depend on the exigencies of wider power struggles between unions, employers and government. Indeed, the association between disciplined, bureaucratically-organized action and *success* in social and economic conflicts was again emphasized by Weber, for, 'as an instrument of rationally organizing authority relations', he claimed that bureaucracy was 'a power instrument of the first order for one who controls the bureaucratic apparatus.'[18] He thus recognized that, when roughly equal conditions prevailed, 'rationally organized and directed action' was superior not only to every other variety of collective behaviour but also to 'social action' which opposed it.[19] The inevitable effect of this in a union context was that the early local trade clubs, relying almost entirely upon voluntary efforts, were no match for a disciplined employer. Indeed, the Webbs also noted that the 'exigencies of their warfare with the employers' were primarily responsible for departures from simple democratic ideals.[20] While, in their view, ample proof of this proposition was to be found in the adoption of centralized financial and policy-making bodies; a move which not only occasioned the emergence of a 'practically irresistible bureaucracy', but at the same time ushered in constitutions which enabled trade unions 'to attain a high degree of efficiency'.[21]

Evolutionary factors

In a further approach, however, the development of modern organizational forms has been viewed as the outcome of a complex historical process of interaction between trade unions and their environment. Moreover, in such an analysis, a lengthy time-scale has been envisaged in which, in response to major changes in the environment, outbursts of 'evolutionary energy' have been directed to the establishment of initial modes of organization or to a fundamental transformation of the essential framework.[22]

The germs of an evolutionary perspective on union internal structure and government originated in the respective works of the Webbs and G.D.H. Cole, but by far the most comprehensive historical and neo-evolutionary theory (in which early origins were viewed as a critical element in explaining the present circumstances of unions) has derived from Turner who employed his familiar classification of 'closed' and 'open' unions to great effect in this context.[23]

Indeed, by way of illustration, Turner demonstrated that there have been three main 'themes' in the evolution of British trade union government. Thus, in the craft amalgamations, there was early support for centralization followed by movements of an opposing character, and here the typical structure consists of a small executive committee subject to re-election. In the 'mass successors' to the new unions, however, authority usually resides in a large annual or biennial assembly of delegates who entrust executive decision to a committee which is in turn responsible for the appointment of full-time officers. Lastly, in federally-organized unions (such as the cotton industry), authority primarily rests in the hands of the union's local and sectoral units.[24]

Pressure towards centralized administration in the craft unions emerged partly then from an obligation to accumulate benefit reserves and partly from attempts to control mobility in crafts to effect a reduction in the 'random' element involved in tramping and other associated practices.[25] But in the adoption of centralized government, the crafts may well have drawn sustenance from a very ancient model, the great urban guild.[26] Gradually, however, external demands for local control gained ascendancy and in the example of the Amalgamated Engineering Union a considerable measure of local autonomy was ceded to back up a traditional pattern of decentralized bargaining.

By contrast, the experience of local autonomy among new unions has been minimal not because of their size *per se* but because, in Turner's judgment, at critical points in their development, they were constructed on national lines by their professional leaders.[27] Above all, in the 1910s, when the governing structure of the new unions began to crystallize, there was an obvious absence of the cohesiveness of purpose and occupational-based solidarity that was of such great moment to craft workers in guaranteeing a high degree of internal self-government. And in such a milieu, of course, the power of professional leaders to shape a particular decision-making structure within their unions was in practice difficult to resist.[28]

The closed-open distinction was also employed by Turner to explicate variations in the practice of union democracy. Taking the view that the day-to-day government of unions depends upon the relationships between full-time officers, lay members who actually take part in union management, and the rank-and-file, Turner noted that craft unions have a propensity towards 'exclusive democracy', that is to say, in these unions lay members exert a strong influence, high membership participation is common, and branches are small with a low ratio of officers to members. By contrast, in unions which have expanded from an originally closed craft base, intense involvement is usually apparent only amongst the aristocracy, whose members, in turn, comprise a high proportion of officialdom. Finally, in open unions, described as 'popular bossdoms', responsibility for government rests with paid officials, membership participation is low, branches are large and meetings poorly attended, and the ratio of officers to members high.[29]

Of course, as Hughes has argued, the notion of 'exclusive democracy' is too pessimistic in stressing the relationship between closed unionism and participatory democracy,[30] especially if shop floor unionism is included in our purview. But what is critical to note, in the works of the Webbs and Cole as well as Turner, is an explicit recognition of the time dimension and its strategic role in the inquiry into the environmental roots of British trade union government. In essence, the inference here is that however entrenched unions appear to be in the modern era their complexities cannot be fully comprehended on this basis, since the heart of their composition is a reflection of a series of adaptations emanating from their earliest days. Similarly, an all-embracing model of trade union organization must perforce take account of a number of 'evolutionary survivals' in contemporary institutional practices. Moreover, even if we eschew the language of the evolutionists, there can be little doubt that early structural and subjective influences, together with past struggles against employers and government, have made a lasting imprint upon the fabric of modern unionism.

'Contextual' variables

The notion of context, while often understood as more restricted than that of environment, is on one view not dissimilar since both relate to the external situation of trade unions. Thus, in the 'contextual' approach, a series of specific economic, political and social variables are enumerated which have implications for the shape of union institutions and, especially, for the extent to which the action and behaviour of the leadership is constrained. On occasions the division between, 'contextual' and 'formal organizational' positions has appeared so wide as to be intractable,[31] but such a synthesis is an indispensible element of any sufficient treatise on union administration and government.

Above all, the contextual approach offers the opportunity to determine, by means of multivariate analyses, the explanatory value of each main dimension affecting union government. A secondary advantage, but one which has factors in common with other environmental perspectives, is that it avoids treating 'the specific patterns of a union's membership composition, the contents of its rule book, and its organizational traditions, as a sufficient explanation of the nature of internal power relations'.[32] Its most obvious weakness stems from the eclecticism which it substitutes for the broad theoretical insights of other environmental schools.

In the British literature, Roderick Martin can claim to have produced the closest approximation to a contextual theory of union democracy.[33]

This work is uniquely thorough in that it also grapples with factors such as membership characteristics and union structure but elsewhere Martin associates himself particularly with the cause of the contextual vis-à-vis formal organization theorists.[34]

Martin perceived democracy in trade unions as depending upon the constraints upon leaders to accept 'healthy' internal opposition based on distinctive factions, and in this he betrayed a commitment to a variant of the civil libertarian interpretation of democracy. But he went somewhat further by postulating that the 'constraint' approach is not only particularly appropriate to 'the study of union politics' but also the most likely to yield 'an adequate theory of union democracy'.[35] Clearly, however, to allude to factions as such constituted a perspective rather than a theory, but it followed that, for Martin, issues such as membership participation in union government, shop-floor participatory democracy, and representative institutions were not in themselves the ultimate determinants of democratic practice.

From a sociological standpoint, the exposition of a series of explanatory variables largely resting in the 'environmental context' of unions was paramount. Martin thus classified restrictions upon executives being able 'to prevent oppositional factions distributing propaganda and mobilizing electoral support' into twelve categories as follows: the political culture, government attitudes and behaviour, the pattern of membership distribution, the industrial setting (including the degree of ownership concentration and collective bargaining), the economic environment, technology and the rate of technical change, the source of union bargaining power, membership characteristics, membership beliefs, opposition expertise and resources, leadership beliefs and union structure.[36] But it was solely in this ultimate group of factors that the issues of formal organizational analysis were accorded any significance.

Yet although Martin recognized the desirability of undertaking more comprehensive investigations to gauge the relative salience of each variable,[37] there remains a danger of excessive eclecticism. Indeed, not linking these dimensions more explicitly to those general societal movements outlined in the first section, or to critical periods in the evolution of the governing structure of trade unions, or even, again, to a number of fundamental categories of organizational analysis, inhibits any conclusions about which of these variables actually accounted for differences in the degree of democracy in these unions and which were associated merely in a fortuitous or random manner.

ENVIRONMENTAL AND ORGANIZATIONAL APPROACHES

It has long been obvious to the analyst that the most successful explanatory models of union government, in particular, have been founded upon a fusion of the combined strengths of environmental and internal organizational models. But before we proceed with our examination of contributions to the study of union administration from organizational theorists, it is worth briefly observing how the insights of these two competing schools can be combined.

In terms of the development of analytical frameworks, the work of Child, Loveridge and Warner, while primarily organizational in focus, has been a cornerstone of the debates so far since, as the authors argued, 'union environment is relevant to the question of administrative and representative rationality'.[38] Hence, on these assumptions, the union administrative structure and the external environment are related in the way set out in Figure 7.2.[39]

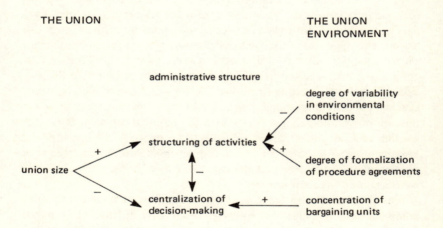

Figure 7.2   *Environmental and organizational factors in trade unionism*
(Source: J. Child, R. Loveridge and M. Warner, *Sociology*, 1973, p. 87)

None the less, the central cycle of union activity combines an administrative and a representative system within the organization itself and this includes the pressures placed on union officials, the strength of expression of members' views received by union leadership, interpretation of members' views, decisions made on behalf of unions and action taken.[40] Moreover, although we shall deal in greater detail with the specific hypotheses which were derived from the general model at a later juncture, the germs of a strategic conceptual integration between the principal schools of labour theory (relating to unions as organizations) is clearly a possibility if a greater specificity of environmental conditions is combined with the internal cyclical processes and structures (see Figure 7.3).[41]

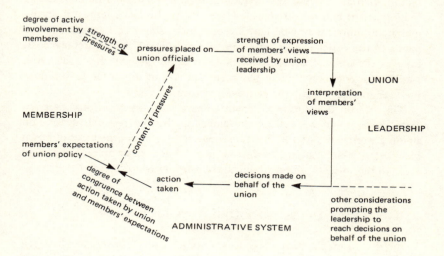

Figure 7.3   *The central cycle of union activity*
(Source: J. Child, R. Loveridge and M. Warner, *Sociology*, 1973, p. 83.)

Furthermore, in a recent study of local union democracy, there has been a valuable attempt to assess the importance 'of the union's external environment, internal processes, and organizational structure in determining the extent of democratic government at the local level'.[42] Drawing upon the work of Strauss,[43] Anderson has affirmed that the criteria of union democracy may be classified into three groups: *legal* (constitutional provisions); *behavioural* (institutionalized opposition, close elections and high participation); and *responsiveness and control* (ability of officers to respond to and reflect members' interests, and to allow a substantial amount of control to reside with the general membership).[44] But, as Anderson has cogently argued, local union democracy may in turn be influenced by *characteristics of the environment, organizational structure*, and *internal processes of the union*.[45]

Among environmental factors, then, union-management relations and environmental uncertainty were both identified as possible influences on internal modes of government. Thus, in periods of intense bitterness between unions and management, increased internal cohesion would be a likely consequence, while uncertainty should produce 'increased decentralization of power and influence throughout the organization, as well as differentiation of structure'.[46] Similarly, Anderson examined internal structural variables (complexity and control mechanisms) and other factors such as electoral and communication processes before considering the important control variables.[47] Moreover, in this latter respect decision-making in unions may well have become increasingly concentrated in the hands of top officials over time, and was considered likely to remain so as long as the union leadership was able to attain membership goals. And similarly, a common finding has been that size of union tends to reduce membership participation in processes of control.[48]

The fruitful integration of environmental and organizational perspectives, then, could be usefully developed in further research designs on union government. At this juncture, however, for the purposes of our own analysis, it is appropriate to proceed with a view to examining contributions to the study of union administration from organizational theorists.

ORGANIZATIONS AND THE SOCIOLOGY OF TRADE UNIONISM

In the first place, therefore, it is usual to observe major differences between trade unions and other varieties of organization. Indeed, Hyman and Fryer have contended that trade unions and other types of association are social units which have been purposefully created (to which we would add, 'by conscious actors under conditions not entirely of their own choosing'). In the second place, they have a measure of continuity over time despite changes in the membership and official personnel. And, third, they have a clearly defined administrative structure.[49]

Notwithstanding these similarities, the differences between trade unions and most other types of 'continuous association' are very marked. In the main this proceeds from their formally democratic character, which, in turn, implies a consideration of their *representative* as well as their *administrative* structures.[50] This democratic potential facilitates a degree of dynamism not necessarily apparent in other organizations and this has the further consequence that goals of the membership may well vary both between different unions and, over a period of time, within the same trade union. Again, to the extent that there are clashes over goals, the outcome will tend to revolve around the internal power struggles at least amongst the more active members. Furthermore, as Hyman and Fryer have also argued, trade unions are in one sense secondary associations in that they presuppose the existence of antecedent structures, and above all, the presence of a substantial number of workers 'by hand or by brain' whose position in a market economy gives them an interest in combination in the first place. They are in this sense *historically specific* organizations whose character, under different economic and social conditions, would be expected to be radically at variance with that which at present obtains.[51] In sum, therefore, Hyman and Fryer emphasized the following similarities and differences between unions and other forms of social organization:[52]

> Certain similarities are almost defining characteristics of organization: unions are social units which have been purposefully created; they exhibit continuity despite changes in membership and officials; and they possess a formally defined structure of decision-making and administration. Two other features of trade unions are empirically to be found in virtually every type of organization (though their implications are normally very different). First, those in positions of leadership face problems of internal and external administration and control which parallel those confronting other types of leaders, managers or officials. (Hence *they* at least may find some value and relevance in 'organization theory'.) Second, the members of a union may experience it in certain situations as an oppressive entity which threatens or constrains them.

Moreover, on such assumptions, trade unions are 'first and foremost a source and medium of power' and hence processes of *'differential distribution of control over and access to resources of sanctions, both material and ideological' must also be incorporated into the analysis.*[53] Once again, therefore, the significance of power as a variable has been acknowledged, but in this sense, it has been viewed as a factor in internal processes of decision-making and government and as a central defining characteristic of organization itself.

ORGANIZATIONAL APPROACHES TO THE STUDY OF TRADE UNIONS

At this point, therefore, our attention will focus more specifically upon the literature on trade unions based upon organizational perspectives. But there are, in fact, three main typologies of organizations which have a bearing upon the study of trade unionism based, first, upon the functions of the associations in question; second, upon their internal modes of regulation; and third, upon their internal structures including the actions of members.

Functions of trade unions

The idea that the internal structures of trade unions may be defined by their functions was of course central to the structural-functionalist analysis. None the less, early British writers on this subject, such as G.D.H. Cole, had reached not dissimilar conclusions well before the acme of this particular sociological movement in the 1950s and early 1960s. But in so far as the *functions* of trade unions are concerned, two main components have usually been detailed in the literature: (1) their economic activities and (2) their role as agents of social change in which the democratic involvement of the membership is a key element.[54]

But to create a sophisticated typology, as Eldridge and Crombie have argued, 'is not an end in itself. It is valuable to the extent that it suggests new hypotheses to guide inquiry, and directs attention to relationships not previously observed.'[55] And, in this respect, it is questionable whether the functions of trade unions can in any event be discussed without focusing upon the orientations and interests of the membership who may themselves be regarded as accountable for determining the functions of their associations albeit, again, in conditions for which they were not necessarily responsible.[56]

In their well-known demonstration of this approach Blau and Scott went to some lengths to surmount problems of reification by detailing the principal *beneficiaries* of given types of organization; the membership, owners or managers, clients and the public at large.[57] This classification, in turn, permitted four categories of organization to be identified, mutual benefit associations (including trade unions), business concerns, service organizations and commercial organizations. Blau and Scott also commented upon the potentially democratic character of mutual benefit associations as a notable component of their internal administration:[58]

> One purpose, just as in the case of other organizations, is the effective accomplishment of the specific objectives of the organization — for example, improving employment conditions in the case of unions. But another distinctive purpose of these associations is to provide their members with a mechanism for arriving at agreements on their common objectives. For to serve the interests of its members a mutual-benefit association must furnish mechanisms for ascertaining what their collective objectives are as well as mechanisms for implementing them, and the ascertaining of objectives requires democratic self-government and freedom of dissent.

If the functions of trade unions are perceived in terms of the collective objectives of the membership, this thesis is clearly not without merit.

After all, the functions are then not regarded, in a reified fashion, as the property of organizations as such, and clearly the potential for democracy itself facilitates a recognition of the role of change and conflict. Moreover, trade unions are at least distinguished in this analysis from business concerns in which other priorities and goals are usually evident.

But it is still unsatisfactory, in our view, to elaborate upon the functions of trade unions (or any other association) on *a priori* grounds alone. Rather, an analysis which is genuinely explanatory must either focus upon structural conditions which make particular patterns of decision-making in organizations intelligible or must address attention to goals, and especially those of the more active members; indeed, a comprehensive model embraces aspects of both perspectives. Furthermore, inasmuch as the functions of trade unions are themselves in dispute, this in turn reflects struggles both within the membership as a whole, and between the membership acting in concord against actors in competing associations. In short, the so-called functions of trade unions that actually become dominant at any given point in time are in fact the product of power struggles which are waged in contexts which constrain and limit the choices of the actors concerned.

Internal modes of regulation

None the less in at least one version of organization theory some reference has been made to the strategic role of power in the analysis of trade unions. Studies emanating from the work of Etzioni are a case in point, for his familiar classifications of organizations essentially revolve around the notion of compliance.[59] This 'refers both to the relations in which an actor behaves in accordance with a directive supported by another actor's power, and to the orientation of the subordinated actor to the power applied.'[60] None the less, despite its potential advantages over, say, typologies rooted in functions, the focus of the analysis itself necessarily avoids confronting the critical issue of democracy in any satisfactory way; indeed the perennial dilemma of organization theory, in which, wittingly or not, the investigator adopts a position which largely embraces the interests of the leadership and of senior administrative personnel is particularly evident in this context.

It was, of course, Etzioni's view that power holders marshalled either physical, material or symbolic sanctions in order to ensure the compliance of subordinates.[61] There are, however, a number of serious deficiencies in this assessment in so far as trade unionism is concerned. In the first place, a *dichotomous* power model is assumed in which power is always in the possession of one group of actors and is thus never capable of being shared, albeit unequally, among the membership as a whole. But it is not true to suggest that this pattern invariably obtains in organizations generally, let alone in trade unions. Indeed, as Wrong has not unreasonably argued:[62]

> People exercise mutual influence and control over one another's behavior in all social interaction — in fact, that is what we *mean* by social interaction. Power relations are asymmetrical in that the power holder exercises greater control over the behavior of the power subject than the reverse, but reciprocity of influence — the defining criterion of the social relation itself — is never entirely destroyed except in those forms of physical violence which, although directed against a human being, treat him as no more than a physical object.

In any event, no guide is offered in this analysis to the *origins* of particular modes of control in organizations and to why certain individuals tend to become incumbents of given administrative positions in the first place. Similarly, there is no systematic argument in support of the claim that specific resources will tend to be marshalled while others will be eschewed, and above all, there is no explanation for why given parties find themselves in possession of particular resources at the outset, even though, of course, structural and subjective factors are likely to be particularly salient in this respect.

Hence, by way of illustration, a well-known study in the British literature on trade unions has been by Moran who employed Etzioni's framework in his investigation of the Union of Post Office Workers.[63] In this analysis, several of the aforementioned problems were avoided, and the author made no pretensions of substantiating any of the principal assumptions of the Etzioni model itself, but both the theoretical bedrock underlying his contribution and its empirical validation were still in certain respects unsatisfactory. In this survey of the post-office workers, three main sets of variables were considered: first, the type of *involvement* in the organization of rank-and-file members; second, the *power bases* mobilized by power holders; and third, the *goals* pursued by the 'organization' itself.[64]

Taking first of all the involvement of members, Moran argued, with reference to trade unions, that this may be either calculative or moral, the latter being composed of two elements: (1) commitment to a political creed, or (2) social moral involvement, in which workgroups rather than wider political norms are of greater salience.[65] Moreover, although 'dual' involvement may be apparent on occasions, there is a propensity for the altruistic member to demonstrate a moral commitment by comparison with his essentially passive colleagues, whose orientations are liable to be of a predominantly calculative character.[66]

Up to this point, then, Moran's position relied heavily on the assumptions of the action frame of reference in which the orientations of members are defined as critical to the shape of the government and internal structure of the union itself. But Moran then adopted a modified version of Etzioni's category of the 'means used by power holders to secure compliance' by introducing the notion of power bases. These, in his conception, refer to the sources of power mobilized by so-called power holders and consist largely of coercive, remunerative and normative components.[67]

Finally, Moran identified certain organizational goals, which he classified in a threefold manner: order goals, economic goals and cultural goals.[68] The first are pursued to ensure that deviant or recalcitrant members can be 'controlled' (as when the closed shop is insisted upon), the second refer to the 'allocation or re-allocation of material resources and services', and the third are adopted by organizations concerned with the creation and promotion of symbolic objects. This, then, results in the typology set out in Table 7.1.[69]

Table 7.1 *Union goals and Etzioni's categories*

Type of organization	Type of goal		
	Order	Economic	Cultural
Coercive	1	2	3
Utilitarian	4	5	6
Normative	7	8	9

But, as we have argued, to identify so-called organizational goals leads almost inevitably to a process of reification in which these are ultimately attributed to the organization and not to the officials and members from whom they originate.

Internal structures and actions of members

Proponents of the third organizational approach to the study of trade unionism have taken a central position in the debate by focusing upon the internal decision-making of these associations themselves. The salient features of an organizational theory of union democracy were originally sketched by Edelstein[70] and then later, in *Comparative Union Democracy*, by Edelstein and Warner[71] who set out to relate the main propositions of this model to the decision-making processes in a number of British and American unions. But from a theoretical standpoint a major breakthrough was also consequent upon the model of Child, Loveridge and Warner who endeavoured to establish a comprehensive explanatory analysis in which the actions of members and environmental variables are considered alongside organizational factors.[72] And this as we have seen offers some prospect of arriving at a more satisfactory explanatory model of union government than one which rests solely upon the assumptions of either the environmental or organizational schools alone.

But in purely descriptive terms, formal organizational scholars have evolved typologies of the shape of the internal structure of associations and here the distinction has commonly been drawn between *geneity* and *nodality*.[73] The concept of geneity has again been reified but is potentially valuable in so far as it refers to the degree to which members have control over their respective organizations. Special attention is paid to the contrast between homogeneous organizations where 'the members function so as to serve the organization's objectives' and heterogeneous ones in which 'the organization exists to further the objectives of its members'.[74] Nodality, by comparison, relates to the way in which authority is actually distributed. A uninodal organization is hierarchically structured and pyramidal in shape; a multinodal one is far more democratic and offers opportunities for relatively autonomous decision-making by members and a multi-centred allocation of authority.[75]

Yet, as we have indicated, the theory expounded by Edelstein and Warner is by far the most sophisticated of its kind. Their intention was to establish the organizational foundations of democracy in large autonomous national unions and they were especially concerned with those components of union structure and procedure which promote competition for top or near top posts. They noted too that with the exception of a handful of common features the constitutions of unions bear little resemblance to the majority of organizations, but at the same time emphasized that:[76]

> The approaches to union democracy in and around the labour
> movement generally neglect the essence of what we would call
> organizational structure — the various subdivisions, conferences,
> committees and posts and how these relate to each other,
> particularly near the pinnacle of the national organization.

In this conception, then, formal democracy (or democratic potential) in trade unions is enhanced by internal structure and procedures such as the allocation to important posts through election, the maintenance of an electorate free from control of contenders for office, active or potentially active rank-and-file leaders, a sufficiently large membership who actually care about national issues, an abundance of aspirants for office, and internal democratic norms.[77]

But which of these several factors were particularly germane to closely fought elections for top positions within a given union? Here a series of twenty-one different propositions were delimited and these in turn represented the main components of an empirically verifiable organizational approach to union democracy.[78] But given a reasonable opportunity to nominate candidates two elements above all appeared vital, namely, the absence of a clear and 'logical' line of succession, and a suitable voting procedure.[79]

The emphasis upon the role of internal structural variables has of course been a valuable corrective to certain forms of environmental determinism. Nevertheless, the organizational perspective remains one-sided in its advocacy of such factors for not only are external environmental factors largely excluded, but also the focus of attention tends to be concentrated upon the official hierarchy rather than upon workshop level. Similarly, the analysis betrays a commitment largely to a civil-libertarian (and ultimately, a pluralist) position in which the importance of internal opposition and the division of powers is viewed as particularly significant for the effective operation of democracy itself.

Recently, too, Clegg has suggested that the particular tests for democracy used by Edelstein and Warner are not wholly suitable in the case of British trade unions.[80] Indeed, Clegg revealed his preference for 'a wider and less precise test' such as 'strong evidence that opposition groups are able to push union administrations into policies or actions which they would not otherwise have favoured.'[81] But equally none of this detracts from the argument that internal organizational variables influence democratic practice: indeed Edelstein and Warner themselves considered that *'formal organization contributes even more to democratic decision-making'* than it was possible to demonstrate from within the corpus of that volume alone.[82]

Yet a comprehensive explanatory framework of union government should, of course, encompass both membership attitudes *and* the origins of internal structures. Child, Loveridge and Warner have attempted to meet such a challenge by developing a comprehensive statement about union character within the aegis of an overall organizational framework.[83] With this end in view, their model incorporated the nature of membership attachment, the twin rationales of unions of goal-formation through representation and of goal-implementation through administration, and an account of the origins of the internal structures of the constituent trade unions.[84]

A number of hypotheses were then suggested to link these with the main independent variables. These included first, that structuring of activities will be encouraged by increasing union size; second, that variability in environmental conditions will however discourage structuring; third, that increased formality in procedural agreements will favour greater structuring of activities; fourth, that a concentration of bargaining units will tend to increase centralization; fifth, that other than matters of overall union policy, however, large unions will tend to have a higher measure of decentralization than smaller ones; and finally, therefore, a negative relationship should be hypothesized between the structuring of activities and centralization of decision-making on operational matters.[85]

This approach, therefore, offered some possibility of linking elements from both the environmental and formal organizational perspectives and in a way which avoided problems of reification. Moreover, an empirical statement on this issue appeared in a study by Donaldson and Warner of six trade unions and one professional association and in so far as dimensions which showed similarities with other organizations were concerned, once again *the size of an organization* was critical.[86] In particular, so-called specialization, standardization, formalization and vertical span were all positively correlated with each other and with size.[87]

In trade unions and other occupational interest-group associations, however, democratic 'rationality' was found to modify this relationship on the dimension of centralization of decision-making. In short, the principal effect of representative or democratic institutions is the tendency for occupational interest-groups to be *more* centralized than business firms.[88]

Moreover, Donaldson and Warner in a subsequent paper detailed another study which examined the effects on the internal structure of trade unions of their representative character and in particular, sought to measure the degree to which decisions about the incumbency of any full-time posts were made by electoral rather than bureaucratic procedures.[89] More specifically, a scale of Electoral Control of Officials was constructed in which four critical decisions were located: appointment to post, continuation in post, promotion to a higher level, and dismissal from post.[90] It emerged from this investigation that electoral control over officials leads to lower levels of overall standardization and functional specialization, or, in other words, 'the election of staff seems to inject a considerable element of uncertainty and unpredictability into the affairs of the association, and the concern for political fortune seems to detract from purely administrative considerations.'[91]

But the elaborate model of union democracy contained in the parent study of Child, Loveridge and Warner has not been fully explored: indeed, research has been largely concerned with demonstrating a reciprocal relationship between the government and internal structure of unions and has as yet not related these to membership heterogeneity and environment.

There is still much to be achieved in this area, then, if we are to understand the relative weight of the key variables which have been isolated to date. But at the same time we should not fail to record the advances which have been made in conceptual sophistication and in the consequent recognition that structural, subjective and 'power' factors (both in the external environment and in the formal organizational framework of trade unions) must be accounted for in any comprehensive analysis of the government and internal structure of unions themselves.

Finally, in theoretical terms it is worth emphasizing how these propositions on trade union democratic and administrative structures find a parallel in ongoing disputation within the organizational literature itself. Hence, as Sorge has pointed out, it is possible to contrast *the determinist approach*, in which the relationship between structure and context in particular has been viewed as operating in a causal relationship largely independent of the motivations of the actors concerned, with the so-called choice argument in which equally rational structures may be envisaged as producing the same results which cannot, therefore, be inferred from such variables as size/technology or the task environment, and with *the 'culturalist perspective* in which interaction patterns and values of the wider culture are highlighted'.[92] Moreover, in the best models, there is a fusion of a number of such strands in order to:[93]

> reconcile the conflicting perspectives of mainstream theory, with its
> sights on administrative 'instrumental rationalities', and of 'culturalism'
> which focuses on national 'value rationality' . . . within a theory that
> bears regard to political choice without letting considerations of
> constraints within different available options fall into oblivion.

CONCLUSION

The objective of this chapter has been to highlight the gradual emergence of distinctively organizational theories of trade unionism. These were originally rooted in the propositions of structural-functionalism and the early traditions of labour theory. Gradually rather different frameworks have emerged, in which, not only have the differences between 'environmental' and 'formal organizational' approaches proved to be of significance for ongoing disputation, but also more complex models have emerged in which a number of insights have been combined in order that the orientations of actors and cultural conditions may be incorporated. Having examined in some depth the 'structuralist' argument, it is apposite that our review of theories of trade unionism should attain its highest point of synthesis with an account of wider cultural and subjective factors and the role of social action in shaping the resulting modes of trade union conduct itself.

8 Culture, values and perception

The fate of an epoch which has eaten of the tree of knowledge is that it must know that we cannot learn the *meaning* of the world from the results of its analysis, be it ever so perfect; it must rather be in a position to create this meaning itself. It must recognize that general views of life and the universe can never be the products of increasing empirical knowledge, and that the highest ideals, which move us most forcefully, are always formed only in the struggle with other ideals which are just as sacred to others as ours are to us.[1]

Within the compass of this theoretical treatise we have frequently drawn attention to the vital role of cultural and other subjective factors in the compound of interconnected causative elements which have shaped trade union growth, structure and policy. In classic sociological scholarship such an insight was naturally a commonplace: indeed, although this emphasis was particularly conspicuous in the works of Max Weber,[2] the problem of 'consciousness' has been a perennial concern in all but the most one-sided structuralist accounts within the Marxian tradition.[3] Similarly, although Durkheim considered that social facts possessed immanent properties which constrained industrial behaviour, the analytical significance attached to normative and ethical criteria was undoubtedly fundamental;[4] while even the late Talcott Parsons not only emphasized action categories in his earliest passages but also, more especially, built these into his later propositions on the nature of social systems and on the saliency of common values as a source of social integration therein.[5] Again, among leading industrial relations theorists, Dunlop referred to the *actors* in the industrial relations system and to their role in the shaping and formulation of rules;[6] while in pluralist accounts, the Webbs,[7] Flanders,[8] and Clegg[9] have all stressed the significance of ethics and morals in securely founded institutional systems. Meanwhile, Turner, in his appreciation of the dynamic propensities of 'open' and 'closed' unions revealed the manifold consequences of the different *policies* expressed in this crucial distinction.[10] More recently, Goodman and his colleagues have amended the Dunlop formula by referring to the concept of a rule-making action system.[11] By the same token, in Bain's exposition of the factors affecting union growth, the significance of recognition by employers and government has been frequently demonstrated;[12] while, even in the neo-Marxist writings of, say, Hyman,[13] Brough,[14] and Fryer,[15] the dangers of reification in other than action-based conceptions has been frequently remarked upon. And finally, of course, the focus on the problem of control *as a condition for creation* derives quintessentially from the fundamental maxims and premises of the corpus of Weber's writings.[16]

In this chapter, then, the main facets of a 'culturalist' or 'subjective' appreciation of trade union character will be enumerated prior to a restatement and recapitulation of those themes to which we attach a special significance. With such objectives to the fore we shall now proceed by way of a systematic examination of five interconnected themes: (1) the general methodological assumptions of the action approach; (2) the role of culture, civilization and values in the comparative analysis of international labour movements; (3) the relationship between politics, party and trade unionism; (4) the problems of control and creation; and (5) the formal analysis of trade unionism based on action categories in which 'end' and 'value' rationality as well as 'affectual' orientations and tradition are all incorporated. Such a review will foreshadow the integration of theoretical and methodological themes based on the main points of emphasis in our general review of classic and modern approaches to labour theory itself.

GENERAL METHODOLOGICAL IMPLICATIONS OF THE ACTION APPROACH

To focus on 'subjective' categories of social action is to formulate radically different theoretical and methodological propositions from the structuralist accounts which have featured prominently in our outline so far. Hence, in perhaps the most influential passage in the entire sociological literature, Weber considered 'action' to encapsulate the very essence of the discipline.[17]

> Sociology (in the sense in which this highly ambiguous word is used here) is a science concerning itself with the interpretive understanding of social action and thereby with a causal explanation of its course and consequences. We shall speak of 'action' insofar as the acting individual attaches a subjective meaning to his behavior — be it overt or covert, omission or acquiescence. Action is 'social' insofar as its subjective meaning takes account of the behavior of others and is thereby oriented in its course.

In this understanding of the nature of sociology, Weber wished to define the subject, together with history, as the *empirical sciences of action* and hence to differentiate them sharply from dogmatic branches of instruction such as 'jurisprudence, logic, ethics, and aesthetics' in which 'objectively' correct meanings of action were sought.[18] Nevertheless, sociology and history were also perceived as differing in certain fundamental respects, for while the former sought to formulate generic type concepts and generalized uniformities of empirical process, the latter was oriented to causal analysis and explanation of individual actions and structures possessing cultural significance.[19] In other words, while the empirical material upon which sociologists and historians drew overlapped considerably, what sociology lacked in terms of 'fullness of concrete content' was more than compensated for by the greater precision and depth of its concepts and its more exacting theoretical standards.[20]

Moreover, on the basis of action categories, the defining quality of social reality became values, their significance and meaning understood in entirely different ways from that envisaged by, say, Durkheim in his exposition of the role of social facts. Instead, therefore, of establishing correlations between, for instance, moral values and union development, such factors as world-views, ethical orientations and individual action were now to be regarded as fused through *'that means-and-end relationship of reasoning [that] gives the structure of action'*[21] (i.e. they became part of a conscious process of action rather than a correlate of behaviour). Indeed, on these assumptions, action consists of motive *and* behaviour, with the latter, therefore, constituting merely a 'fragment' of action.[22] By extension, too, the establishment of observable correlations constitutes only a preliminary step in the analysis which requires subsequent development to be construed in a causal fashion.[23]

In classic Weberian scholarship, then, as will be familiar, causal analysis and adequacy at the level of meaning were essential parts of advanced and systematic sociological theory. That is to say, the establishment of structural causes must be supplemented by a focus on the *meanings* actors give to the process of interaction and an examination of the orientations of action itself. Also, on such formulations, explanation is not linear or cumulative but *simultaneous* (i.e. the delineation of both causal and meaningful associations).[24]

Of course, Weber's most influential contributions were never one-sidedly 'culturalist' in emphasis. On the contrary, as Rex has insisted, much of *Economy and Society* was unmistakably structuralist in content.[25] However, for the comparative analysis of economic, historical and sociological forms, the principal methodological device was the ideal-type; although this was to be established only after correlations had been formulated.[26] Moreover, ideal-types consisted of a complex of elements associated in historical reality which we unite into a conceptual whole from the standpoint of their cultural significance.[27] As such, then, as Sahay has noted, there are logically four modes of ideal-type corresponding to different levels of explanation and generality: *'individualizing' forms* (a) making the characteristics of a unique action or event explicit (b) making the ideas of an action clear and consistent; and *'generalizing' forms* (a) organizing correlated facts to allow the imputation of a causal relationship between them (b) conceptualizing the basic, general characteristics of a social action in its pure form.[28]

Of course, in view of their one-sided accentuation of reality and the tendency to encourage the method of comparative statics, modifications are required in the use of ideal-types in order to facilitate a satisfactory analysis of social forms. But, in trade union studies, they are potentially useful and remain crucial for avoiding reification. This property is particularly valuable in the context of evaluations of the ways in which social movements become institutionalized (e.g. in consequence of the transference of actors' orientations from 'value' to 'end' or to 'traditional' rationality).

CULTURE, CIVILIZATION AND VALUES

Turning more specifically, then, to trade unions themselves, the potential role of culture, civilization and values in informing union purpose had been first formulated, of course, by the 'ethical' school. Moreover, as Flanders, in particular, subsequently argued, the pursuit of 'the sword of justice' has been historically a central feature of securely-founded labour movements.[29] On one view, however, increasing rationalization, the growth of bureaucratic administrative forms, and structural differentiation within industrial societies has resulted in a progressive abandonment of any commitment to absolute values and to their substitution by the narrower confines of 'vested interest'. None the less, in action terms, even assuming the validity of this prognosis, no trend of this kind should be regarded as irreversible; while, for analytical purposes, the significance of cultural and institutional variations in the comparative study of labour movements has proved to be a particularly interesting departure in contemporary studies of the phenomena under review.

The revival of 'culturalist' modes of explanation, then, has been evident in a number of different if theoretically cognate studies (see, for example, Dore,[30] Sorge[31] and Warner[32]). But in trade union terms, a particularly fruitful and worthwhile illustration may be identified in the work of Gallie on the petrochemical industries of Britain and France; for the principal purpose of this study was to demonstrate that common technological systems may be institutionalized in substantially different ways in divergent cultural milieux.[33] Hence:[34]

> Advanced automation proved perfectly compatible with radically
> dissimilar levels of social integration, and fundamentally different
> institutions of power and patterns of trade unionism . . . our evidence
> indicates the critical importance of the wider cultural and social

structural patterns of specific societies for determining the nature of social interaction within the advanced sector.

Moreover, as Gallie again revealed, the nature of the trade union movement in Britain and France had in turn radically affected the institutionalization of work roles and relationships in the refineries in the two countries. That is to say, 'powerful trade unions in the wider society, with long established traditions and well-set modes of ideology and organization, had succeeded in penetrating into the advanced sector, and had been assimilated into the wider patterns of society.'[35] More specifically, too, the principal unions in the French and British refineries[36]

> had fundamentally different conceptions of the role of trade unions in the workplace; and this difference had important implications for their method of operation on the shop floor, the nature of the relationship between the workplace and central union organization, the type of demand that was made on management, and the quality of the relationship between the unions and the workers themselves.

There was thus a divergence between the emphasis on *mobilization* in French unions and on *regulation* of the relationship between employers and workmen in British unions with the consequent focus on control over *workplace* relationships and immediate benefits in the latter case.[37] And more generally:[38]

> while the Western nations share a common capitalist mode of production that generates similar conflicts of interest between employers and employed, this underlying system contradiction can have very different consequences at the level of social integration. The crucial mediating variables, we would suggest, are factors like the managerial ideology, the typical structure of power in social institutions, and the ideology and mode of action of the trade union movement characteristic of the specific society. Moreover, if we are to understand the differences between the working classes of the various Western societies, we will need to look much more closely at their pattern of historical development, and examine the way in which different historical experiences have generated distinctive cultural and social structural patterns.

POLITICS, PARTY AND INSTITUTIONALIZATION

The significance of unique cultural and historical experiences and of the theoretical importance of the action approach in this context may be further highlighted by an examination of the salience of 'party' as an analytical construct. Naturally, in the British case, this has a particular poignancy on account of the historical links between trade unions and the Labour Party enshrined in the very conception of a labour movement comprising industrial and political wings. Although in a theoretical treatise it is not of relevance to examine the substantive aspects of this relationship, it is pertinent to note that 'party' may be construed not only as a structural concept in terms of social divisions in society, but more especially as a conscious attempt by social actors *to control the environment in which union action in the industrial context takes place* and hence indirectly to impose their own definitions on the ultimate morphology, internal structure, governance, and primary objectives of their associations.

For Weber, of course, the term 'party' was deployed to designate associations in which membership rested 'on formally free recruitment'[39] and, in particular, two main types were identified: 'patronage' parties (concerned with 'the attainment of power for their leaders and with securing positions in the administrative staff for their own members') and 'ideological' parties (which consciously 'act in the interests of a status group or a class or of certain objective policies or of abstract principles').[40] Interestingly, too, the evolution of ideological parties into patronage parties was hinted at by Weber; for, even in the former type, a secondary aim had always been 'the attainment of positions in the administrative staff for members' and hence, in such circumstances, 'often merely a means of persuading outsiders to participate'.[41] Moreover, in terms of the relationships of power and influence between trade unions and political parties *the method of finance* of political organs (mass contributions, direct payments from interested bodies, and taxation) could have major implications 'for the economic aspect of the distribution of power and for the determination of party policy'.[42]

Yet clearly social *action* at opportune historical moments has been absolutely vital in shaping the political and industrial connection between the Labour Party and the trade unions (the *growth* of the Labour Representation Committee in 1901 (following its inception in the previous year) was thus in no small measure a consequence of an active initiative following the Taff Vale judgment).[43] Similarly, as we have already seen in the debates on corporatism, writers such as Schmitter have viewed the growth of state intervention, ostensibly occasioned by structural change, as having been substantially determined by the very emergence of intermediate associations such as unions, with their leaders demanding a more active and interventionist state role in order to produce a favourable milieu for successful bargaining and the pursuit of members' interests in the economic and industrial fields.[44] Again, the growth of enacted rules in the area of employment protection, health and safety at work and so on, can in part be attributed to successful *trade union pressure* for legislation which may be expedited through Labour Party connections and by the forging of links between political and industrial modes of action. More- over, it is interesting how different unions have responded variously throughout their history to the use of political or industrial methods (the open 'generals' being far more favourably disposed to political interven- tion than the closed 'crafts'); a situation which again indicates a substantial measure of social choice in these respects.[45]

PROBLEMS OF CONTROL AND CREATION

Above all, the action approach has focused the attention of industrial relations scholars and sociologists on the problem of control. Indeed, Dawe's familiar and graphic statement in this regard is worth quoting at length:[46]

> There are, then, two sociologies: a sociology of social system and a sociology of social action. They are grounded in the diametrically opposed concerns with two central problems, those of order and control. And, at every level, they are in conflict. They posit antithetical views of human nature, of society and of the relationship between the social and the individual. The first asserts the paramount necessity, for societal and individual well-being, of external constraint; hence the notion of a social system ontologically and methodologically prior to its participants. The key notion of the second is that of autonomous man, able to realize his full potential and to create a truly human social order only when freed from external constraint. Society is thus the creation of its members; the product of their construction of meaning, and of the action and relationships through which they attempt to impose that meaning on their historical situations.

Yet, in classic formulations, control (which has been avowed in a number of recent trade union analyses) was a *means* to secure the free develop- ment of all socially useful human attributes rather than in any way consti- tuting an ultimate end of action itself. And, on such assumptions, the higher *purpose* of a control strategy was precisely to develop or to re-establish the conditions of human creativity and to secure a new dawn in which the capacities of sensibility and intellect of the populace would be based on *cultural or value premises* rather than on the narrow '*end*' *rationality and economic objectives* which modern administrative and bureaucratic systems had inexorably produced. Moreover, in Weber's own conception, the real cause of alienation and the destruction of human creativity and dignity rested not upon capitalism *per se* but upon bureaucratic structures consequential upon dominant rationalization tendencies, the result of which was that the role of markets, discretionary authority and so on had been continuously circumscribed.[47] And on this view the public ownership of the means of production and socialism would merely speed up the process of bureaucratization and the emergence of the 'iron cage of serfdom' in which 'all forms of value-oriented social conduct would be suffocated by the almighty bureaucratic structures and by the tightly knit networks of formal-rational laws and regulations, against which the individual would stand no chance at all.'[48] Moreover, although in contemporary union analysis the idea that the ultimate purposes of union activity should be to establish the conditions for *freedom* and for *value decisive rational* action would seldom seem to surface, it was still a preoccupation of early union leaders and was espoused perhaps most memorably by William Straker in his presentation of the case of the Miners' Federation to the Sankey Commission in 1919:[49]

> In the past workmen have thought that if they could secure higher wages and better conditions they would be content. Employers have thought that if they granted these things the workers ought to be contented. Wages and conditions have improved; but the discontent and the unrest have not disappeared. Many good people have come to the conclusion that working people are so unreasonable that it is useless trying to satisfy them. The fact is that the unrest is deeper than pounds, shillings and pence necessary as they are. The root of the matter is the straining of the spirit of man to be free.

PERCEPTIONS OF TRADE UNIONISM AND THE CATEGORIES OF SOCIAL ACTION

Turning more specifically, then, to the formal elaboration of action categories and the perception of unionism it is worth emphasizing that in Weber's own interpretation, trade unions were to be understood as specific types of economic organization.[50] Hence, the trade union constituted a major instance of an 'economically regulative organization' (*wirtschafts-regulierender Verband*) in which the 'autocephalous economic activity of the members is directly oriented to the order governing the group' and in which regulation of ends and procedures of economic activities are sought by the directing authorities.[51] None the less, Weber himself considered it vital to distinguish between *economic action* (or a conscious primary orientation to economic considerations) and *economically oriented action* in which both political struggle and power conflict could be discerned.[52] Thus, in this latter respect, two main instances were cited in which a direct concern for economic objectives was not necessarily predominant; namely, action which though primarily oriented to other ends takes account in the pursuit of them of economic considerations, and action which, though oriented to economic ends, makes use of physical force as a principal means.

In short, in *Economy and Society*, Weber defined and interpreted trade unionism in a manner which was clearly sensitive to both economic and political purposes, even though his main emphasis was unmistakably upon the former. But, in any comprehensive modern analysis of trade unions, such propositions have to be modified and refined in order to encompass three primary explanatory dimensions: (1) at a structural level, the impact of economic, organizational, political and technological change upon union growth and character; (2) at a level of values, the subjective perceptions of members in so far as these inform and guide union activities to given goals, objectives and purposes; and (3) the power of 'actors' in industrial and labour relations including that of not only employers and trade unions but also the legislature, political parties, and the state.

Contemporary accounts of trade unionism thus differ from Weber's own formulation in three major aspects. In the first instance, economic movements and technical changes are usually construed as structural variables which constrain social action itself, a view sharply at odds with Weber's understanding of such developments as either the outcome or means of social action. Indeed, Weber referred to the latter particularly as the 'technique' of an action; 'to the means employed as opposed to the meaning or end to which action is, in the last analysis, oriented'.[53] Second, the bulk of sociological interpretations eschew any notion of essentialism and, while countenancing the role of structural variables, seek to extend Weber's *method* by discovering union purposes in terms of the goals of leading 'actors' within the labour movement. Third, modern analyses are more likely to include references to the environing influence of agencies of the state upon union growth and character than is immediately apparent from within the corpus of Weber's treatise.

At the same time, however, Weber's sensitivity to the issue of power in industrial and labour relations and his recognition of its significance in social action should in no way be minimized. On the contrary, in this regard Weber was especially concerned with the 'power of control and dispersal' (*Verfügungsgewalt*), which included the possibility of control over the actor's own labour power.[54] Thus, on one view, he clearly anticipated a series of contemporary discussions on the character, nature, and possibility of industrial democracy and of the associated practices of autonomous working groups and of self-governance of enterprise itself. Moreover, Weber's ultimate recognition of 'the ethical nature of the individual's orientation, even in the economic sphere' could be clearly discerned in his familiar delineation of social action categories, which revealed 'not a substantive coincidence between economic and social action, but the similarity and difference in the nature of concepts to be employed in the analysis of end-rational economic action, and value-rational social action'.[55]

Table 8.1   *Categories of social action and perceptions of trade unionism*

General categories of social action	*Perceptions of trade unionism*
1 *Instrumental or 'end' rational* (*zweckrational*), that is, determined by expectations as to the behaviour of objects in the environment and of other human beings; these expectations are used as 'conditions' or 'means' for the attainment of the actor's own rationally pursued and calculated ends.	1 Instrumentally rational orientation to a variety of union objectives such as safety and welfare, wages and working conditions, job regulation and control and the democratic governance of industry itself.
2 *Value rational* (*wertrational*), that is, determined by a conscious belief in the value for its own sake of some ethical, aesthetic, religious or other form of behaviour independently of its prospects of success.	2 Value rational orientation to the principle of trade unionism as an end in itself and to the advancement of *workers'* rights.
3 *Affectual* (especially emotional), that is, determined by the actor's specific affects and feeling states.	3 Affectual orientation to the community and solidarity of union and workgroup.
4 *Traditional*, that is, determined by ingrained habituation.	4 Traditional orientation to union activities and to the habituation of 'custom and practice' in the workplace.

Yet, to what extent, it may be reasonably asked, does such an approach to members' perceptions offer sharply defined analytical and empirical advantages over other explanatory formulations? To begin with, therefore, its very basis in Weberian scholarship not only facilitates a secure anchorage in classic sociological literature, but also, more especially, enables general properties to be enunciated that can be applied to a whole class of instances of the phenomenon under review. This, in turn, avoids the problem intrinsic in the very nature of the random *ad hoc* categories which have emerged in much of the empirical literature so far, since their specificity prevents a systematic accumulation of knowledge on this subject. Similarly, the identification of ideal-typical properties allows the comparative method to be used to make 'the means-end relationship' of a given 'action, event, process or interpretation of ideas, unambiguous' and hence to realize 'the principle of sociological rationality'.[56] Furthermore, so long as the analysis is sufficiently flexible and encompasses, for example, the effects of structural variables, it becomes possible, in turn, to evaluate a variety of expectations of unions which may surface in a complex fashion on account of economic or technical change, the internal structure of unions, the initiatives of the legislature, political parties and the state, and alterations in the balance of power between 'actors' in industrial and labour relations more generally. Finally, of paramount importance, the absence of any postulated antithesis between such union goals as improvements in wages and working conditions on the one hand, and workers' participation in management on the other, enables the analyst to interpret accurately any parallel concern for both so-called 'economistic' and 'control' issues.

The formal elaboration of subjective variables in so far as trade union action is concerned may thus be adumbrated under the principal heads of: (a) *instrumental or 'end'-rational action*; (b) *value rational action*; (c) *'affectual' or solidaristic action*; and (d) *'traditional' action*. Each of these categories logically incorporates general and individual variants and also, sociologically, a number of intermediate or middle range propositions associated with social imagery and orientations to unionism and union modes of activity respectively.

Instrumental or 'end'-rational action

At its most general level, then, instrumental or 'end'-rational action may be viewed as having gained ascendancy in industrial societies as economic and technical objectives have become progressively more dominant accompanying rationalization and the institutional advance of bureaucracy. On one view, too, within trade unions the expansion of instrumental and economic considerations at the expense of value-oriented criteria would appear to have reflected similar exigencies. But the upshot of these departures has been that economic development has become not just a principal concern of the modern era but also a primary source of legitimacy of the social order itself. Of course, the processes of institutionalization of the *idea* of economic development have been considerably complex with the result that when such ideas have been transferred to different social contexts their ultimate form has by no means closely mirrored that of the Western European experience. Yet this in no way invalidates the contemporary significance of the preoccupation with instrumentally rational objectives and with sensate as opposed to idealist impulses.[57]

In such milieux, however, the role of labour movements would appear to have had paradoxical results; a situation especially evident in the extent to which bureaucratic or democratic administrative procedures have in practice surfaced. For while the value-rational commitment to 'social democracy' has undoubtedly at times assisted democratic growth and, more especially, a questioning of the legitimacy of managerial domination at workplace level, by contrast, the concern within trade unions for economic development has facilitated economic planning and a concomitant extension of bureaucracy. On the one hand, then, the power of labour movements has increased the demand for workers' participation and control and for the more general ideal of industrial democracy. However, on the other hand, no less insistent has been the countervailing pressure for economic security, steadily rising living standards and so on, which have helped to foster more state control and intervention, the increasingly 'rational' use of resources towards these ends and hence, ultimately, an encouragement of bureaucratic patterns of administration.[58]

Moreover, these analytical and empirical observations may be augmented from the accounts of 'middle range' conceptions of social imagery and orientations. Hence the significance of so-called 'images of society' (or how workers themselves subjectively understand the social environment and the patterns of class formation therein) has rested upon their salience in evaluating the potentialities for radical action and, by extension, the dominant attitudes and behaviour of trade unionists in the post-Second World War period. The most influential of these statements appeared in Lockwood's classic paper, 'Sources of Variation in Working Class Images of Society', in which, it will be recalled, a threefold classification of working-class social imagery was formulated which took account of the substantial variation in workplace and community milieux that existed within modern urban and industrial populations.[59] These embraced the 'deferential' proletarian image, in which the patterns of social hierarchy were largely legitimated (in small firms and/or small workplaces); the 'traditional' proletarian image, in which a substantial measure of opposition to the social order existed (especially common among geographically segregated communities such as miners, shipyard workers and dockworkers); and finally, the 'pecuniary' image of social differentiation of the 'privatized' worker (the 'prototypical' consciousness of modern mass production industries and heterogeneous urban populations).[60]

This classification permitted certain major inferences to be drawn with respect to the character of British trade unionism and its evolutionary development during the period in question. Hence, the first type of social image was assumed to decline in overall importance (as the industries and communities which supported traditional deferential identities became increasingly eroded by technical advance and geographical social mobility respectively), and as a result one impediment to the development of trade unionism would thus gradually be lifted. Equally the highly cohesive bonds of community and kinship associated with solidaristic working-class communities were also perceived to be slackening because of major reductions in the labour force in the industries concerned. It was thus hypothesized that the typical image of 'class formation' would in the long-term be associated especially with that emerging from the *prototypical* mass industrial complexes and largely fragmented urban communities, in which 'pecuniary' or economic forms of consciousness appeared to be a dominant feature.[61] As Goldthorpe and his colleagues argued:[62]

> The prevalence of an outlook of this kind is, in our view, both confirmed and elucidated by the fact that among the workers we studied the idea of society as fundamentally divided into opposing classes was only very rarely advanced. The class structure was not, as they described it, a historically created system of domination which had to be overthrown, or at any rate combatted, in order for men such as themselves to achieve their legitimate objectives.

Since these ideas were first formulated, however, a number of research investigations, together with certain strategic changes in industrial relations and in the economy, have served to cast doubt on certain aspects of this particular hypothesis. Thus, valuable work undertaken by Brown and his colleagues (of the shipbuilding industry in North East England) revealed that the traditional shipbuilding working-class community was not in fact homogeneous at all, but rather was sharply divided on the basis of skills, enterprise traditions, and small-scale geographical neighbourhoods.[63] That is to say, one of the key environments of the traditional proletarian worker did not accord well with the descriptive characteristics of the industrial and community milieux which were supposed to induce traditional proletarian forms of consciousness. Moreover, although the craft-based divisions in the industry concerned were gradually being eroded by developments in modern industrialism and especially in the socio-technical systems of work organization in the shipyards involved,[64] these data still served to question any thesis which rests on the straightforward linking of ideas and social action bereft of an understanding of social structural considerations. In addition there was a marked upswing in militancy in the early 1970s and a parallel emergence of interest in the ideal of industrial democracy and in a variety of specific forms of workers' participation and control.[65] These developments, again, could not be easily accommodated by a model in which largely 'pecuniary' issues were regarded as prototypical of the future.

However, in the industrial sociological literature, investigations into working-class images of society have been matched by the correspondingly close attention to the nature and origins of orientations to work. Advocates of this approach can trace their ideas, more or less directly to Weber's original understanding of the nature of social action, and indeed their essential theoretical premises closely impinge upon the perspectives of the social action framework as, indeed, Brown has suggested.[66]

> Advocates of an action approach suggest that analysis should begin
> with the orientations to work of the actors concerned, with the way in
> which workers order their wants and expectations relative to their
> employment, with the meaning work has for them. Such orientations,
> wants, expectations, and meanings are of importance because they
> are not to be seen as varying randomly from individual to
> individual but as being socially shared.

The most explicit account of this position was developed, of course, by Goldthorpe and his colleagues who set out in 'ideal-typical' form three contrasting orientations to work which were associated with the affluent worker, the salaried employee, and the traditional worker. These were instrumental, bureaucratic and solidaristic respectively.[67] An instrumental orientation to work was thus conceived as having four major distinguishing characteristics: the primary meaning of work was as a means to an end, the workers' involvement in the organization was primarily calculative, the ego-involvement of workers in their jobs was weak, and the workers' lives were sharply dichotomized between work and non-work.[68] Hence, among affluent workers, the authors deduced that unionism 'had lost its emotional appeal, its moral force, and its ability to extend men's social and political horizons,' because:[69]

> The orientation of workers towards trade unionism reflects their
> orientation towards their employment generally; and where the latter
> is predominantly instrumental, it is not expected that unionism, any
> more than work itself, will be seen as a way of satisfying other
> than economic needs.

Moreover, whatever the specific empirical reservations there may be about this thesis, it is theoretically interesting in terms of the growth of instrumental or 'end'-rational action. Analytically, too, this type of action may also be gauged at an individual level in terms of the orientation of members to *specific trade union objectives*. On this view, therefore, members' perceptions may be interpreted in terms of a rational calculation of the advantages of unionism in respect of issues such as welfare and safety, hours and holidays, wages, working conditions, job regulation and participation in management.[70]

Silverman has also argued that an action analysis of social relationship in the factory might proceed as follows:[71]

1 Establish the ends held by different groups and the degree of conflict between the ends;
2 Understand how these ends related to the social situations which groups face;
3 Examine the means used to achieve these ends, and, for example, whether collective (trade union) approaches or individual ones are used;
4 Attempt to explain why certain means are used by groups at certain times;
5 Examine the consequences of action for the social situation of the group concerned;
6 Consider the likely cause of change by examining how ends may be modified and the availability and effectiveness of how given means may vary.

In short he attempted to draw up a comprehensive, if almost entirely *Zweckrational*, account of action in the workplace.

Finally, again at the industrial level, the *variations* in outlook and objective of unionists have been frequently stressed. Indeed, on this view, the idea that workers develop distinctive orientations to work that provide them with an opportunity to evaluate their circumstances consistently in the light of dominant purposes, is itself of dubious validity. Thus drawing upon his research on productivity bargaining, Daniel argued that, in different contexts, workers frequently had 'quite different priorities in what was demanded of work, quite different implicit definitions of the nature even of work itself, and quite different definitions of the relationship between management and labour'.[72] Thus when negotiations took place on the actual components of the productivity bargain concerned, there was marked antipathy between management and worker, a high saliency of instrumental goals, and a great deal of dissatisfaction expressed about the work involved. But once the proposals were implemented, the work environment was judged to have improved markedly, management-worker relations were less hostile, and the relative emphasis on instrumental and intrinsic goals respectively had been reversed.[73]

However, the idea that meanings and objectives may be inconsistent and constantly negotiated is associated less with the classic social action approach than with phenomenology as developed by Husserl and Schutz and with ethnomethodology.[74] After all, the purpose of the social action perspective is to analyse trade union activities through the construction of ideal-types (such as the instrumental) and produce logically coherent models based explicitly upon the premise of substantive rationality and consistency in any particular case. None the less, the argument that orientations are totally dependent upon context and are inherently unstable over time was not entirely satisfactorily established by Daniel, even though his work was useful in highlighting the major variations in perspective which obtain in any given industrial situation, and by inference, in the recognition that members' orientations to their unions are not necessarily one-dimensional.

Value rational action

Yet the development of mature civilizations has been conventionally understood in terms of the prior advance of so-called *value rational action*. Thus the preconditions for such 'cultural leaps' would appear to be: first, economic and political objectives being a means for the accomplishment of higher cultural purposes; and second, the absence of any displacement of moral and ethical codes by ideologies (i.e. the use of ideas for the coercive exercise of power). Certainly these cardinal points were clearly understood by the earliest labour theorists, for the significance of the pursuit of justice (the moral or ethical position) was sharply contrasted with both instrumental or economic orientations and the ideological modes of action envisaged in the revolutionary and to a lesser extent the political schools. But the earliest theorists of labour recognized the role of value-ideas in shaping union purpose and, while clearly establishing that these were not autonomous entities independent of the objective reality of the environment,[75] still pointed to their cardinal role at crucial moments in labour history. After all, when anchored in precepts of justice, the moral force of unionism has been at its greatest and it has, on such occasions, correspondingly reflected not just the aesthetic and ethical qualities of values but also their encapsulation of the criterion of truth upon which the growth of science and civilization themselves have depended. Thus, as Durkheim observed, 'of all the elements of civilization, science is the only one which, under certain conditions, presents a moral character.'[76] For although, strictly, it should be classified as outside the moral sphere, science was in Durkheim's view 'nothing else than conscience carried to its highest point of clarity.'[77] Similarly, as Bottomore has pointed out, the cardinal weakness of conventional Marxism has been the absence of an ethical theory since 'It has become increasingly evident, in the controversies that have gone on since the end of the nineteenth century, that some of the fundamental propositions of Marxist theory — concerning the development of the working-class movement, its engagement in political action, and the nature of the transition from capitalist to socialist society — need to be subjected to both scientific and ethical criticism.'[78] At the highest and most general level of perception, therefore, a basic disjunction between ethics and ideologies has been perennially manifest. The first, concerned with moral principles and rules of conduct, have at times been reflected in union affairs in 'the sword of justice'[79] but such advances, however, have often been vitiated either by an excessive instrumentalism (i.e. a drift towards 'vested interest') or by the degeneration of ethics into ideologies, by the replacement of morally by politically informed modes of action, and by the advent of 'determinist theories of social development' which cannot be easily reconciled with the possibility of moral choice.[80] Again, as Bottomore has further insisted, the basic question remains[81]

> whether a transition to socialism is possible at all unless bourgeois society has already attained an advanced stage of development with high levels of production and consumption, strongly established democratic practices and widespread experience of the exercise of democratic rights, and a widely diffused scientific and humanistic culture, which would provide a reliable foundation for an extension of human freedom.

Moreover, of further significance in this respect would appear to be the development and deployment of language and the enhancement of its *communicative* as well as *instrumental* objectives.[82] After all, among the most notable of subjective influences on unionism would appear to be the differential development of *syntactic* as well as *semantic* components of values. In particular, the fundamental disjunction in outlook between intellectuals and trade union members may well reside in their use of different precepts of language, a conclusion which has received support in countries with such contrasting economic and political systems as Britain and Hungary.[83] On this view, therefore, there are differences in the capacity of trade unionists to adopt clear-cut and consistent forms of consciousness in which specific issues and situations can be firmly grounded, and this may be in part a consequence of the limited social roles that modern manufacturing processes engender for the bulk of factory employees. In other words, fragmented and meaningless work situations can encourage a *restricted use of general concepts and hinder the development of fully fledged ethics and values as well as ideologies.*

But a paradox in the labour movement context is that union members have at times elaborated these wider value-rational modes of action; a situation which in turn suggests a certain autonomy for subjective influences. Moreover, in recent literature there has been an interesting attempt to measure value-rationality by Withers based on Rawlsian principles of justice,[84] while even the recent McCormick analysis of trade unionism is ultimately action-based.[85] Hence, as part of a dynamic, normative model of trade union and bargaining relationships focused on the idea of social co-operation for mutual advantage, Withers has acknowledged the potential benefits of social contract policies while at the same time observing that:[86]

> while the ideal of equality has played a noble role in overcoming oppression in human societies, its continued dogmatic pursuit runs the risk of perverting justice. In the first place, the more policy concentrates on eliminating disparities, the more intolerable they seem — as noted by Freud in his 'Narcissism of Small Differences'. Secondly, and more importantly, there is no ultimate satisfaction possible in the pursuit of equality because, as De Jouvenal says, 'Every allocation of reward which is founded on equality under a certain aspect, will be hierarchical and contrary to equality under another aspect'.
>
> Thus to the extent that we fail in developing a superior conception of justice in terms of mutual benefit there will be those for whom society represents not a true community, but a relationship among people founded on force and all members of such a society are likely to share in the disadvantages of the ensuing conflict and antagonism.

Yet, in the more specific debates on the factors which have helped to shape the character of the British trade union movement, it is of course usual to argue that, historically, there was once a profound influence of ethical values but that, by contrast with continental labour movements, ideologies have been less fundamental an influence. Indeed, it is the absence of a coherent ideology that is often held responsible for the apparent unwillingness on the part of trade union leaders and their members to use the labour movement as a vehicle for a radical transformation of British society. But the significance of *values*, by way of contrast, was well understood by the Webbs, who differentiated between values arising from religious 'emotion', from humanistic ideals, and from deliberate planning for efficiency in the carrying out of social purposes.[87] Moreover, in view of their interest in trade unionism, it is worth briefly examining at least the first two of these forces.

In contemporary Britain the trade union movement appears, on the face of it, less dependent in its character upon religion than corresponding organizations in, say, Italy or France. This superficial analysis is only in part correct, however, because historically there is the evidence that the impact of Methodism and of other Nonconformist creeds upon the outlook of working people in Great Britain was once profound.[88] Yet, the humanistic ideals of democracy and socialism have probably exerted a greater impact upon the shape of unionism than has religion. Again it is worth reiterating that it is precisely when trade unions have pursued the 'sword of justice' that they have evoked the greatest public sympathy and that, by contrast, whenever they are perceived to pursue 'narrow sectional interests' or these purposes have been vitiated by ideology, or they have lacked a coherent moral stance, hostility to the labour movement has been at its most acute.[89] Furthermore, when humanistic ideals have taken precedence over ideological vituperation, the dual identity of trade unions emphasized by Herberg has been at its most evident:[90]

> A modern labor union is, at one and the same time, (1) a business-like service organization, operating a variety of agencies under a complicated system of industrial relations; and (2) an expression and vehicle of the historical movement of the submerged laboring masses for social recognition and democratic self-determination.

Of course there have been writings on the British labour movement in which the authors concerned have specifically sought to replace moral and ethical by ideological precepts. From an analytical point of view, to be sure, there remains a great deal of common ground since such remarks are usually premised by the concession that for the most part the British Labour Party and, above all, the trade unions have 'never been in more than a tenuous sense a vehicle for oppositional ideology'.[91] Apart, then, from some of the recent studies on trade unions and the media, where the role of ideology has been openly discussed,[92] Hyman and Brough's *Social Values and Industrial Relations* is an obvious case in point, for while the authors observed that 'it is evident that conflict over prevailing norms of fairness in industrial relations is not primarily the outcome of a clash of opposing ideologies: *for no clear counter-ideology to the prevailing values* is purveyed in the main institutions of the labour movement',[93] equally, 'the notion of "a reconstruction of the normative order" in industrial relations which leaves intact the basic structure of the political economy' was regarded as 'a singularly futile goal'.[94] Yet leaving aside the obviously assertive nature of such a proposition what is seldom evident in this and in comparable analyses is the most transparent of all conclusions, that ideological premises have never and *can* never form the basis of a genuine *labour* movement. For the goal of creation of productive labour and of material or ethical progress which this suffuses can only be the outcome of purposive action designed to accomplish these and not the radically different *political* objectives of *ideological* premises. In short, any anchorage of union purposes in political objectives by definition depresses the internal cohesion and character of a *labour* movement and empirically ensures a displacement of original aims by the ceaseless turmoil and necessarily unproductive character of political conflict and factionalism themselves. The most fundamental of all contradictions, then, is the sacrifice of the creative essence of labour, which provides the moral basis for effective organization and action (as well as public and ultimately legislative support) in the first place, for the quicksands of ideology which necessarily vitiates the prospects for long-term survival of genuinely independent trade union and labour movements.

But the *analytical* significance of social justice as an explanatory category is nowhere better revealed than in the series of social surveys which suggest that, *at an individual level*, the commitment of members to their unions pursuing principles of justice (if necessary at the expense of material ends) remains deeply entrenched. Certainly Roberts and his colleagues found an approximately 3:1 preference amongst members of their sample of white-collar and manual workers for their unions to act as vehicles for social justice rather than as a means solely for the material advance of the membership.[95] Hence, the orientation of the individual member would appear to be decisively *ethical*: a principle which elsewhere has been described as 'much more empirical as well as comprehensive than the deterministic clichés of coercion, function, class-consciousness or ideology'.[96]

By extension, too, this evidence clearly reflects the two cardinal premises of Weber's methodology: value-relevance and means-end relationships.[97] For after all, values are clearly significant here in orienting social action, while a means-end relationship involves appreciation of the conscious selection of possibilities, which in turn undermines the claims to validity of exclusively behaviourist and determinist formulae. Indeed, by way of further illustration, the models of socialism which would appear to achieve the most widespread support at an individual level are very much the compound of the ideals of freedom and self-government, coupled with the desire for greater equity and fairness in material distribution, and seldom encapsulate blueprints for ideologically based social reconstruction. This, too, conforms closely to the personal vision of the early classic writers on British labour such as G.D.H. Cole:[98]

> By Socialism I mean fundamentally, not a particular economic arrangement by which the State owns and runs industry, but the entire body of principles. . . . The public ownership of the essential means of production . . . is itself a means towards making them

effective, not an end in itself, or to be pursued save to the extent to which it is a means. There is nothing sacred about nationalization; but. . . . Without a high degree of economic equality, we cannot have either freedom and self-government for all, or a satisfactory standard of living for all.

'Affectual' orientations

But in analytical terms, trade unions are also of course interesting as focal points for 'affectual' or 'solidaristic' attachments and allegiances and for the generation of so-called sentiments (i.e. the feelings towards certain ideas, things and acts).[99] Indeed, on one view, sentiments help us to understand the historical acceptance and persistence of the compounds of feelings and action (i.e. beliefs) and give a subjective *significance* to reality.[100] Hence, if 'values emphasize the conviction of truth which an individual has to have to believe in certain ideas; sentiments emphasize the manifestation and reinforcement of this conviction in the cultural and social reality which is the context of human experiences.'[101] Moreover, they can further serve to provide a deeper attachment of the individual to ethical values themselves.

In Max Weber's classical account, then, social action was construed not only in terms of the pursuit of specific objectives and as the reflection of broader values and ethical purposes, but also in respect of solidaristic and emotional loyalties, and especially the 'actor's specific affects and feeling states'.[102] Furthermore, although such modes of action were not regarded by Weber as entirely rational in the specific sense of reflecting an integration of behaviour and orientations within a means-end relationship, this does not invalidate their potentially far-reaching importance within any given industrial milieu.

In trade unionists' perceptions, this category of action is reflected most obviously in solidaristic orientations in which work tends to be experienced as a group activity, involvement in work is strong although often taking the form of opposition against an employer, ego involvement in work is also at a high level, and 'work experiences and relationships' help to 'form the basis of workers' out-plant social existence'.[103] But such orientations may in turn be conceived as having fundamental implications for trade unionism, since solidaristic sentiments would tend to induce the strongest possible bonds of affiliation to the union, which would thus constitute a source of collective identification, and a focal point for action against employers whether in private or publicly-owned industries.

Yet historically, it is usual to posit that there has been a progressive decline in solidaristic loyalties to the union. None the less, evidence from previous investigations provides no unequivocal conclusions on such questions. After all, whereas Goldthorpe and his colleagues argued that, on the basis of their data, it was difficult to gainsay the view that trade unionism had lost its 'emotional appeal',[104] studies of miners[105] and dock-workers[106] have revealed very strong occupational loyalties with communities displaying elements of *gemeinschaft* societies.[107] To be sure, some 'secularization' of union affairs is almost an inevitable concomitant of the structural division of work and non-work activities associated with industrialization itself. Nevertheless, this general condition is entirely consistent with the incidence of major variations in different trade unions and occupational groups. However, there may be an increasing gulf between union allegiance and emotional identification with the union, as indeed Sayles and Strauss have argued on the basis of their data:[108]

> A distinction can be made between 'intellectual acceptance' of the union and 'emotional identification' with it. Almost all workers were convinced of its value as a form of job security; only a minority showed 'emotional identification' with its organizational goals.

Traditional orientations

At a number of points in this study we have observed how processes of institutionalization have served to consolidate certain formative developments in trade unions and to ensure a traditional basis for conduct and behaviour in which historical experiences are transmitted into contemporary actions through institutionalized customs and practices. Traditions, therefore, are to do with particular presuppositions and habits of thought and action and the unity in traditions and cultures may thus be transmitted via individual 'habituated' forms of action.[109] Hence, in sociological terms, 'the problem of understanding and communication is basically a problem of understanding the relativity of traditions, the dependence of institutions on traditions, and above all the formation of traditions.'[110] Moreover, in this latter aspect we have already seen the importance attached by Sorge, in particular, to understanding the forces which shape institutions at crucial phases in development for interpreting and explaining the *emergence* of deeply-rooted traditions themselves.[111] But traditions also form part of the continuity of individual consciousness and a link between practices otherwise separated temporally and spatially.

Traditional forms of action and behaviour are thus occasioned by 'habituation' of 'custom and practice',[112] although in trade union affairs these may be understood in two rather different senses: the adherence to established workplace practices (such as demarcational rules, manning levels, and seniority in promotion to shop floor and supervisory posts); and the propensity for union membership itself to be a long-established mode of conduct which may be traced back within individual working-class families over a number of generations. Indeed, in British trade unionism, a twin, if paradoxical, commitment to the preservation of traditional 'job rights' and an affirmation of the desirability of social change associated with *wertrational* orientations has long been evident. Moreover, it is a phenomenon with deep historical roots identifiable not just at the time of the formation of 'new model' unions in the 1850s, but also at other key phases in the development of the labour movement. Thus as Hinton has recalled in the context of the emergence of the first shop stewards' movement in the 1910s:[113]

> The shop-stewards' movement was primarily a movement of skilled engineering workers, their militancy reflected the breakdown, in wartime conditions of vastly expanded demand for the products of their labour, of their traditional security as a privileged section of the working class. . . . The leaders of the movement were revolutionaries who saw in the craftsmen's militant revolt against bureaucratic trade unionism the germs of a revolutionary spirit on which they could build. But the movement contained, as well, the germs of a merely sectional struggle for the restoration of lost status. Its development hung between these possibilities.

Yet, in so far as the maintenance of traditional practices is concerned, it was once assumed that these were largely a reflection of craft union consciousness. Indeed, as Turner emphasized in his familiar distinction between 'closed' and 'open' unions, members of the former associations characteristically have enforced a series of 'restrictionist' practices encompassing not only the recruitment and training of new members but also their deployment in specific enterprise tasks themselves.[114] None the less, from the evidence of the Fawley researches onwards, it has become clear that workers in open unions are by no means averse to establishing, say, demarcational and other traditionally-based rules.[115] Traditional practices are thus firmly rooted in trade union consciousness in general; a proposition which can be further justified from the members' own trade union experience within family and community. Indeed, there is considerable intergenerational union experience in contemporary Britain and while, on certain assumptions, these very attachments to traditional aspects of union behaviour have been identified as a major stumbling block to efficient utilization of manpower and to the emergence of those radical initiatives in, say, the socio-technical system design of work practices at shop floor level,[116] this in no way invalidates their significance in so far as the perceptions of ordinary trade unionists are concerned.

The emerging synthesis

This outline of the patterning of union character by forces of a 'subjective' character thus brings to a close our review of the main approaches to labour theory. But to focus upon cultural elements and the social action perspective is to add a final crucial dimension, which alongside structural movements, organizational and institutional exigencies and the power of the respective parties to industrial relations, binds together the various segments of modern theorizing about trade unionism. For, after all, an indispensible minimum in any explanatory synthesis is to incorporate the distinctively human capacity of groups of workers to develop certain meanings (whether context-independent or context-specific) about their social experiences since, in action, these produce a rich cultural variety manifest in an array of cognate institutional forms.

During the course of our survey, then, we began by observing that modern theories of trade unionism had originally evolved from five disparate schools (moral and ethical, revolutionary, defensive or conservative, economic, and political). In the first approach, the character of trade unionism was seen to depend upon cultural adaptations and especially upon the consequential elevation of principles of justice within civilized communities. But to this was counterpoised the revolutionary tradition in which, in the so-called 'optimistic' and 'pessimistic' schools of thought, the potential role of unions as vehicles for politically based, ideologically informed social transformations has been variously assessed. Similarly, in other perspectives, the emphasis upon the defensive or conservative elements of unionism (the saliency of job control), upon economic foundations (i.e. structural) and economic purposes of unions (i.e. subjective), and upon the political implications of the role of unions as instruments of industrial governance and of the exercise of power in union-management-government relations could be readily discerned.

But although these various paradigms have lines of filiation in modern perspectives, a major shift in emphasis was undoubtedly occasioned by the publication of J.T. Dunlop's *Industrial Relations Systems*. After all,

187

this seminal study brought a synthetic breadth to otherwise discrete formulations; although, equally, being the offspring of structural-functionalism a number of consequent problems were to arise from its widespread adoption (notably in terms of teleological explanation, comparative statics, the placement of power and ideology in the overall model and a number of specific lacunae such as on process, conflict and change). Yet Dunlop ushered in the vogue for advanced analytical models which encompassed structural constraints upon action, the conceptualization of actors in the industrial relations system, and a recognition of the saliency of power and ideology in union-management relations that is now such a commonplace of contemporary theorizing.

But in British research on labour the 'Oxford' and now 'Warwick' schools of thought have undoubtedly been dominant in industrial relations analysis. Moreover, despite certain superficial affinities with the Dunlop model in the emphasis on rules, in all the most important respects of epistemology and methodology, radically different premises have undoubtedly informed such perspectives. Indeed, the ultimate theoretical roots are to be discovered in Durkheimian scholarship and in the British empirical theory and historiography of the Webbs rather than in Parsonian categories: a situation clearly evident in the focus on moral and ethical considerations rather than ideology, in the development of an explanatory rather than teleological mode of structuralism, and a focus upon institutions of collective bargaining rather than upon industrial relations systems *per se*. In the British literature, furthermore, a major challenge from the so-called radical school to the dominant liberal-pluralism of the traditional Oxford framework has also been a feature of recent literature. None the less, despite an avowedly Marxist emphasis, in trade union terms, as we have seen, power rather than class would appear to be the most crucial factor of inequality affecting trade union action itself. And this, together with the operational distinction between the exercise of power and the resources upon which its successful deployment is based, derives ultimately from the corpus of Weberian scholarship.

Yet in addition to the obvious significance of power as an explanatory variable it was also found possible to piece together the elements of a structural model which incorporated not only the familiar macro-micro distinction but also primary and secondary levels of structural constraint. The former encompassed the deeper levels of structural explanation and embraced politico-economic conditions, technology and the division of labour, while the latter consisted of higher order constraints embodying the class and occupational structure, the size of the enterprise, community variables and micro-structural forces. Moreover, when the insights of organizational and institutional theorists (in which power, structure and action were all central ingredients) were added to this framework, the main foci of modern theorizing began to be substantially clarified. For after all, not only has the institutional structure of collective bargaining profoundly shaped union action and behaviour in pluralist industrial systems, but also organizational constraints have been similarly relevant. To be sure, the latter 'school' has been conventionally divided between the 'environmental' and 'internal' organizational approaches (the first, covering general societal conditions, evolutionary variables, and contextual influences; and the second, the functions, internal modes of regulation, and internal structures and actions of members), but an emerging interpenetration of the two paradigms seems to be an imminent possibility.

But the summit of our theoretical exposition, the accomplishment of which enabled a considerable clarification of the main point at issue, awaited the final acknowledgment of the significance of subjective capacities not least because of the very possibilities that these were to demonstrate of human control (over the physical, natural, and ultimately social environment) as a condition for creation which could be accomplished through advanced and systematic knowledge. Furthermore, in this review, not only were the distinctive methodological implications of the action approach alluded to, but also we examined the role of culture, civilization and values, of political parties, of control as a basis for creation and of the formal elaboration of categories to accommodate 'end', 'value', 'affectual' and 'traditional' orientations.

Yet if all conclusions are in one sense inevitably a consummation of previous endeavour they also embrace points of departure for further studies and analyses and in such a vein, therefore, we would wish to isolate four particular insights which may prove to be signposts for future researches:

1   the importance of attaching or assigning weights to the main
    determinants;
2   the need to distinguish a series of dependent as well as independent
    variables in this particular field of inquiry;
3   a preliminary outline of hypothesized relationships between the
    complex ensemble of independent and dependent variables; and
4   the role of knowledge in enhancing human subjectivity in all
    contexts but not least in so far as trade union action is concerned.

First, then, the comprehensive delineation of variables affecting trade union action should clearly be a prelude to attaching weights to significant associations and not become in any way a shallow, *a priori* and ultimately descriptive eclecticism. For undoubtedly a mere listing of relevant variables is no substitute for rigorous analytical and empirical studies of key structural, subjective, internal organizational, or, indeed, power factors which have affected the development, growth, internal structure and policy formation and implementation within modern unionism.

Yet such an objective is amplified by the parallel requirement of isolating a series of key *dependent* variables, since the manifold specific influences upon the phenomenon under review may in turn have *differential* effects upon specific aspects of unionism itself (e.g. growth or character). Indeed, it is evident that at least seven main dependent variables should be isolated for analytical purposes: (1) trade union growth; (2) trade union structure (especially morphology); (3) internal structure (administration and government); (4) perceptions of unions and of unionism; (5) differential rates of participation in unions; (6) interaction relations *within* unions encompassing relations between rank-and-file members, representatives and leaders; and (7) relationships with employers and managers, the state and the legislature.

Moreover, preliminary indications would appear to be that while trade union growth has almost certainly been occasioned principally by a number of crucial structural variables (employment levels, prices and enterprise size) punctuated at times by recognition policies, union character and membership aspiration are more the product of 'subjectivist' influences, while the relationship with employers and government seems to be particularly affected by the overall balance of power. Furthermore, it is in the analyses of union government and of democratic potential that the contributions of the institutional and organizational theorists have been most relevant. To be sure, these are only general associations but they indicate the utility of more complex models which admit the establishment of a series of dependent as well as independent variables for theoretical and for analytical purposes.

None the less, it remains the case that, in the long-term, considerations of 'value' could gradually predominate in this field of inquiry because detailed knowledge of structural constraints can itself facilitate purposive conduct and even inspire collective action to transform given conditions at source; a situation which is especially so under circumstances of enhanced union power. In other words, whereas in the nineteenth century social scientific knowledge and union power were both rudimentary and, in consequence, many initiatives proved to be hopelessly utopian or foundered on the superior strength of opposed forces, both these considerations are far less applicable in the twilight years of the current century. Our conclusion must be, therefore, that whatever may be the future of the labour movement, its ultimate contours will be shaped less by the exigencies of structure or so-called 'contradictions' of modern political economies than by a series of conscious decisions that will not only impinge upon the concrete manifestations of union character but also, more especially, upon the prospects of enhancing those civilized values which alone enable the free development of all socially useful potentialities and which encourage the concomitant creation of truly humanitarian social orders in which an unleashing of the talents and aptitudes of the working population may yet produce one of the most satisfying and productive epochs in the history of the British people.

Notes

Point of departure

1. G.S. Bain and F. Elsheikh, *Union Growth and the Business Cycle*.
2. J.D. Edelstein and M. Warner, *Comparative Union Democracy*.
3. M. Perlman, *Labor Union Theories in America*.
4. J.T. Dunlop, *Industrial Relations Systems*.
5. See, e.g. A.N.J. Blain and J. Gennard, 'Industrial Relations Theory — A Critical Review'.
6. See for an acknowledgment H.A. Clegg, *Trade Unionism Under Collective Bargaining*, especially Preface.
7. For a review and a critique, however, see G.S. Bain, D. Coates and V. Ellis, *Social Stratification and Trade Unionism*.
8. P. Abell, 'The Many Faces of Power and Liberty'.
9. M. Weber, *The Methodology of the Social Sciences*.
10. T. Parsons and E.A. Shils (eds), *Towards a General Theory of Action*.

Chapter 1   Early theories of the labour movement

1. H.A. Clegg, *Trade Unionism Under Collective Bargaining*, 1.
2. M. Perlman (ed.), *Labor Union Theories in America*, x-xi. For another general collection see E.W. Bakke, C. Kerr and C.W. Anrod, *Unions, Management and the Public*, and C. Kerr, *Labor and Management in Industrial Society*.
3. M. Perlman (ed.), *Labor Union Theories in America*, op. cit., i.
4. Ibid., 18-31. Perlman also mentions the 'social history approach' and certain psychological approaches, 31-42.
5. W. Galenson and S.M. Lipset, *Labor and Trade Unionism*, 395-7.
6. M. Perlman (ed.), *Labor Union Theories in America*, op. cit., ix.
7. Ibid., x-xi.
8. Ibid., i.
9. Ibid., 46-65.
10. Ibid., 47.
11. Ibid., 48. See also R.A. Levitas, 'Some Problems of Aim-Centred Models of Social Movements'.
12. G.K. Chesterton, 'Notebooks', in M. Perlman (ed.), *Labor Union*

Theories in America, op. cit., 46-7.

13 J. Rawls, *A Theory of Justice*, 302.

14 Ibid., 303.

15 E. Durkheim, *The Division of Labor in Society*, 381-2.

16 A. Flanders, *Management and Unions*, 15.

17 Ibid., 39.

18 E. Halévy, *A History of the English People in 1815*, 410-28; and E. Halévy, *The Birth of Methodism in England*.

19 B. Semmel, *The Methodist Revolution*.

20 E.P. Thompson, *The Making of the English Working Class*, Chapter 11, 350-400.

21 R. Moore, *Pit-Men, Preachers and Politics*.

22 E. Halévy, *A History of the English People in 1815*, op. cit., 363 and 410-28.

23 B. Semmel, *The Methodist Revolution*, op. cit., 198.

24 E.P. Thompson, *The Making of the English Working Class*, op. cit., Chapter 11, 350-400.

25 R. Moore, *Pit-Men, Preachers and Politics*, op. cit., 26.

26 Ibid., 10.

27 J.L. Hammond and B. Hammond, *The Town Labourer 1760-1832*, 268-87 and 328-9. The Hammonds deal very sensitively with the paradoxical effects of Methodism and the extent of its impact.

28 E.J. Hobsbawm, *Labouring Men*, 23-33.

29 H. Pelling, *A History of British Trade Unionism*, 15.

30 R.A. Levitas, 'Some Problems of Aim-Centred Models of Social Movements', op. cit., 47-63.

31 J.A. Banks, *Marxist Sociology in Action*, 47.

32 R. Hyman, *Marxism and the Sociology of Trade Unionism*, 4-37.

33 See V.L. Allen, *The Sociology of Industrial Relations*, 1-11.

34 For a further review of Marx's account of trade unions see A. Lozovsky, *Marx and the Trade Unions*, and especially J.A. Banks, *Marxist Sociology in Action*, op. cit., 47.

35 J.A. Banks, *Marxist Sociology in Action*, op. cit., 67.

36 Ibid., 117.

37 R. Hyman, *Marxism and the Sociology of Trade Unionism*, op. cit., 8.

38 Ibid., 8-9.

39 K. Marx, *Value, Price and Profit*, 94.

40 V.I. Lenin, 'What is to be done?', in V.I. Lenin, *Collected Works*, vol. 5, 375.

41 R. Michels, *Political Parties*, 277-92 and 342-56.

42 See L. Trotsky, 'Marxism and Trade Unionism', in T. Clarke and L. Clements (eds), *Trade Unions under Capitalism*, 77-92.

43 R. Hyman, *Marxism and the Sociology of Trade Unionism*, op. cit., 37.

44 S. Perlman, *A Theory of the Labor Movement*, 4-5.

45 Ibid., 5.

46 Ibid., 6.

47 Ibid.

48 Ibid., 7.

49 Ibid., 9.
50 Ibid., 9-10.
51 R. Hoxie, *Trade Unionism in the United States.*
52 C.H. Parker, *The Casual Labourer and Other Essays.*
53 F. Tannenbaum, *A Philosophy of Labor.*
54 L. Brentano, *On the History and Development of Gilds and the Origin of Trade Unions*; see especially Chapters 4 and 5, 114-98.
55 G. Howell, *The Conflicts of Capital and Labour* and G. Howell, *Trade Unionism: New and Old.*
56 H.A Turner, *Trade Union Growth Structure and Policy*, especially 139-68 and 254-64.
57 S. Webb and B. Webb, *The History of Trade Unionism.*
58 Ibid., 5-6.
59 Ibid., 24.
60 Ibid., 25.
61 J.R. Commons, *et al., History of Labor in the United States*, 10-11.
62 H.B. Davis, 'The Theory of Union Growth', 617-20.
63 J.T. Dunlop, 'The Development of Labor Organization', in R.A. Lester and J. Shister (eds), *Insights into Labor Issues*, 163-93.
64 I. Bernstein, 'The Growth of American Unions'.
65 J. Shister, 'The Direction of Unionism, 1947-1967: Thrust or Drift?'.
66 G.S. Bain and F. Elsheikh, *Union Growth and the Business Cycle*, 58-70.
67 G.S. Bain and R. Price, 'Union Growth and Employment Trends in the United Kingdom 1964-1970'. R. Price and G.S. Bain, 'Union Growth Revisited: 1948-1974 in Perspective'; see especially 345-7 and 348-54.
68 J.H. Goldthorpe, D. Lockwood, F. Bechhofer and J. Platt, *The Affluent Worker: Industrial Attitudes and Behaviour*, 176.
69 Ibid., 177.
70 N.W. Chamberlain and J.W. Kuhn, *Collective Bargaining*, 191-209.
71 J.R. Commons, *Industrial Goodwill.*
72 H.C. Adams, 'An Interpretation of the Social Movements of Our Time', especially 45-7.
73 A. Flanders, *Management and Unions*, op. cit., especially 38-47 and 220-40.
74 N.W. Chamberlain and J.W. Kuhn, *Collective Bargaining*, op. cit., 121.
75 M. Perlman (ed.), *Labor Union Theories in America*, op. cit., 189.
76 H.C. Adams, 'An Interpretation of the Social Movements of Our Time', op. cit., especially 38-40. See also M. Perlman, *Labor Union Theories in America*, op. cit., 160-213, for an extended view.
77 A.M. Ross, *Trade Union Wage Policy*, 12. Cf. also J.T. Dunlop, *Wage Determination Under Trade Unions.*
78 A.M. Ross, op. cit., Chapters 2 and 3. See also H.M. Levinson, *Determining Forces in Collective Wage Bargaining*, for an excellent summary of these debates.
79 G.D.H. Cole, *Short History of the British Working Class Movement 1789-1937*. See also by the same author *British Trade Unionism*

Today; *Organised Labour*; *Self-Government in Industry*; and *The World of Labour*.
80   A. Flanders, *Management and Unions*, 42.
81   Ibid., 42-7.

Chapter 2   System models of labour relations

1   J.T. Dunlop, *Industrial Relations Systems*, vi.
2   Ibid.
3   See e.g. D. Fatchett and W.M. Whittingham, 'Trends and Developments in Industrial Relations Theory', 50.
4   J.T. Dunlop, *Industrial Relations Systems*, op. cit., Chapter 1.
5   K. Menzies, *Talcott Parsons and the Social Image of Man*, 110-22.
6   W.C. Mitchell, *Sociological Analysis and Politics: The Theories of Talcott Parsons*, 10.
7   T. Parsons, *The Social System*, 36-45; see also K. Menzies, *Talcott Parsons and the Social Image of Man*, op. cit., especially 36-7, 56 and 110.
8   T. Parsons and N.J. Smelser, *Economy and Society*, 19.
9   Dunlop's own analysis closely parallels that of T. Parsons and N. Smelser, ibid., see especially Chapter 2, 46-51. The quotation is on page 51.
10   J.T. Dunlop, *Industrial Relations Systems*, op. cit., 28-9.
11   Ibid.
12   Ibid., 30.
13   Ibid., 31.
14   Ibid.
15   Ibid., 32.
16   The debates between Parsons and Mills on this issue were once central in the sociological literature on power (see also notes 17 and 18 to this chapter).
17   Talcott Parsons has of course been the main exponent of this thesis. See T. Parsons, *Structure and Process in Modern Societies*, 41-4; T. Parsons, 'On the Concept of Influence', 37-62; A. Giddens, 'Power in the Recent Writings of Talcott Parsons'.
18   See especially C.W. Mills, *The Power Elite*; and R. Dahrendorf, *Class and Class Conflict in Industrial Society*, especially Chapters 1, 11 and 12.
19   A. Touraine, 'Towards a Sociology of Action', in A. Giddens (ed.), *Positivism and Sociology*, 82.
20   T. Parsons, *Structure and Process in Modern Societies*, op. cit., 187.
21   J.A.A. Van Doorn, 'Sociology and the Problem of Power', 16-18.
22   A. Giddens, 'Power in the Recent Writings of Talcott Parsons', op. cit., 257-72.
23   T. Parsons, *Sociological Theory and Modern Society*, 353. Indeed, to achieve a harmonious social system, power and influence, according to Parsons, should be ordered as set out in Table N.1:

Table N.1   *Parsons's model of power and influence*

	Value-principle	Co-ordination standard	Factors controlled	Products controlled
Influence	Solidarity	Consensus	Commitments to valued association Policy decisions	Commitment to common values Political support
Power	Effectiveness	Success	Interest demands Control of productivity	Leadership responsibility Control of fluid resources

This is particularly to avoid a power deflation. See also K. Menzies, *Talcott Parsons and the Social Image of Man*, op. cit., 68-89.

24   J.T. Dunlop, *Industrial Relations Systems*, op. cit., 11-12.
25   Neil Smelser's work was thus most important in this respect. T. Parsons and N. Smelser, *Economy and Society*.
26   J.T. Dunlop, *Industrial Relations Systems*, op. cit., 4.
27   Ibid.
28   Ibid., 7.
29   Ibid., 5-7.
30   Ibid., 9.
31   Ibid., 7.
32   Ibid., 11-13, my italics.
33   Ibid., 16.
34   Ibid., 17.
35   Ibid., 16-18.
36   Ibid., 18.
37   Ibid., 9-13.
38   Ibid., 10.
39   Ibid., 10-13.
40   Ibid., 16.
41   N.W. Chamberlain, *Collective Bargaining*.
42   J.R. Commons, *Industrial Goodwill*.
43   J.T. Dunlop, *Industrial Relations Systems*, op. cit., 13.
44   Ibid., 13-14.
45   Ibid., 388.
46   A. Flanders, *Management and Unions*, op. cit., 86.
47   G.S. Bain and H.A. Clegg, 'A Strategy for Industrial Relations Research in Great Britain'. See also H.A. Clegg, *The Changing System of Industrial Relations in Great Britain*.
48   K.F. Walker, 'Towards Useful Theorising About Industrial Relations'.
49   G.G. Somers (ed.), *Essays in Industrial Relations Theory*, 39-53.
50   J.C. Anderson, 'Bargaining Outcomes: An IR System Approach'.
51   A.N.J. Blain, *Pilots and Management: Industrial Relations in the U.K. Airlines*.

52 J.F.B. Goodman, E.G.A. Armstrong, J.E. Davis and A. Wagner, *Rule Making and Industrial Peace*.
53 J.C. Anderson, 'Bargaining Outcomes: An IR System Approach', op. cit., 129.
54 A.N.J. Blain, *Pilots and Management*, op. cit. See 'Theoretical Framework', Chapter 2.
55 J.F.B. Goodman, *et al.*, *Rule Making and Industrial Peace*, p. 15.
56 P.S. Cohen, *Modern Social Theory*, 47-56.
57 S.J. Wood *et al.*, 'The "Industrial Relations System Concept" as a Basis for Theory', op. cit., 296.
58 Ibid., cf. J.T. Dunlop, *Industrial Relations Systems*, op. cit., 30-2.
59 See J.T. Dunlop, ibid., 57-8 and Chapter 7.
60 A.N.J. Blain and J. Gennard, 'Industrial Relations Theory — A Critical Review'.
61 G.G. Somers (ed.), *Essays in Industrial Relations Theory*, op. cit., especially 49-53 in his general model of power.
62 A.W.J. Craig, 'A Framework for the Analysis of Industrial Relations Systems', in B. Barrett, E. Rhodes and J. Beishon (eds), *Industrial Relations and the Wider Society*.
63 R. Singh, 'Systems Theory in the Study of Industrial Relations: Time for a Reappraisal?'.
64 A. Craig, 'A Framework for the Analysis of Industrial Relations Systems', op. cit., 9.
65 Ibid., 19.
66 R. Singh, 'Systems Theory in the Study of Industrial Relations', op. cit., 61.
67 Ibid., 67.
68 Ibid., 68. See also R. Singh, 'Theory and Practice in Industrial Relations'.
69 J.F.B. Goodman, *et al.*, *Rule Making and Industrial Peace*, op. cit., 19.
70 A.N.J. Blain and J. Gennard, 'Industrial Relations Theory — A Critical Review', op. cit., 394-5.
71 Ibid., 394.
72 Ibid.
73 S.J. Wood, A. Wagner, E.G.A. Armstrong, J.F.B. Goodman and J.E. Davis, 'The "Industrial Relations System" Concept as a Basis for Theory in Industrial Relations', 297.
74 H.G. Heneman, Jr, 'Toward A General Conceptual Scheme of Industrial Relations', in G.G. Somers (ed.), *Essays in Industrial Relations Theory*, op. cit., 11.
75 P.S. Cohen, *Modern Social Theory*, op. cit., 52.
76 A.N.J. Blain and J. Gennard, 'Industrial Relations Theory — A Critical Review', op. cit., 401-2 and 405-7.
77 Ibid., 401.
78 Ibid.
79 A.N.J. Blain, *Pilots and Management*, op. cit., 46.
80 Ibid.
81 Ibid.
82 J. Gill, 'One Approach to the Teaching of Industrial Relations', 269.

83   S. Hill and K. Thurley, 'Sociology and Industrial Relations', 154.
84   R. Hyman, *Industrial Relations: A Marxist Introduction*; his criticisms of Dunlop are contained on pp. 10-15.
85   R. Singh, 'Systems Theory in the Study of Industrial Relations', op. cit., 62-3.
86   G.S. Bain and H.A. Clegg, 'A Strategy for Industrial Relations Research in Great Britain', op. cit., 92.
87   J. Gill, 'One Approach to the Teaching of Industrial Relations', op. cit., 269.
88   T. Parsons and E.A. Shils (eds), *Towards a General Theory of Action*.
89   Ibid., see also S.J. Wood *et al.*, 'The "Industrial Relations System" Concept as a Basis for Theory', op. cit., 292.
90   Cf. again S.J. Wood *et al.*, 'The "Industrial Relations System" Concept as a Basis for Theory', op. cit., 292-3.
91   J.F.B. Goodman *et al.*, *Rule Making and Industrial Peace*, op. cit., 19.
92   Ibid.
93   S.J. Wood *et al.*, 'The "Industrial Relations System" Concept as a Basis for Theory', op. cit., 292.
94   A.N.J. Blain, *Pilots and Management*, op. cit., 44.
95   Ibid.
96   Problems of comparison are dealt with by A.N.J. Blain and J. Gennard, 'Industrial Relations Theory — A Critical Review', op. cit., 405-6 and P.S. Cohen, *Modern Social Theory*, op. cit., 53-6.
97   G.G. Somers (ed.), *Essays in Industrial Relations Theory*, op. cit., 43.
98   G.S. Bain and H.A. Clegg, 'A Strategy for Industrial Relations Research in Great Britain', op. cit., 107-8.
99   A.N.J. Blain and J. Gennard, 'Industrial Relations Theory — A Critical Review', op. cit., 405.
100   Ibid., 405-6.
101   K.F. Walker, 'Towards Useful Theorising About Industrial Relations', op. cit., 311.
102   Ibid., 311-2.
103   J.T. Dunlop, *Industrial Relations Systems*, op. cit., 8.
104   Ibid.
105   See e.g. G.S. Bain, *The Growth of White Collar Unionism*, 124-5 and 181-2.
106   R. Hyman, *Industrial Relations: A Marxist Introduction*, op. cit., 11.
107   J.A. Banks, *Trade Unionism*, 17-18.
108   E.g. G.S. Bain and H.A. Clegg, 'A Strategy for Industrial Relations Research in Great Britain', op. cit., 95-6.
109   C.J. Margerison, 'What do we mean by Industrial Relations? A Behavioural Science Approach'. See especially Model 1, p. 276.
110   G.S. Bain and H.A. Clegg, 'A Strategy for Industrial Relations Research in Great Britain', op. cit., 93.
111   Ibid., 95.
112   There are several writers who have mentioned this issue but A.N.J. Blain and J. Gennard, 'Industrial Relations Theory — A Critical

Review', op. cit., 406, and S. Shimmin and R. Singh, 'Industrial Relations and Organizational Behaviour: A Critical Appraisal', are particularly important instances.

113 Ibid., 38.
114 A.N.J. Blain and J. Gennard, 'Industrial Relations Theory — A Critical Review', op. cit., 406.
115 Ibid.
116 G.S. Bain and H.A. Clegg, 'A Strategy for Industrial Relations Research in Great Britain', op. cit., 95.
117 W. Brown, 'A Consideration of "Custom and Practice" ', 42-61.
118 A. Flanders, *Management and Unions*, op. cit., 86-94.
119 J.F.B. Goodman, *et al.*, *Rule Making and Industrial Peace*, op. cit., 16-18.
120 G.S. Bain and H.A. Clegg, 'A Strategy for Industrial Relations Research in Great Britain', op. cit., 92-3.
121 W. Brown, 'A Consideration of "Custom and Practice" ', op. cit., 42.
122 J.F.B. Goodman *et al.*, 'Rules in Industrial Relations Theory: A Discussion', 14-30.
123 Ibid., 16-18.
124 J.T. Dunlop, *Industrial Relations Systems*, op. cit., 14-16.
125 See e.g. D.H. Zimmerman, 'The Practicalities of Rule Use', in J.T. Douglas (ed.), *Understanding Everyday Life*, 221-38.
126 J.F.B. Goodman *et al.*, *Rule Making and Industrial Peace*, op. cit., 17.
127 Ibid., 16-18.
128 J.T. Dunlop, *Industrial Relations Systems*, op. cit., 13.
129 J.F.B. Goodman, *et al.*, *Rule Making and Industrial Peace*, op. cit., 17.
130 Ibid., 17-18.
131 Ibid., 18.
132 Ibid.
133 Ibid.
134 S.J. Wood, *et al.*, 'The "Industrial Relations System" Concept as a Basis for Theory', op. cit., 300-3.
135 J.C. Anderson, 'Bargaining Outcomes: An IR System Approach', op. cit., 128.
136 A.N.J. Blain, *Pilots and Management*, op. cit., 47.
137 G.S. Bain and H.A. Clegg, 'A Strategy for Industrial Relations Research in Great Britain', op. cit., 95.
138 Ibid., 91-7.
139 A.N.J. Blain and J. Gennard, 'Industrial Relations Theory — A Critical Review', op. cit., 398-407.
140 G.G. Somers (ed.), *Essays in Industrial Relations Theory*, op. cit., 42-53.
141 S.J. Wood *et al.*, 'The "Industrial Relations System" Concept as a Basis for Theory', op. cit., 300-5.
142 Ibid., 304.
143 Ibid.
144 Ibid., 302.
145 J.T. Dunlop, 'Political Systems and Industrial Relations', 104.

146   Ibid. See also pp. 101-2 for Dunlop's definition of political systems. Quoted also in S.J. Wood *et al.*, 'The "Industrial Relations System" Concept as a Basis for Theory', op. cit., 302.
147   J.F.B. Goodman *et al.*, *Rule Making and Industrial Peace*, op. cit., 18.
148   S.J. Wood *et al.*, 'The "Industrial Relations System" Concept as a Basis for Theory', op. cit., 303.
149   G.S. Bain and H.A. Clegg, 'A Strategy for Industrial Relations .Research in Great Britain', op. cit., 94-5.
150   R. Hyman, *Industrial Relations*, op. cit., especially Chapter 11.
151   C.J. Margerison, 'What do we mean by Industrial Relations? A Behavioural Science Approach', op. cit., 273.
152   K. Laffer, 'Industrial Relations, Its Teaching and Scope: An Australian Experience', 9-26 and 21-2.
153   J.F.B. Goodman *et al.*, *Rule Making and Industrial Peace*, 16.
154   S.J. Wood, 'Ideology in Industrial Relations Theory', 55.
155   J.T. Dunlop, *Industrial Relations Systems*, 380.

Chapter 3   The theoretical foundations of the 'Oxford school'

1   S.J. Wood, 'The Radicalisation of Industrial Relations Theory', 52.
2   R. Hyman, 'Pluralism, Procedural Consensus and Collective Bargaining', 22.
3   So far as can be ascertained the epithet 'Oxford school' derived from the cognate expression 'Oxford Line' which was coined by the Montagu Burton Professor of Industrial Relations at Cambridge to refer (somewhat disparagingly) to the contribution of those Oxford scholars who had been influential in shaping the researches and ultimate recommendations of the Donovan Commission on Trade Unions and Employers' Associations. In an oft-quoted passage, H.A. Turner ('The Royal Commission Research Papers', 359) drew attention to the essentially pragmatic considerations which had informed this approach and although its tenor no longer wholly captures the analytical advances of the 1970s, at the time it was indicative of the dearth of serious contribution to theory. None the less, despite major differences in perspective, Flanders, Clegg and Fox have of course all produced major works of significance for trade union theorizing and hence, given obvious inaccuracies of geography and institutional position, and allowing for substantial academic disagreements among these scholars, we shall follow the convention of deploying the term 'Oxford school' to delineate the influential 'pluralist perspective' and other related theoretical propositions that, originally, at least, were developed by members of that University.
4   S.J. Wood and R. Elliott, 'A Critical Evaluation of Fox's Radicalisation of Industrial Relations Theory', 106-7.
5   Both Bain and Clegg have worked on the outlines of theories initially formulated by Flanders. See H.A. Clegg, *Trade Unionism Under Collective Bargaining*, ix.
6   S. Giner, *Sociology*, 91.

7 Ibid., 218.
8 E. Durkheim, *The Division of Labor in Society*, especially 364-8 and 398-9, 401.
9 Ibid., 197 and 266-75.
10 Ibid., 386-7.
11 Ibid., 374-88, especially 377.
12 S. and B. Webb, *Industrial Democracy*, 454-527 on the entrance to a trade and the right to a trade contain many examples.
13 A. Flanders, *Management and Unions*, especially 15, 41-2 and 239-40.
14 J.H. Goldthorpe, 'Social Inequality and Social Integration in Modern Britain', in D. Wedderburn (ed.), *Poverty, Inequality and Class Structure*, 217-39; and A. Fox, *Beyond Contract: Power, Work and Trust Relations*.
15 E. Durkheim, *The Division of Labor in Society*, op. cit., 270.
16 Ibid., Chapter 1.
17 Ibid., 50.
18 See the importance attached to occupation by Bain in G.S. Bain, *The Growth of White Collar Unionism*, 11-13.
19 J.A. Banks, *Marxist Sociology in Action*, especially 37 and 306-9.
20 A. Fox, *Beyond Contract*, op. cit., 207-47.
21 E. Durkheim, *The Division of Labor in Society*, op. cit., 354-7.
22 See e.g. R. Hyman, *Industrial Relations*, especially 21-4 and 178-80; and A. Fox, *Beyond Contract*, op. cit., 241-3 and 274-96.
23 A. Fox and A. Flanders, 'The Reform of Collective Bargaining: From Donovan to Durkheim'.
24 A. Fox, *Beyond Contract*, op. cit., 229-36 and 274-96.
25 S. and B. Webb, *The History of Trade Unionism*, 5-6.
26 E. Durkheim, *The Division of Labor in Society*, op. cit., 354-6.
27 Ibid.
28 See chapter 6 and J. Curran and J. Stanworth, 'Worker Involvement and Social Relations in the Small Firm', especially 317-23.
29 E. Durkheim, *The Division of Labor in Society*, op. cit., 368.
30 Ibid., 374-88.
31 Ibid., 375.
32 Ibid., 405-9.
33 Ibid., 389-96.
34 Ibid., 389.
35 E. Durkheim, *Suicide*, 384.
36 E. Durkheim, *The Division of Labor in Society*, op. cit.
37 E. Durkheim, *Sociology and Philosophy*, especially 35-62.
38 E. Durkheim, *Suicide*, op. cit., 379.
39 A. Fox, *Beyond Contract*, op. cit., and A. Fox and A. Flanders, 'The Reform of Collective Bargaining: From Donovan to Durkheim', op. cit., 173-80.
40 H.A. Clegg, 'Pluralism in Industrial Relations', 312-16.
41 Ibid., 309.
42 E. Durkheim, *Suicide*, op. cit., 378-84.
43 P.S. Cohen, *Modern Social Theory*, 2-6.
44 S. and B. Webb, *The History of Trade Unionism*, op. cit.; and S. and

B. Webb, *Industrial Democracy*, 2 vols.

45   H.A. Turner, *Trade Union Growth Structure and Policy*, see especially 201.
46   A. Flanders, *Management and Unions*, 213.
47   S. and B. Webb, *Industrial Democracy*, op. cit., 603-850.
48   Ibid., see e.g. 'The Assumptions of Trade Unionism', Chapter XIII.
49   Ibid., 654-702, and Chapter IV.
50   Ibid., 572.
51   Ibid., Part 2.
52   Ibid., 560 and 715-40.
53   Ibid., 566-8.
54   Ibid., 560-1.
55   Ibid., 715-40.
56   Ibid., 748.
57   Ibid., 749-60.
58   Ibid., 747. See also 746-9, 792.
59   Ibid., especially 809 and 846-50.
60   Ibid., 590.
61   Ibid., especially 809. See also T. Keenoy, 'From the Webbs to Corporatism', 23-54.
62   S. and B. Webb, *Industrial Democracy*, op. cit., 825.
63   Ibid., Chapter IV.
64   A. Flanders, *Management and Unions*, op. cit.
65   N.W. Chamberlain, *Collective Bargaining*.
66   M. Derber, *Plant Union Management Relations: From Practice to Theory*.
67   A.M. Ross, *Trade Union Wage Policy*.
68   A. Flanders, *Management and Unions*, op. cit., 213-40.
69   Ibid., especially 228-30.
70   G.S. Bain and F. Elsheikh, *Union Growth and the Business Cycle*.
71   H.A. Clegg, *Trade Unionism Under Collective Bargaining*, ix.
72   A. Flanders, *Management and Unions*, op. cit., 13-47.
73   Ibid., 41-2.
74   Ibid., 91-2.
75   Ibid., 215.
76   Ibid., 41-2.
77   Ibid., 215-16.
78   A. Fox, 'Collective Bargaining, Flanders and the Webbs', 170.
79   A. Flanders, *Management and Unions*, op. cit., 216.
80   Ibid., 233-8.
81   Ibid., 213-26. For the evaluation of 'economism' see M. Mann, *Consciousness and Action Among the Western Working Class*, 24-33.
82   A. Flanders, *Management and Unions*, op. cit., 239-40.
83   A. Fox and A. Flanders, 'The Reform of Collective Bargaining: From Donovan to Durkheim', in A. Flanders, *Management and Unions*, op. cit., 241-76.
84   Ibid., but see also A. Fox, *Beyond Contract*, op. cit.
85   A. Fox and A. Flanders, op. cit., 247.
86   Ibid., 246-60.

87   Ibid., especially 253-5.
88   Ibid., 262-3.
89   A. Flanders, *Management and Unions*, op. cit., see especially 213-40.
90   Ibid., for example, 236-8.
91   Ibid.
92   Ibid., 233-8.
93   N.W. Chamberlain, *Collective Bargaining*. Criticized in A. Flanders, *Management and Unions*, op. cit., 235.
94   G.S. Bain and H.A. Clegg, 'A Strategy for Industrial Relations Research in Great Britain'.
95   H.A. Clegg, *The Changing System of Industrial Relations in Great Britain*, 451.
96   A. Flanders, *Management and Unions*, op. cit., 44.
97   H.A. Turner, *Trade Union Growth, Structure and Policy*, 14.
98   A. Flanders, *Management and Unions*, op. cit., 279.
99   Ibid.
100   Ibid., 288-94.
101   Ibid., 24-37 especially 31.
102   Ibid., 30-1.
103   R. Hyman, *Marxism and the Sociology of Trade Unionism*, 8-9.
104   A. Flanders, *Management and Unions*, op. cit. See e.g. 27 and 278-85.
105   Ibid., 100-1.
106   Ibid., 94-103.
107   Ibid., 38-47, and 94-9.
108   Ibid., 103-13.
109   Ibid., 114.
110   See e.g. C. Crouch, *Class Conflict and the Industrial Relations Crisis*; and R.E. Pahl and J.T. Winckler, 'The Coming Corporatism'.

Chapter 4   Pluralism and trade unionism

1   H.A. Clegg, 'Pluralism in Industrial Relations'.
2   A. Fox, *Beyond Contract, Man Mis Management*, and also J.H. Goldthorpe, 'Social Inequality and Social Integration in Modern Britain', in D. Wedderburn (ed.), *Poverty, Inequality and Class Structure*, 217-38, reflect principal modifications.
3   R. Hyman, 'Pluralism, Procedural Consensus and Collective Bargaining', 16.
4   Ibid., 17-20.
5   Ibid., 20.
6   H.A. Clegg, 'Pluralism in Industrial Relations', op. cit., 309-16.
7   H.A. Clegg, *A New Approach to Industrial Democracy*, 19-30.
8   H.A. Clegg, 'Pluralism in Industrial Relations', op. cit., 310-12; and H.A. Clegg, *The Changing System of Industrial Relations in Great Britain*, Chapter 11.
9   Ibid., and H.A. Clegg, 'Pluralism in Industrial Relations', op. cit., 311.
10   H.A. Clegg, *The Changing System of Industrial Relations in Great*

Britain, op. cit., 455.

11   H.A. Clegg, 'Pluralism in Industrial Relations', op. cit., 316.
12   Ibid., 311.
13   H.A. Clegg, *The Changing System of Industrial Relations in Great Britain*, 450-6.
14   Ibid., 455-6.
15   Ibid., 456.
16   H.A. Clegg, *Trade Unionism under Collective Bargaining*.
17   A. Fox, *Beyond Contract*, op. cit., 274-96.
18   S.J. Wood and R. Elliott, 'A Critical Evaluation of Fox's Radicalisation of Industrial Relations Theory'.
19   A. Fox, 'A Note on Industrial Relations Pluralism', 105-9.
20   A. Fox, *Industrial Sociology and Industrial Relations*, 3-15.
21   A. Fox, *A Sociology of Work in Industry*, 57-62 and Chapters 4 and 5.
22   N.S. Ross, 'Organized Labour and Management in the UK', in E.M. Hugh-Jones (ed.), *Human Relations and Management*, 101.
23   A. Fox, 'Industrial Relations: A Social Critique of the Pluralist Ideology', in J. Child (ed.), *Man and Organization*, 205-31.
24   A. Fox, *Beyond Contract*, op. cit., 274-96.
25   A. Fox, *Man Mis Management*, op. cit., 15-20.
26   S. Wood and R. Elliott, 'A Critical Evaluation of Fox's Radicalisation of Industrial Relations Theory', op. cit., 120.
27   A. Fox, *Man Mis Management*, op. cit., 15.
28   Ibid., see also 15-20.
29   A. Fox, 'A Note on Industrial Relations Pluralism', op. cit., 105.
30   These distinctions are further elaborated in chapters 5-8 inclusive.
31   A. Fox, *Beyond Contract*, op. cit., 274-96.
32   Ibid., 255-74.
33   Ibid., Chapter 7.
34   Ibid., 290-6.
35   Ibid., 338-47.
36   Ibid., especially Chapter 8.
37   Ibid., Chapter 6.
38   Ibid., 293.
39   Ibid., 292-4.
40   Ibid., 317-22.
41   S.J. Wood and R. Elliott, 'A Critical Evaluation of Fox's Radicalisation of Industrial Relations Theory', op. cit., 121.
42   Ibid., 122.
43   A. Fox, *Beyond Contract*, op. cit., 277.
44   Ibid., 276-80.
45   A. Flanders, *Management and Unions*, 94.
46   E. Durkheim, *The Division of Labor*, 110-32, 364-6 and especially Appendix 411-35.
47   S. and B. Webb, *Industrial Democracy*, 807-50.
48   G.S. Bain and H.A. Clegg, 'A Strategy for Industrial Relations Research in Great Britain', 91-3.
49   J.T. Dunlop, *Industrial Relations Systems*, 13-16.
50   R. Hyman, *Industrial Relations*, 11.

51 H.A. Clegg, 'Pluralism in Industrial Relations', op. cit.

52 R. Hyman, *Industrial Relations*, op. cit., 11-31.

53 H.A. Clegg, *The Changing System of Industrial Relations in Great Britain*, op. cit., 452.

54 A. Flanders, *Management and Unions*, op. cit., 213.

55 A. Fox, 'Collective Bargaining, Flanders and the Webbs'.

56 Ibid., 170.

57 I.e. S. and B. Webb.

58 A. Fox, 'Collective Bargaining, Flanders and the Webbs', op. cit., 156-7.

59 Ibid., 156.

60 Ibid.

61 Ibid., 162.

62 Ibid.

63 Ibid., 164.

64 Ibid., 171.

65 The term 'behaviour' remains awkward though Clegg admits the difficulty but 'action' would still be preferable. H.A. Clegg, *Trade Unionism Under Collective Bargaining*, ix.

66 Ibid., 11.

67 Ibid., 4. My italics.

68 Ibid.

69 Ibid., 8-11.

70 Ibid.

71 Ibid., 10.

72 Ibid.

73 Ibid., Chapters 2-8 inclusive.

74 A.N.J. Blain and J. Gennard, 'Industrial Relations Theory — A Critical Review'.

75 H.A. Clegg, *Trade Unionism Under Collective Bargaining*, op. cit., 12-28.

76 Ibid., 7-8.

77 Ibid., Chapter 3, especially 39.

78 Ibid., Chapters 4 and 5.

79 Ibid., 54.

80 Ibid., Chapter 6.

81 Ibid., Chapter 7.

82 Ibid., Chapter 8.

83 M. Warner, review of H.A. Clegg, *Trade Unionism Under Collective Bargaining*.

84 H.A. Clegg's own comments in the Preface to *Trade Unionism Under Collective Bargaining*, op. cit., x, are pertinent here.

85 A. Flanders and H.A. Clegg (eds), *The System of Industrial Relations in Great Britain*, see especially v, and Chapters 3, 4 and 5.

86 H.A. Clegg, *The Changing System of Industrial Relations in Great Britain*, op. cit., 450.

87 Ibid.; and A. Flanders, *The Fawley Productivity Agreements*, 21-64 and especially 43-9.

88 H.A. Clegg, *The Changing System of Industrial Relations in Great Britain*, op. cit., 451.

89   Ibid.
90   Ibid., 451-2.
91   S.N. Eisenstadt, 'Social Institutions', in D. Sills (ed.), *International Encyclopedia of Social Sciences*, 418.
92   A. Sorge, 'The Evolution of Industrial Democracy in the Countries of the European Community', 281-9.
93   Ibid., 281-2.
94   Ibid., 282-3.
95   Ibid., 283.
96   R.A. Lester, *As Unions Mature*, 23-34. The reference is to American trade unionism.

Chapter 5   Social inequality and trade union behaviour

1   K. Marx, London, 18 March 1872. Quoted in the opening of L. Althusser and E. Balibar, *Reading Capital*.
2   N. Elias, 'Problems of Involvement and Detachment', 226-52.
3   M. Perlman (ed.), *Labor Union Theories in America*, 66-143, 160-213.
4   M. Weber, *The Theory of Social and Economic Organization*; and H.H. Gerth and C.W. Mills, *From Max Weber*, 180.
5   R. Crompton and J. Gubbay, *Economy and Class Structure*, 167-9.
6   J.H. Goldthorpe, 'Social Inequality and Social Integration in Modern Britain', in D. Wedderburn (ed.), *Poverty, Inequality and Class Structure*, 217-34.
7   K. Prandy, *Professional Employees*, 37.
8   J.H. Goldthorpe and D. Lockwood, 'Affluence and the British Class Structure', 146.
9   P. Abell, 'The Many Faces of Power and Liberty'.
10   P. Bowen, *Social Control in Industrial Organizations*, 1-77.
11   C. Edwards, 'Measuring Union Power: A Comparison of Two Methods Applied to the Study of Local Union Power in the Coal Industry'.
12   R. Martin, *The Sociology of Power*.
13   See chapter 4.
14   R. Hyman, *Industrial Relations*, 12.
15   G.S. Bain, D. Coates and V. Ellis, *Social Stratification and Trade Unionism*, 160.
16   H.H. Gerth and C.W. Mills, *From Max Weber*, op. cit., 181.
17   Ibid. See also R. Crompton and J. Gubbay, *Economy and Class Structure*, op. cit., 5-19.
18   Ibid. See also M. Weber, *The Theory of Social and Economic Organization*, op. cit., and H.H. Gerth and C.W. Mills, *From Max Weber*, op. cit., 180-95.
19   Ibid., 181.
20   Ibid., 180.
21   R. Crompton and J. Gubbay, *Economy and Class Structure*, op. cit., 140-66.
22   V.L. Allen, *The Sociology of Industrial Relations*, especially 8-11.
23   H. Braverman, *Labor and Monopoly Capital*.

24 R. Crompton, 'Approaches to the Study of White Collar Unionism', especially 413-23.
25 R. Crompton and J. Gubbay, *Economy and Class Structure*, op. cit., Chapter 2, 12-15 and 39-40.
26 K. Marx, letter to J. Weydemeyer 5 March 1852, in K. Marx and F. Engels, *Selected Correspondence 1843-1895*, 86.
27 R. Crompton and J. Gubbay, *Economy and Class Structure*, op. cit., 167.
28 Ibid., 71.
29 K. Marx, *Capital*, vol. 1, 180.
30 K. Marx, *Capital*, vol. 3, 885-6.
31 M. Weber, *The Theory of Social and Economic Organization*, op. cit., and H.H. Gerth and C.W. Mills, *From Max Weber*, op. cit., 180-95.
32 Ibid., 184.
33 Ibid., 183.
34 Ibid., 184.
35 Ibid., 186.
36 Ibid., 186-7.
37 Ibid., 193.
38 Ibid., 193-4.
39 K. Marx, *Value, Price and Profit*, 94.
40 R.M. Blackburn, *Union Character and Social Class*; J.H. Goldthorpe and D. Lockwood, 'Affluence and the British Class Structure', op. cit.; D. Lockwood, *The Blackcoated Worker*; K. Prandy, *Professional Employees*, op. cit.; and M. Scheler, *Die Wissensformen und die Gesellschaft*.
41 Referred to in W. Stark, *The Sociology of Knowledge*, 77-8.
42 J.H. Goldthorpe and D. Lockwood, 'Affluence and the British Class Structure', op. cit., 153.
43 H. Popitz, H.P. Bahrdt, E.A. Jueres and A. Kesting, 'The Worker's Image of Society', reprinted in T. Burns (ed.), *Industrial Man*, 281-317.
44 Ibid., 294.
45 Ibid., 290-1.
46 G.S. Bain, D. Coates and V. Ellis, *Social Stratification and Trade Unionism*, op. cit., 9.
47 Ibid., 160.
48 D. Lockwood, *The Blackcoated Worker*.
49 R.M. Blackburn, *Union Character and Social Class*.
50 K. Prandy, *Professional Employees*, op. cit.
51 G.S. Bain, D. Coates and V. Ellis, *Social Stratification and Trade Unionism*, op. cit., 134 and 159.
52 Ibid., 154.
53 Ibid., Chapter 4.
54 J.H. Goldthorpe, 'Social Inequality and Social Integration in Modern Britain', op. cit., 218.
55 Ibid.
56 Ibid., 233.
57 R. Hyman, *Industrial Relations*, op. cit.

58 Ibid., 4.
59 These have developed from a wide range of Marxist writings which cannot be fully listed here but see e.g. T.B. Bottomore, *Marxist Sociology*.
60 Ibid., 75.
61 T. Parsons, *Essays in Sociological Theory*, 334.
62 R. Hyman, *Industrial Relations*, op. cit., 12.
63 S.J. Wood, 'The Radicalisation of Industrial Relations Theory', 54.
64 H.A. Clegg, *The Changing System of Industrial Relations in Great Britain*, 452.
65 R. Hyman, *Industrial Relations*, op. cit., 19-20.
66 Ibid., 31.
67 Ibid., 26.
68 Ibid., 27.
69 Ibid., 28-31.
70 M. Weber, *Economy and Society*, op. cit.; H.H. Gerth and C.W. Mills, *From Max Weber*, op. cit., 180-95.
71 S. and B. Webb, *Industrial Democracy*, 173-221.
72 A. Flanders, *Management and Unions*, especially 38-47 and 238-40.
73 R. Martin, *The Sociology of Power*, op. cit., 100.
74 J.H. Goldthorpe, 'Social Inequality and Social Integration in Modern Britain', op. cit., 217-19.
75 R. Martin, *The Sociology of Power*, op. cit., 118-19.
76 Ibid., 115.
77 G.S. Bain, *The Growth of White Collar Unionism*, 183-4.
78 Ibid., 185; see also R. Adams, 'Bain's Theory of White Collar Union Growth: A Conceptual Critique'.
79 D. Lockwood, *The Blackcoated Worker*, op. cit., 39-133.
80 K. Prandy, *Professional Employees*, op. cit., especially 30-47.
81 D. Lockwood, *The Blackcoated Worker*, op. cit., 15.
82 K. Prandy, *Professional Employees*, op. cit., 30-47.
83 R. Crompton, 'Approaches to the Study of White Collar Unionism', op. cit., 413-16.
84 Ibid., 416-17.
85 Ibid., 423.
86 J.A. Banks, 'A Comment on Rosemary Crompton's "Approaches to the Study of White Collar Unionism" ', 141-2.
87 R. Dubin, 'Power and Union-Management Relations'.
88 W.E.J. McCarthy and S.R. Parker, 'Shop Stewards and Workplace Relations'.
89 R. Hyman, *Industrial Relations*, for example 18-28; R. Hyman and I. Brough, *Social Values and Industrial Relations*, especially 62-92.
90 C. Goodrich, *The Frontier of Control*. See the various distinctions developed in Chapter 12, 253-66.
91 Ibid., 253-66.
92 R. Herding, *Job Control and Union Structure*, 1-14.
93 Ibid., 3-12.
94 P. Abell, 'The Many Faces of Power and Liberty'.
95 Ibid., 3.
96 Ibid.

97 S. Lukes, *Power: A Radical View*, 11-25.
98 P. Abell, 'The Many Faces of Power and Liberty', op. cit., 3. (See also P. Abell (ed.), *Organizations as Bargaining and Influence Systems*.)
99 Ibid., 9.
100 Ibid., 11-13.
101 Ibid., 13-21. Also C. Edwards, 'Measuring Union Power: A comparison of two methods applied to the study of Local Union Power in the Coal Industry', op. cit., 1-2.
102 R. Dubin, 'Power and Union-Management Relations', op. cit., 62.
103 Ibid.
104 Ibid.
105 R. Bierstedt, 'An Analysis of Social Power'.
106 R. M. Blackburn, *Union Character and Social Class*, 14-17.
107 M. Poole, 'A Power Analysis of Workplace Labour Relations'.
108 Ibid., 34.
109 R. Bierstedt, 'An Analysis of Social Power', op. cit., 737 (also includes 'natural resources').
110 R. M. Blackburn and K. Prandy, 'White-Collar Unionization: A Conceptual Framework', 112-15.
111 Ibid., 112.
112 K. Prandy, A. Stewart and R. M. Blackburn, 'Concepts and Measures', especially 432-43.

Chapter 6   Modern structuralist approaches

1 M. Weber, *The Methodology of the Social Sciences*, 68.
2 R. K. Merton, 'Structural Analysis in Sociology', in P. M. Blau (ed.), *Approaches to the Study of Social Structure*, 32.
3 P. M. Blau, 'Introduction' in Ibid., 7.
4 There are many varieties of structuralist account of course but most stem either from Durkheimian or Marxian scholarship. See E. Durkheim, *The Rules of Sociological Method*; and K. Marx, Preface to *A Contribution to the Critique of Political Economy*. For a recent valuable reader see P. M. Blau (ed.), *Approaches to the Study of Social Structure*; and for the structuralist critique of Weberian sociology see B. S. Turner, 'The Structuralist Critique of Weber's Sociology'. The quotation is from B. S. Turner, op. cit., 1.
5 P. M. Blau (ed.), *Approaches to the Study of Social Structure*, op. cit., 2.
6 Ibid., 3-18. See also R.K. Merton, 'Structural Analysis in Sociology', in P.M. Blau (ed.), *Approaches to the Study of Social Structure*, op. cit., 31-7.
7 P.M. Blau, Introduction in ibid., 9-15.
8 This was of course Durkheim's view, which was set out clearly in the *Rules of Sociological Method*, op. cit. (especially 1-46) and on the whole consistently developed in his various empirical researches.
9 This corresponds to Gurvich's view analysed by T.B. Bottomore in P. M. Blau (ed.), *Approaches to the Study of Social Structure*, 159-71, especially 160-1.

10   See especially R.A. Lester, *As Unions Mature*, 105-26; and A.M. Ross and P.T. Hartman, *Changing Patterns of Industrial Conflict*, 42-61.

11   This view has been developed in many writings which are usefully summarized in R. Hyman, *Strikes*, 66-73.

12   T.B. Bottomore, in P.M. Blau (ed.), *Approaches to the Study of Social Structure*, op. cit., 159-71.

13   Ibid., 159 and 161-3.

14   Ibid., 167-71.

15   L. Althusser, *For Marx*; and L. Althusser and E. Balibar, *Reading Capital*.

16   Ibid.

17   M. Godelier, 'Structure and Contradiction in Capital', in R. Blackburn (ed.), *Ideology in Social Science*, 334-68; see e.g. B. S. Turner, 'The Structuralist Critique of Weber's Sociology', op. cit., 2.

18   B.S. Turner, ibid.

19   Ibid.

20   Ibid.

21   Ibid., 3.

22   B. Brewster, Glossary in L. Althusser and E. Balibar, *Reading Capital*, op. cit., 310.

23   Ibid.

24   M. Godelier, 'Structure and Contradiction in Capital', op. cit., 335.

25   Ibid.

26   Ibid., 335-6. See also L. Althusser and E. Balibar, *Reading Capital*, op. cit.

27   T.B. Bottomore, *Marxist Sociology*, 72-3.

28   E. P. Thompson, *The Poverty of Theory*.

29   T. B. Bottomore, *Marxist Sociology*, op. cit., 72-3.

30   Ibid., 20.

31   G. Lenski, 'Social Structure in Evolutionary Perspective', in P. M. Blau (ed.), *Approaches to the Study of Social Structure*, op. cit., 135-53.

32   M. Godelier, 'System Structure and Contradiction in Capital'.

33   For a useful recent study of the tendencies towards industrial concentration see S. Holland, *The Socialist Challenge*.

34   See especially G.S. Bain, *The Growth of White Collar Unionism*, op. cit., Chapter 6.

35   G. Lenski, 'Social Structure in Evolutionary Perspective', op. cit., 138-9.

36   This is usually expressed by the formula $p = \frac{s}{v} + c$; where p = the rate of profit, s = surplus value, c = constant capital and v = variable capital. See K. Marx, *Capital*, vol. 1, 209. Also vol. 3.

37   C. Crouch, *Class Conflict and the Industrial Relations Crisis*, 271.

38   H. Gospel, 'European Managerial Unions: An Early Assessment', 360-71. See also: G. Bamber, 'Trade Unions for Managers?'; H. Hartmann, 'Managerial Employees: New Participants in Industrial Democracy'; B. J. McCormick, 'Managerial Unionism in the Coal Industry'; K. Prandy, 'Professional Organization in Great Britain'; A. Sturmthal (ed.), *White-Collar Trade Unions*; D. Weir, 'Radical Managerialism: Middle Managers' Perceptions of Collective Bargaining'.

39   H. Gospel, 'European Managerial Unions : An Early Assessment', op. cit., 360.

40 Ibid., 361.
41 Ibid., 364.
42 Ibid., 366.
43 B.J. McCormick, 'Managerial Unionism in the Coal Industry', op. cit., 367.
44 B.J. McCormick, *Industrial Relations in the Coal Industry*, 69.
45 R.E. Pahl and J.T. Winckler, 'The New Corporatism', 72. See also J. T. Winckler, 'The Corporate Economy: Theory and Administration', in R. Scase (ed.),*Industrial Society: Class, Cleavage and Control*, 43-58.
46 L. Panitch, *Social Democracy and Industrial Militancy*, and 'The Development of Corporatism in Liberal Democracies'.
47 R. Jessop, 'Capitalism and Democracy: the best political shell?', in G. Littlejohn (ed.), *Power and the State*.
48 P.C. Schmitter, 'Modes of Interest Intermediation and Models of Societal Change in Western Europe', and 'Still the Century of Corporatism?', 103.
49 Ibid., 107-8.
50 Ibid., 108 and 111-12.
51 L. Panitch, 'The Development of Corporatism in Liberal Democracies', op. cit., 67.
52 R. Jessop, 'Capitalism and Democracy: the best possible political shell?', op. cit., 10-14 and 40-7.
53 C. Offe, *Industry and Inequality*.
54 C. Crouch, *Class Conflict and the Industrial Relations Crisis*, op. cit.
55 C. Offe, *Industry and Inequality*, op. cit., 8.
56 Ibid., 17.
57 Ibid., 14 and 33-9.
58 Ibid., 25-7.
59 C. Crouch, *Class Conflict and the Industrial Relations Crisis*, op. cit., 262-8.
60 Ibid., 263.
61 C. S. Bain and F. Elsheikh, *Union Growth and the Business Cycle*; see also C. Mulvey, *The Economic Analysis of Trade Unions*, especially 58-70.
62 G. S. Bain and F. Elsheikh, *Union Growth and the Business Cycle*, op. cit., 58-81.
63 Ibid., 68-9.
64 H. B. Davis, 'The Theory of Union Growth', 617-20.
65 G. S. Bain and F. Elsheikh, *Union Growth and the Business Cycle*, op. cit., 62-7.
66 R. Price and G.S. Bain, 'Union Growth Revisited: 1948-1974 in Perspective', 350.
67 Thus between 1970 and 1976 in percentage terms the fastest growing unions in Britain were all largely in the white-collar or public sector or both (these involved: ASTMS, 201.6 per cent increase; COHSE, 114.1 per cent; NUPE, 91.5 per cent; NALGO, 57.4 per cent; APEX, 34.7 per cent; and the CPSA, 24.3 per cent). See *Annual Reports of the TUC*, 1970 and 1976. For a general account of the change towards

the public sector see R.W. Bacon and W.A. Eltis, *Britain's Economic Problem: Too Few Producers*.

68   R. Richardson, 'Trade Union Growth'.
69   F. Elsheikh and G. S. Bain, 'Trade Union Growth : A Reply';
      R. Richardson, 'Trade Union Growth: A Rejoinder'.
70   R. Richardson, 'Trade Union Growth', op. cit., 279-82.
71   F. Elsheikh and G.S. Bain, 'Trade Union Growth: A Reply', op. cit., 99.
72   G. S. Bain and F. Elsheikh, 'An Inter-Industry Analysis of Unionisation in Britain'.
73   Ibid., 138-43.
74   Ibid., 153.
75   R. Blauner, *Alienation and Freedom*.
76   L. R. Sayles, *Behavior of Industrial Work Groups*.
77   J. Woodward, *Industrial Organization: Theory and Practice*.
78   B. Blauner, *Alienation and Freedom*, op. cit., 6-8.
79   H. Braverman, *Labor and Monopoly Capital*.
80   T. Nichols and H. Beynon, *Living with Capitalism*, especially xi-xvi.
81   R. Blauner, *Alienation and Freedom*, op. cit., 182.
82   J. Woodward, *Industrial Organization : Theory and Practice*, op. cit., 50-67.
83   Ibid., Chapter 4.
84   On attitudes to technical change see O. Banks, *The Attitudes of Steelworkers to Technical Change*, especially 89-121.
85   D. Gallie, *In Search of the New Working Class*, 239-82.
86   S. Mallet, *The New Working Class*.
87   R. Blauner, *Alienation and Freedom*, op. cit., 143-87.
88   E. Durkheim, *The Division of Labor in Society*, especially 233-55.
89   K. Marx, *Capital*, op. cit., vols 1 (318-47) and 3 (266). See also Z. A. Jordan (ed.), *Karl Marx: Economy, Class and Social Revolution*, 244-58.
90   A. Giddens, *Capitalism and Modern Social Theory*, 229-30.
91   S. Lukes, *Emile Durkheim*, 174.
92   G. Friedmann, *The Anatomy of Work*, Part 2 and 373-99.
93   R. Crompton, 'Approaches to the Study of White Collar Unionism'.
94   R. Crompton and J. Gubbay, *Economy and Class Structure*.
95   R. Crompton, 'Approaches to the Study of White Collar Unionism', op. cit., 418-23.
96   G. S. Bain, *The Growth of White Collar Unionism*, op. cit., 1.
97   This argument has been developed in a number of studies of course. See J. A. Banks, *Marxist Sociology in Action*, 291-309.
98   G. S. Bain, *The Growth of White Collar Unionism*, op. cit., 72-81.
99   G. K. Ingham, *Size of Industrial Organization and Worker Behaviour*, especially 117-25.
100   G. S. Bain, *The Growth of White Collar Unionism*, op. cit., 124-5 and 181-2.
101   Report of the Committee of Inquiry on Small Firms (Bolton Report).
102   E.F. Schumacher, *Small is Beautiful: A Study of Economics as if People Mattered*.
103   E. V. Batstone, 'Deference and the Ethos of Small Town Capitalism',

in M. Bulmer (ed.), *Working Class Images of Society*.

104   J. Curran and J. Stanworth, 'Worker Involvement and Social Relations in the Small Firm', 318.

105   Ibid., 337-8.

106   G. Salaman, *Community and Occupation*.

107   C. Kerr and A. Siegel, 'The Inter-industry Propensity to Strike – An International Comparison', in A. Kornhauser, R. Dubin and A. Ross (eds), *Industrial Conflict*, 189-212.

108   P. K. Edwards, 'A Critique of the Kerr-Siegel Hypothesis of Strikes and the Isolated Mass'.

109   J. L. Nelson and R. Grams, 'Union Militancy and Occupational Communities'.

110   R. Moore, *Pit-Men, Preachers and Politics*, 214-21.

111   See S. R. Parker, R. K. Brown, J. Child and M. A. Smith, *The Sociology of Industry*, Chapter 6. For background details see F.J. Roethlisberger and W.J. Dickson, *Management and the Worker*; E. Mayo, *The Social Problems of an Industrial Civilization*.

112   S.R. Parker, *et al.*, *The Sociology of Industry*, op. cit., 101.

113   L. R. Sayles, *Behavior of Industrial Work Groups*, op. cit., Chapter 5.

114   Ibid., Chapter 2.

115   J.H. Goldthorpe, *et al.*, *The Affluent Worker: Industrial Attitudes and Behaviour*, op. cit., Chapter 5.

116   Ibid., 100-6.

117   T. Lupton, *On the Shop Floor*, 194-201.

118   S. Cunnison, *Wages and Work Allocation*, especially 33-5.

119   See H. Beynon, *Working for Ford*, 187-208; T. Nichols and P. Armstrong, *Workers Divided*, 98-110; and E. Batstone, I. Boraston and S. Frenkel, *Shop Stewards in Action*, 99-130.

120   Ibid., 99.

121   Ibid., 100.

122   H. M. Levinson, *Determining Forces in Collective Wage Bargaining*.

123   R.E. Walton and R.B. McKersie, *A Behavioral Theory of Labor Negotiations*.

124   H. M. Levinson, *Determining Forces in Collective Wage Bargaining*, op. cit., 17-18.

125   R.E. Walton and R.B. McKersie, *A Behavioral Theory of Labor Negotiations*, op. cit., 4.

126   Ibid., 4-6.

Chapter 7   Organizations, institutions and their environments

1   J. Child, R. Loveridge and M. Warner, 'Towards an Organizational Study of Trade Unions'.

2   J. D. Edelstein and M. Warner, *Comparative Union Democracy*.

3   H. A. Clegg, *Trade Unionism Under Collective Bargaining*, 8.

4   Ibid., Chapters 3-7.

5   To be sure, the antecedents of this approach belonged to a different era and were founded upon bureaucratic analysis, on the one hand, and the early scientific management movements, on the other. But

the flowering of organization 'theory' more generally was a later phenomenon. See N. P. Mouzelis, *Organization and Bureaucracy* (especially 7-37 and 79-96) for an account of the earlier developments.

6   That major inequalities still persisted in this era has been argued and well illustrated by J. H. Westergaard and M. Resler, *Class in a Capitalist Society*, 31-140.

7   Early textbooks on industrial sociology such as D. C. Miller and W. H. Form, *Industrial Sociology: An Introduction to the Study of Work Relations*, and E. V. Schneider, *Industrial Sociology*, contrast sharply with, say, J. E. T. Eldridge, *Sociology and Industrial Life*.

8   A. M. Pettigrew, *Politics of Organizational Decision-Making*.

9   A. Sorge and M. Warner, 'The Societal and Organizational Context of Industrial Relations: A Comparison of Great Britain and West Germany'.

10   Ibid., 18.

11   D. Silverman, 'Formal Organizations or Industrial Sociology: Towards a Social Action Analysis of Organizations', 223.

12   A. Sorge and M. Warner, 'The Societal and Organizational Context of Industrial Relations', op. cit., 9.

13   D. Silverman, 'Formal Organizations or Industrial Sociology', op. cit., 234.

14   This is a common finding in the literature on unions as organizations. See e.g. J. Child, R. Loveridge and M. Warner, 'Towards an Organizational Study of Trade Unions', op. cit., 87-8.

15   M. Weber, *Economy and Society*, 1002-3.

16   Ibid., 983.

17   Ibid., 990.

18   Ibid., 987.

19   Ibid.

20   S. Webb and B. Webb, *Industrial Democracy*, 8-9.

21   Ibid., 28.

22   G. Lenski, 'Social Structure in Evolutionary Perspective', in P. M. Blau (ed.), *Approaches to the Study of Social Structure*, 135.

23   H. A. Turner, *Trade Union Growth Structure and Policy*, 139-68.

24   Ibid., 228-9.

25   Ibid., 211.

26   Ibid., 214.

27   Ibid., 215 and 220-4.

28   Ibid., 215-20.

29   Ibid., 289-91.

30   J. Hughes, 'Trade Union Structure and Government', Paper no. 5, Part 1, Royal Commission on Trade Unions and Employers' Associations, especially 4-6.

31   See for example the debate in R. Martin, 'Edelstein, Warner and Cooke on Union Democracy'; and J. D. Edelstein and M. Warner, 'On Measuring and Explaining Union Democracy: a Reply to Dr. Martin's Critique'.

32   R. Hyman, *Industrial Relations*, op. cit., 69.

33   R. Martin, 'Union Democracy: an Explanatory Framework'.

34   R. Martin, 'Edelstein, Warner and Cooke on Union Democracy',

op. cit., 243-4.

35   R. Martin, 'Union Democracy: an Explanatory Framework', op. cit., 205-7.

36   Ibid., 207.

37   Ibid., 207-14.

38   J. Child, R. Loveridge and M. Warner, 'Towards an Organizational Study of Trade Unions', op. cit., 81.

39   Ibid., 87.

40   Ibid., 82-4.

41   Ibid., 83.

42   J.C. Anderson, 'A Comparative Analysis of Local Union Democracy', 278.

43   G. Strauss, 'Union Government in the U.S. : Research Past and Future', 240.

44   J. C. Anderson, 'A Comparative Analysis of Local Union Democracy', op. cit., 279.

45   Ibid., 280-4.

46   Ibid., 281.

47   Ibid., 281-4.

48   Ibid., 283-4.

49   R. Hyman and R.H. Fryer, 'Trade Unions: Sociology and Political Economy', in J.B. McKinley (ed.), *Processing People: Cases in Organizational Behaviour*, 156-60.

50   See J. Child, R. Loveridge and M. Warner, 'Towards an Organizational Study of Trade Unions', op. cit., 71-91.

51   R. Hyman and R. H. Fryer, op. cit., 158.

52   Ibid., 159.

53   Ibid., 160.

54   J. Child, R. Loveridge and M. Warner, op. cit., 71.

55   J.E.T. Eldridge and A.D. Crombie, *A Sociology of Organizations*, 38.

56   Ibid., 38-42.

57   P.M. Blau and W.R. Scott, *Formal Organizations: A Comparative Approach*, 42-5 and 45-9.

58   Ibid., 252.

59   A. Etzioni, *A Comparative Analysis of Complex Organizations*, 5.

60   Ibid., 3.

61   Ibid., 4-5.

62   D. H. Wrong, 'Some problems of defining social power', *American*, 673.

63   M. Moran, *The Union of Post Office Workers*.

64   Ibid., 2.

65   Ibid., 2-4.

66   Ibid.

67   Ibid., 4-5.

68   Ibid., 5-7.

69   Ibid.

70   J.D. Edelstein, 'An Organizational Theory of Union Democracy'.

71   J.D. Edelstein and M. Warner, *Comparative Union Democracy*.

72   J. Child, R. Loveridge and M. Warner, op. cit.

73   See R. L. Ackoff, *A Concept of Corporate Planning*; R. L. Ackoff and

F.E. Emery, *On Purposeful Systems*, 227-29. Also J.E.T. Eldridge and A.D. Crombie, *A Sociology of Organizations*, op. cit., 49.
74 J. E. T. Eldridge and A. D. Crombie, *A Sociology of Organizations*, ibid.
75 Ibid., 49-50.
76 J. D. Edelstein and M. Warner, *Comparative Union Democracy*, op. cit., 54.
77 Ibid., 65-8.
78 Ibid., 68-81.
79 Ibid., 81-2.
80 H. A. Clegg, *The Changing System of Industrial Relations in Great Britain*, 208-9.
81 Ibid., 209.
82 J. D. Edelstein and M. Warner, *Comparative Union Democracy*, op. cit., 340.
83 J. Child, R. Loveridge and M. Warner, 'Towards an Organizational Study of Trade Unions', op. cit., 71-91.
84 Ibid., 72-88.
85 Ibid., 87-8.
86 L. Donaldson and M. Warner, 'Structure of Organization in Occupational Interest Associations'.
87 Ibid., 729-33.
88 Ibid., 736.
89 L. Donaldson and M. Warner, 'Bureaucratic and Electoral Control in Occupational Interest Associations'.
90 Ibid., 49.
91 Ibid., 54.
92 A. Sorge, 'The Cultural Context of Organization Structure: Administrative Rationality, Constraints and Choice', in M. Warner (ed.), *Organizational Choice and Constraint: Approaches to the Sociology of Enterprise Behaviour*, 57-78.
93 Ibid., 74.

Chapter 8   Culture, values and perception

1   M. Weber, *The Methodology of the Social Sciences*, 57.
2   M. Weber, *Economy and Society*. For a useful review of the action approach to industrial relations see also M. P. Jackson, *Industrial Relations*, Chapter 1.
3   See e.g. K. Marx, *Value, Price and Profit*, 94.
4   E. Durkheim, *The Rules of Sociological Method*, especially 411-55.
5   T. Parsons, *Action Theory and the Human Condition*; T. Parsons, *The Social System*; T. Parsons, *The Structure of Social Action*, 12; and T. Parsons and E.A. Shils (eds), *Towards a General Theory of Action*.
6   J.T. Dunlop, *Industrial Relations Systems*, 3-16.
7   S. and B. Webb, *Industrial Democracy*, especially 807-50.
8   A. Flanders, *Management and Unions*, 38-47.
9   H. A. Clegg, 'Pluralism in Industrial Relations', 310-11.
10 H. A. Turner, *Trade Union Growth, Structure and Policy*, 139-68.

11 J. F. B. Goodman, E. G. A. Armstrong, J. E. Davis and A. Wagner, *Rule Making and Industrial Peace*, Chapter 1.

12 G. S. Bain, *The Growth of White Collar Unionism*, 122-33 and 183-6.

13 R. Hyman, *Strikes*, 16.

14 R. Hyman and I. Brough, *Social Values and Industrial Relations*, 154.

15 R. Hyman and R.H. Fryer, 'Trade Unions: Sociology and Political Economy', in J.B. McKinley (ed.), *Processing People*, 171.

16 See A. Dawe, 'The Two Sociologies', *The British Journal of Sociology*; and 'The Relevance of Values', in A. Sahay (ed.), *Max Weber and Modern Sociology*, Chapter 3.

17 M. Weber, *Economy and Society*, op. cit., 4.

18 Ibid.

19 Ibid., 19 and 29. See also A. Giddens, *Capitalism and Modern Social Theory*, 145.

20 Ibid. For a development see A. Sahay, 'Introduction', in *Max Weber and Modern Sociology*, 6-7 and 13; and M. Weber, *The Methodology of the Social Sciences*, op. cit., 78-9.

21 A. Sahay, 'Introduction', op. cit., 5. My italics.

22 Ibid., and A. Sahay, 'The Importance of Weber's Methodology', in *Max Weber and Modern Sociology*, op. cit., 68.

23 A. Sahay, 'Introduction', op. cit., 5-6.

24 A. Sahay, 'The Importance of Weber's Methodology', op. cit., 68.

25 J. Rex, 'Typology and Objectivity: A Comment on Weber's Four Sociological Methods', in A. Sahay (ed.), *Max Weber and Modern Sociology*, op. cit., 27.

26 A. Sahay, 'Introduction', *Max Weber and Modern Sociology*, op. cit., 6.

27 A. Sahay, 'The Importance of Weber's Methodology', op. cit., 72-4.

28 Ibid., 72. My italics.

29 See Chapter 1; A. Flanders, *Management and Unions*, op. cit., 15.

30 R.P. Dore, *British Factory — Japanese Factory*.

31 A. Sorge and M. Warner, 'The Societal and Organizational Context of Industrial Relations'.

32 Ibid.

33 D. Gallie, *In Search of the New Working Class*.

34 Ibid., 295.

35 Ibid., 313.

36 Ibid., 239.

37 Ibid., 257.

38 Ibid., 317-18.

39 M. Weber, *Economy and Society*, op. cit., 284.

40 Ibid., 285.

41 Ibid.

42 Ibid., 286.

43 H. Pelling, *A History of British Trade Unionism*, 117-30.

44 P.C. Schmitter, 'Modes of Interest Intermediation and Models of Societal Change in Western Europe', 108 and 111-12.

45 See e.g. H.A. Clegg, A. Fox and A.F. Thompson, *A History of British Trade Unions Since 1889*, vol. 1, 55-96.

46 A. Dawe, 'The Two Sociologies', op. cit., 214.

47   W. Mommsen, *The Age of Bureaucracy*, 55-8.
48   Ibid., 57.
49   W. Straker, quoted in C. Goodrich, *The Frontier of Control*, 3.
50   M. Weber, *Economy and Society*, op. cit., 74.
51   Ibid., 74-5.
52   Ibid., 64.
53   Ibid., 65.
54   Ibid., 67.
55   Ibid., see notably discussions pp. 136-7. Also see A. Sahay, Introduction in *Max Weber and Modern Sociology*, op. cit., 14.
56   A. Sahay, 'The Importance of Weber's Methodology', *Max Weber and Modern Sociology*, op. cit., 72-3.
57   M.J.F. Poole, 'Ideas, Institutions and Economic Development'.
58   Ibid., 335.
59   D. Lockwood, 'Sources of Variation in Working Class Images of Society'.
60   Ibid., 250.
61   J.H. Goldthorpe *et al.*, *The Affluent Worker: Industrial Attitudes and Behaviour*, op. cit., 176-7.
62   J. H. Goldthorpe, D. Lockwood, F. Bechhofer and J. Platt, *The Affluent Worker in the Class Structure*, 154.
63   R.K. Brown and P. Brannen, 'Social Relations and Social Perspectives amongst Shipbuilding Workers – A Preliminary Statement, Part I'; R.K. Brown, P. Brannen, J.M. Cousins, and M.L. Samphier, 'The Contours of Solidarity: Social Stratification and Industrial Relations in Shipbuilding'; J. Cousins and R.K. Brown, 'Patterns of Paradox: Shipbuilding Workers' Images of Society', in M. Bulmer (ed.), *Working Class Images of Society*, op. cit., 55-82.
64   R.K. Brown and P. Brannen, 'Social Relations and Social Perspectives', op. cit., especially 207-9.
65   For an evaluation of these developments see M.J.F. Poole, *Workers' Participation in Industry*.
66   R. K. Brown, 'Sources of Objectives in Work and Employment', in J. Child (ed.), *Man and Organization*, 19-20.
67   J.H. Goldthorpe *et al.*, *The Affluent Worker: Industrial Attitudes and Behaviour*, op. cit., 38-42.
68   Ibid., 38-9.
69   Ibid., 114.
70   Ibid., 114-15 and 176-7.
71   D. Silverman, 'Formal Organizations or Industrial Sociology: Towards a Social Action Analysis of Organizations', 233-4.
72   W. W. Daniel, 'Industrial Behaviour and Orientation to Work: a Critique'; 'Productivity Bargaining and Orientation to Work – a rejoinder to Goldthorpe'; and 'Understanding Employee Behaviour in its Context', in J. Child (ed.), *Man and Organization*. For Goldthorpe's replies see J.H. Goldthorpe, 'The Social Action Approach to Sociology: A Reply to Daniel'; and 'Daniel on orientations to work – a final comment'.
73   W. W. Daniel, 'Productivity Bargaining and Orientation to Work', op. cit., 329-30.

74 There is of course a wide-ranging literature here. See especially
    E.G.A. Husserl, *The Crisis of European Sciences and Transcendental
    Ethnomethodology*; A. Schutz, *The Phenomenology of the Social
    World*; R. Turner (ed.), *Ethnomethodology*.
75 See Chapter 1. M. Perlman (ed.), *Labor Union Theories in America*,
    especially 18-25 and 46-65.
76 E. Durkheim, *The Division of Labor in Society*, 76-52.
77 Ibid., 52.
78 T. B. Bottomore, *Marxist Sociology*, 56-7.
79 A. Flanders, *Management and Unions*, 15.
80 T. B. Bottomore, *Marxist Sociology*, op. cit., 55.
81 Ibid., 58.
82 Ibid., 56-7.
83 B. Bernstein, *Class, Codes and Control*. For an opposing view, see
    N. Keddie, *Tinker, Tailor . . . The Myth of Cultural Deprivation*; and
    M. Pap and C. Pléy, 'Social Class Differences in the Speech of Six-
    Year-Old Hungarian Children'.
84 G.A. Withers, 'Social Justice and the Unions: A Normative Approach
    to Cooperation and Conflict under Interdependence'.
85 B. J. McCormick, *Industrial Relations in the Coal Industry*, see
    Appendix, 233-49.
86 G. Withers, 'Social Justice and the Unions', op. cit., 333.
87 S. and B. Webb, *Methods of Social Study*, 25-30.
88 J. H. Wilson, *The Relevance of British Socialism*.
89 A. Flanders, *Management and Unions*, op. cit., 15.
90 W. Herberg, 'Bureaucracy and Democracy in Labor Unions'.
91 R. Hyman and I. Brough, op. cit., 212.
92 Hoggart's introduction to *Bad News* (ix-xiii) is a valuable checkweight
    against crude ideological determinism for, as he points out, news
    selects itself through four main filtering processes: (1) constraint of
    time and movement; (2) traditions of news values; (3) television values
    and 'material' and (4) 'the cultural air we breathe, the whole
    ideological atmosphere of society'. Moreover, as was demonstrated in
    Bad News, considerable differences in the approach of unions to the
    media could be discerned. See Glasgow Media Group, *Bad News*, 221.
    Also G. Philo and J. Hewitt, 'Trade Unions and the Media'.
93 R. Hyman and I. Brough, *Social Values and Industrial Relations*,
    op. cit., 222. My italics.
94 Ibid., 253.
95 K. Roberts, F. G. Cook, S. C. Clark and E. Semeonoff, *The Fragmen-
    tary Class Structure*, 133.
96 A. Sahay, Introduction to *Max Weber and Modern Sociology*, op. cit.,
    12.
97 Ibid.
98 G. D. H. Cole, *The Intelligent Man's Guide to the Post-War World*, 38.
99 A. Sahay, 'Knowledge, values and sentiments', 292.
100 Ibid., 292.
101 Ibid., 293.
102 M. Weber, *Economy and Society*, op. cit., 25.
103 J. H. Goldthorpe, *et al.*, *The Affluent Worker: Industrial Attitudes*

and Behaviour, op. cit., 40-1.
104   Ibid.
105   N. Dennis, F. Henriques and C. Slaughter, *Coal is Our Life*, see especially 171-250.
106   S. Hill, *The Dockers*, 163-77.
107   Ibid., Chapter 9.
108   L. R. Sayles and G. Strauss, *The Local Union*, 132.
109   M. Weber, *Economy and Society*, op. cit., 25 and 215-16. See also A. Sahay, 'Knowledge, Values and Sentiments', op. cit., 290.
110   A. Sahay, 'Knowledge, Values and Sentiments', op. cit., 298.
111   A. Sorge, 'The Evolution of Industrial Democracy in the Countries of the European Community', 281-9.
112   See M. Weber, *Economy and Society*, op. cit., and also e.g. W. Brown, 'A Consideration of "Custom and Practice" '.
113   J. Hinton, Introduction to J.T. Murphy, *The Workers' Committee*, 3; and J. Hinton, *The First Shop Stewards' Movement*.
114   H. A. Turner, *Trade Union Growth Structure and Policy*, op. cit., 94, 139-68 and 197.
115   A. Flanders, *The Fawley Productivity Agreements*, 43-9.
116   W.A. Pasmore and J.J. Sherwood, *Sociotechnical Systems: A Sourcebook*, 313-65.

Bibliography

Abell, P., (ed.), *Organizations as Bargaining and Influence Systems*, London, Heinemann, 1975.

Abell, P., 'The Many Faces of Power and Liberty: Revealed Preference Autonomy and Teleological Explanation', *Sociology*, vol. 11, 1977, 3-24.

Ackoff, R. L., *A Concept of Corporate Planning*, New York, Wiley, 1970.

Ackoff, R. L. and Emery, F. E., *On Purposeful Systems*, London, Tavistock, 1972.

Adams, H.C., 'An Interpretation of the Social Movements of Our Time', *International Journal of Ethics*, vol. II, 1891-2, 32-50.

Adams, R., 'Bain's Theory of White Collar Union Growth: A Conceptual Critique', *British Journal of Industrial Relations*, vol. 15, 1977, 317-21.

Allen, V.L., *Power in Trade Unions: A Study of Their Organization in Britain*, London, Longmans Green, 1954.

Allen, V. L., *Trade Union Leadership: Based on a Study of Arthur Deakin*, London, Longmans Green, 1957.

Allen, V. L., *The Sociology of Industrial Relations: Studies in Method*, London, Longman, 1971.

Althusser, L., *For Marx*, London, New Left Books, 1969.

Althusser, L., and Balibar, E., *Reading Capital*, London, New Left Books, 1970.

Anderson, J. C., 'A Comparative Analysis of Local Union Democracy', *Industrial Relations*, vol. 17, 1978, 278-95.

Anderson, J. C., 'Bargaining Outcomes: An IR System Approach', *Industrial Relations*, vol. 18, 1979, 127-43.

Armstrong, K. J., Bowers, D. and Burkitt, B., 'The Measurement of Trade Union Bargaining Power', *British Journal of Industrial Relations*, vol. 15, 1977, 91-100.

Aspinall, A. (ed.), *The Early English Trade Unions: Documents from the Home Office Papers in The Public Record Office*, London, Batchworth, 1949.

Atherton, J., 'Trade Unions and the Law: the Problem, Necessity and Possibility of Law in an Industrial Context', *Manchester Business School Review*, vol. 3, no. 3, 1979, 23-25.

Atkinson, A. B., *The Economics of Inequality*, Clarendon Press, 1975.

Bachrach, P. and Baratz, M. S., 'Two Faces of Power', *American Political*

Science Review, vol. 56, 1962, 947-52.

Bacon, R. W. and Eltis, W. A., *Britain's Economic Problem: Too Few Producers*, London, Macmillan, 1976.

Bagwell, P. S., 'The Triple Industrial Alliance 1913-1922', in A. Briggs and J. Saville (eds), *Essays in Labour History*, London, Macmillan, 1971.

Bain, G. S., *The Growth of White Collar Unionism*, Clarendon Press, 1970.

Bain, G. S. and Clegg, H. A., 'A Strategy for Industrial Relations Research in Great Britain', *British Journal of Industrial Relations*, vol. 12, 1974, 91-113.

Bain, G. S., Coates, D. and Ellis, V., *Social Stratification and Trade Unionism*, London, Heinemann, 1973.

Bain, G.S. and Elsheikh, F., *Union Growth and the Business Cycle: An Economic Analysis*, Oxford, Blackwell, 1976.

Bain, G. S. and Elsheikh, F., 'An Inter-Industry Analysis of Unionisation in Britain', *British Journal of Industrial Relations*, vol. 18, 1979, 137-57.

Bain, G. S. and Price, R., 'Union Growth and Employment Trends in the United Kingdom 1964-1970', *British Journal of Industrial Relations*, vol. 10, 1972, 366-81.

Bakke, E. W., *The Unemployed Man: A Social Study*, London, Nisbet, 1933.

Bakke, E. W., Kerr, C. and Anrod, C. W., *Unions, Management and the Public*, 3rd edn, Harcourt Brace & World, 1967.

Bamber, G., 'Trade Unions for Managers?', *Personnel Review*, vol. 5, no. 4, 1976, 36-41.

Banks, J.A., *Industrial Participation, Theory and Practice: A Case Study*, Liverpool University Press, 1963.

Banks, J. A., *Marxist Sociology in Action: A Sociological Critique of the Marxist Approach to Industrial Relations*, London, Faber & Faber, 1970.

Banks, J. A., *Trade Unionism*, London, Collier-Macmillan, 1974.

Banks, J. A., 'A Comment on Rosemary Crompton's "Approaches to the Study of White Collar Unionism" ', *Sociology*, vol. 12, 1978, 141-2.

Banks, J. A., Halsey, A. H. and Lupton, T., *Technical Change and Industrial Relations*, Liverpool University Press, 1952.

Banks, O., *The Attitudes of Steelworkers to Technical Change*, Liverpool University Press, 1960.

Bass, B. M. and Shackleton, V. J., 'Industrial Democracy and Participative Management: A Case for a Synthesis', *Academy of Management Review*, vol. 4, 1979, 393-404.

Batstone, E., Boraston, I. and Frenkel, S., *Shop Stewards in Action: The Organization of Workplace Conflict and Accommodation*, Oxford, Blackwell, 1977.

Batstone, E. and Davies, P. L., *Industrial Democracy: European Experience*, London, HMSO, 1976.

Beaumont, P. B., 'Union Membership and the Coverage of Collective Agreements in Britain', Discussion Papers in Economics, no. 28, University of Glasgow, 1978.

Beaumont, P.B., Thomson, A.W.J. and Gregory, M.B., 'The Determinants of Bargaining Structure in Britain: An Exploratory Exercise', Discussion Papers in Economics, no. 23, University of Glasgow, 1978.

Beharrel, P. and Philo, G., *Trade Unions and the Media*, London, Macmillan, 1977.

Bernstein, B., *Class, Codes and Control*, London, Paladin, 1973.

Bernstein, I., 'The Growth of American Unions', *American Economic Review*, vol. 64, 1954, 301-18.

Bevan, A., *In Place of Fear*, London, Heinemann, 1952.

Beynon, H., *Working for Ford*, Harmondsworth, Penguin, 1973.

Beynon, H. and Blackburn, R. M., *Perceptions of Work: Variations Within a Factory*, Cambridge University Press, 1972.

Biasatt, L.L. and Martin, J.E., 'A Measure of the Quality of Union-Management Relationships', *Journal of Applied Psychology*, vol. 64, 1979, 387-390.

Bierstedt, R., 'An Analysis of Social Power', *American Sociological Review*, vol. 15, 1950, 730-8.

Blackburn, R. M., *Union Character and Social Class: A Study of White-Collar Unionism*, London, Batsford, 1967.

Blackburn, R. M. and Prandy, K., 'White-Collar Unionization: A Conceptual Framework', *British Journal of Sociology*, vol. 16, 1965, 111-22.

Blain, A. N. J., *Pilots and Management: Industrial Relations in the U.K. Airlines*, London, Allen & Unwin, 1972.

Blain, A.N.J. and Gennard, J., 'Industrial Relations Theory — A Critical Review', *British Journal of Industrial Relations*, vol. 8, 1970, 389-407.

Blau, P. M. (ed.), *Approaches to the Study of Social Structure*, London, Open Books, 1976.

Blau, P. M. and Scott, W. R., *Formal Organizations: A Comparative Approach*, London, Routledge & Kegan Paul, 1963.

Blauner, R., *Alienation and Freedom: The Factory Worker and his Industry*, London, University of Chicago Press, 1964.

Blumler, J.G. and Ewbank, A.J., 'Trade Unionists, The Mass Media and Unofficial Strikes', *British Journal of Industrial Relations*, vol. 8, 1970, 32-54.

Booth, C., *Labour and Life of the People*, London, Williams & Northgate, 1889.

Booth, C., *Life and Labour of the People in London*, London, Macmillan, 1902.

Boraston, I., Clegg, H. A., and Rimmer, M., *Workplace and Union : A Study of Local Relationships in Fourteen Unions*, London, Heinemann, 1975.

Bottomore, T. B., *Marxist Sociology*, London, Gollancz, 1963.

Bowen, P., *Social Control in Industrial Organizations: Industrial Relations and Industrial Sociology: A Strategic and Occupational Study of British Steelmaking*, London, Routledge & Kegan Paul, 1976.

Bowen, P., Shaw, M. and Smith, R., 'The Steelworker and Work Control', *British Journal of Industrial Relations*, vol. 12, 1974, 249-67.

Braverman, H., *Labor and Monopoly Capital: The Degradation of Work in the Twentieth Century*, New York, Monthly Review Press, 1974.

Brentano, L., *On the History and Development of Gilds and the Origin of Trade Unions*, London, Trubner, 1870.

Briggs, A. and Saville, J. (eds), *Essays in Labour History*, London, Macmillan, 1971.

Brown, R.K., 'From Donovan to Where? Interpretation of Industrial Relations in Britain Since 1968', *British Journal of Sociology*, vol. 29, 1978, 439-60.

Brown, R.K., 'Sources of Objectives in Work and Employment', in J. Child (ed.), *Man and Organization: The Search for Explanation and Social Relevance*, London, Allen & Unwin, 1973.

Brown, R. K. and Brannen, P., 'Social Relations and Social Perspectives Amongst Shipbuilding Workers – A Preliminary Statement', part 1, *Sociology*, vol. 4, 1970, 71-8.

Brown R.K. and Brannen, P., 'Social Relations and Social Perspectives Amongst Shipbuilding Workers – A Preliminary Statement', part 2, *Sociology*, vol. 4, 1970, 197-211.

Brown, R. K., Brannen, P., Cousins, J. M. and Samphier, M. L., 'The Contours of Solidarity: Social Stratification and Industrial Relations in Shipbuilding', *British Journal of Industrial Relations*, vol. 10, 1972, 12-41.

Brown, W., 'A Consideration of "Custom and Practice" ', *British Journal of Industrial Relations*, vol. 10, 1972, 42-61.

Brown, W., Ebsworth, R., and Terry, M., 'Factors Shaping Shop Steward Organization in Britain', *British Journal of Industrial Relations*, vol. 16, 1978, 139-59.

Bullock, A., *The Life and Times of Ernest Bevin*, London, Heinemann, 1967.

Bullock, A., *Report of the Committee of Inquiry on Industrial Democracy*, London, HMSO, 1977, Cmnd 6706.

Bulmer, M. (ed.), *Working Class Images of Society*, London, Routledge & Kegan Paul, 1975.

Burkitt, B., 'Are Trade Unions Monopolies?', *Industrial Relations Journal*, vol. 8, 1977, 17-21.

Burkitt, B., Bowers, D., and Armstrong, K.J., 'The Relationship between Money Wages and Unionization: A Reappraisal', *Bulletin of Economic Research*, vol. 30, 1978, 95-107.

Calder, A., *The People's War: Britain 1939-45*, London, Panther, 1971.

Campbell, A., *The Industrial Relations Act: An Introduction*, London, Longman, 1971.

Carew, A., *Democracy and Government in European Trade Unions*, London, Allen & Unwin, 1976.

Carter, G. R., *The Tendency Towards Industrial Combination*, London, Constable, 1913.

Carter, R., 'Class, Militancy and Union Character: A Study of the Association of Scientific, Technical and Managerial Staffs', *Sociological Review*, vol. 27, 1979, 297-316.

Chamberlain, N.W. and Kuhn, J.W., *Collective Bargaining*, New York, McGraw-Hill, 1951.

Cherns, A.B., and Wacker, G.J., 'Analysing Social Systems: An Application of Parsons' Macrosystem Model to the Organizational Level and the Sociotechnical Perspective', *Human Relations*, vol. 31, 1978, 823-842.

Chesterton, G. K., 'Notebooks', in M. Perlman (ed.), *Labor Union Theories in America*, Illinois, Row Peterson, 1958.

Child, J. (ed.), *Man and Organization: The Search for Explanation and Social Relevance*, London, Allen & Unwin, 1973.

Child, J., 'Class Perceptions and Social Identification of Industrial Supervisors', Working Paper no. 100, Aston, the University of Aston Management Centre, 1978.

Child, J., Loveridge, R., and Warner, M., 'Towards an Organizational Study of Trade Unions', *Sociology*, vol. 7, 1973, 71-91.

Clarke, T. and Clements, L. (ed.), *Trade Unions Under Capitalism*, Glasgow, Fontana/Collins, 1977.

Clegg, H. A., *A New Approach to Industrial Democracy*, Oxford, Blackwell, 1960.

Clegg, H.A., *The System of Industrial Relations in Great Britain*, Oxford, Blackwell, 1970.

Clegg, H. A., 'Pluralism in Industrial Relations', *British Journal of Industrial Relations*, vol. 13, 1975, 309-16.

Clegg, H. A., *Trade Unionism Under Collective Bargaining: A Theory Based on Comparisons of Six Countries*, Oxford, Blackwell, 1976.

Clegg, H. A., *The Changing System of Industrial Relations in Great Britain*, Oxford, Blackwell, 1979.

Clegg, H.A., Fox, A. and Thompson, A.F., *A History of British Trade Unions since 1889*, vol. 1, Clarendon Press, 1964.

Clegg, H.A., Killick, A.J. and Adams, R., *Trade Union Officers: A Study of Full-time Officers, Branch Secretaries and Shop Stewards in British Trade Unions*, Oxford, Blackwell, 1961.

Clegg, S., *Power, Rule and Domination*, London, Routledge & Kegan Paul, 1975.

Cohen, P. S., *Modern Social Theory*, London, Heinemann, 1968.

Cohen, S., 'Does Public Employee Unionism Diminish Democracy?', *Industrial and Labour Relations Review*, vol. 32, 1979, 189-95.

Cole, G. D. H., *The World of Labour: A Discussion of the Present and Future of Trade Unionism*, London, Bell, 1913.

Cole, G. D. H., *Self-Government in Industry*, London, Bell, 1918.

Cole, G. D. H., *Organized Labour: An Introduction to Trade Unionism*, London, Allen & Unwin, 1924.

Cole, G. D. H., *Short History of the British Working Class Movement 1789-1937*, London, Allen & Unwin, 1937.

Cole, G. D. H., *British Trade Unionism Today*, London, Gollancz, 1939.

Cole, G. D. H., *The Intelligent Man's Guide to the Post War World*, London, Gollancz, 1947.

Committee of Inquiry on Small Firms, (Bolton Report), London, HMSO, 1971, Cmnd 481.

Commons, J. R., *Industrial Goodwill*, New York, McGraw-Hill, 1919.

Commons, J. R., *Labor and Administration*, New York, Macmillan, 1917.

Commons, J. R., *et al.*, *History of Labor in the United States*, New York, Macmillan, 1918.

Cook, F. G., Clark, S. C., Roberts, K. and Semeonoff, E., 'White and Blue Collar Attitudes to Trade Unionism and Social Class', *Industrial Relations Journal*, vol. 6, 1975/6, 47-58.

Cousins, J., 'The Non-Militant Shop Steward', *New Society*, 3 February

1972, 226.

Cousins, J. and Brown, R. K., 'Patterns of Paradox: Shipbuilding Workers' Images of Society', in M. Bulmer (ed.), *Working Class Images of Society*, London, Routledge & Kegan Paul, 1975.

Craig, A. W. J., 'A Framework for the Analysis of Industrial Relations Systems', in B. Barrett, E. Rhodes and J. Beishon (eds), *Industrial Relations and the Wider Society*, London, Collier-Macmillan, 1975.

Crompton, R., 'Approaches to the Study of White Collar Unionism', *Sociology*, vol. 10, 1976, 407-26.

Crompton, R. and Gubbay, J., *Economy and Class Structure*, London, Macmillan, 1977.

Crouch, C., *Class Conflict and the Industrial Relations Crisis: Compromise and Corporatism in the Policies of the British State*, London, Heinemann, 1975.

Cunnison, S., *Wages and Work Allocation: A Study of Social Relations in a Garment Workshop*, London, Tavistock, 1966.

Curran, J. and Stanworth, J., 'Worker Involvement and Social Relations in the Small Firm', *Sociological Review*, vol. 27, 1979, 317-42.

Dahl, R. A., *'Who Governs? Democracy and Power in an American City'*, Yale University Press, 1961.

Dahrendorf, R., *Class and Class Conflict in Industrial Society*, London, Routledge & Kegan Paul, 1959.

Daniel, W. W., 'Industrial Behaviour and Orientation to Work: A Critique', *Journal of Management Studies*, vol. 6, 1969, 366-75.

Daniel, W. W., 'Productivity Bargaining and Orientation to Work : a Rejoinder to Goldthorpe', *Journal of Management Studies*, vol. 8, 1971, 329-35.

Daniel, W. W., 'Understanding Employee Behaviour in its Context: Illustration from Productivity Bargaining', in J. Child (ed.), *Man and Organization : The Search for Explanation and Social Relevance*, London, Allen & Unwin, 1973.

Davis, H. B., 'The Theory of Union Growth', *Quarterly Journal of Economics*, vol. 55, 1941, 611-37.

Dawe, A., 'The Two Sociologies', *The British Journal of Sociology*, vol. 21, 1970, 207-18.

Dawe, A., 'The Relevance of Values', in A. Sahay (ed.), *Max Weber and Modern Sociology*, London, Routledge & Kegan Paul, 1971.

Dennis, N., Henriques, F., and Slaughter, C., *Coal is Our Life*, London, Eyre & Spottiswode, 1956.

Department of Employment and Productivity, *In Place of Strife: A Policy for Industrial Relations*, London, HMSO, 1969, Cmnd 3888.

Derber, M., *Plant Union Management Relations: From Practice to Theory*, University of Illinois Press, 1965.

Diamond, Lord, Royal Commission on the Distribution of Income and Wealth, report no. 5, London, HMSO, 1977, Cmnd 6999.

Donaldson, L. and Warner, M., 'Structure of Organization in Occupational Interest Associations', *Human Relations*, vol. 27, 1973, 721-38.

Donaldson, L. and Warner, M., 'Bureaucratic and Electoral Control in Occupational Interest Associations', *Sociology*, vol. 8, 1974, 47-57.

Donovan, Lord, report of Royal Commission on Trade Unions and

Employers' Associations, London, HMSO, 1968, Cmnd 3623.

Dore, R., *British Factory – Japanese Factory: The Origins of National Diversity in Industrial Relations*, London, Allen & Unwin, 1973.

Driscoll, J. W., 'Coping with Role Conflict: Implications from an Explanatory Field Study of Union-Management Co-operation', Working Paper no. 1012-78, Massachusetts, Massachusetts Institute of Technology, Alfred P. Sloan School of Management, 1978.

Dubin, R., *The World of Work: Industrial Society and Human Relations*, Englewood Cliffs, Prentice Hall, 1958.

Dubin, R., 'Power and Union-Management Relations', *Administrative Science Quarterly*, vol. 2, 1957, 60-81.

Dunlop, J. T., *Wage Determination Under Trade Unions*, New York, Macmillan, 1944.

Dunlop, J. T., 'The Development of Labor Organization', in R. A. Lester and J. Shister (eds), *Insights into Labor Issues*, New York, Macmillan, 1949.

Dunlop, J. T., *Industrial Relations Systems*, New York, Holt, 1958.

Dunlop, J. T., 'Political Systems and Industrial Relations', *International Institute for Labour Studies Bulletin*, no. 9, 1972, 99-116.

Durkheim, E., *The Division of Labor in Society*, Illinois, Free Press, 1947.

Durkheim, E., *Suicide*, London, Routledge & Kegan Paul, 1952.

Durkheim, E., *Sociology and Philosophy*, London, Cohen & West, 1953.

Durkheim, E., *The Rules of Sociological Method*, New York, Free Press, 1962.

Edelstein, J. D., 'An Organizational Theory of Union Democracy', *American Journal of Sociology*, vol. 67, 1968, 19-39.

Edelstein, J. D. and Warner, M., 'On Measuring and Explaining Union Democracy: A Reply to Dr. Martin's Critique', *Sociology*, vol. 5, 1971, 398-408.

Edelstein, J. D. and Warner, M., *Comparative Union Democracy: Organization and Opposition in British and American Unions*, London, Allen & Unwin, 1975.

Edelstein, J. D. and Warner, M., 'Research Areas in National Union Democracy', *Industrial Relations*, vol. 16, 1977, 186-98.

Edwards, C., 'Measuring Union Power: A Comparison of Two Methods Applied to the Study of Local Union Power in the Coal Industry', *British Journal of Industrial Relations*, vol. 16, 1978, 1-15.

Edwards, P.K., 'A Critique of the Kerr-Siegel Hypothesis of Strikes and the Isolated Mass: A Study of the Falsification of Sociological Knowledge', *Sociological Review* vol. 25, 1977, 551-74.

Eisenstadt, S. N., 'Social Institutions', in D. Sills (ed.), *International Encyclopedia of Social Sciences*, Macmillan and Free Press, 1968.

Eldridge, J.E.T., *Sociology and Industrial Life*, London, Nelson, 1971.

Eldridge, J. E. T. and Crombie, A. D., *A Sociology of Organizations*, London, Allen & Unwin, 1974.

Elias, N., 'Problems of Involvement and Detachment', *British Journal of Sociology*, vol. 7, 1956, 226-52.

Elsheikh, F. and Bain, G.S., 'Trade Union Growth: A Reply', *British Journal of Industrial Relations*, vol. 16, 1978, 99-102.

Etzioni, A., *A Comparative Analysis of Complex Organizations: On Power*

Involvement and their Correlates, New York, Free Press, 1961.

Evans, E. O., 'Cheap at Twice the Price? Shop Stewards and Workshop Relations in Engineering', in M. Warner (ed.), *The Sociology of the Workplace: An Interdisciplinary Approach*, London, Allen & Unwin, 1973.

Fatchett, D. and Whittingham, W. M., 'Trends and Developments in Industrial Relations Theory', *Industrial Relations Journal*, vol. 7, 1976, 50-60.

Flanders, A., *The Fawley Productivity Agreements*, London, Faber & Faber, 1964.

Flanders, A., *Trade Unions*, London, Hutchinson, 1968.

Flanders, A., *Management and Unions: The Theory and Reform of Industrial Relations*, London, Faber & Faber, 1970.

Flanders, A. and Clegg, H. A. (eds), *The System of Industrial Relations in Great Britain, Its History, Law and Institutions*, Oxford, Blackwell, 1954.

Fox, A., *Industrial Sociology and Industrial Relations*, Royal Commission on Trade Unions and Employers' Associations, Research Paper 3, London, HMSO, 1966.

Fox, A., *A Sociology of Work in Industry*, London, Collier-Macmillan, 1971.

Fox, A., *Beyond Contract: Power, Work and Trust Relations*, London, Faber & Faber, 1974.

Fox, A., *Man Mis Management*, London, Hutchinson, 1974.

Fox, A., 'Collective Bargaining, Flanders and the Webbs', *British Journal of Industrial Relations*, vol. 13, 1975, 151-74.

Fox, A., 'Industrial Relations: A Social Critique of the Pluralist Ideology', in J. Child (ed.), *Man and Organization*, 205-31.

Fox, A., 'A Note on Industrial Relations Pluralism', *Sociology*, vol. 13, 1979, 105-9.

Fox, A. and Flanders, A., 'The Reform of Collective Bargaining: From Donovan to Durkheim', *British Journal of Industrial Relations*, vol. 7, 1969, 241-80.

Friedmann, G., *The Anatomy of Work: The Implication of Specialisation*, London, Heinemann, 1961.

Galenson, W. and Lipset, S. M., *Labor and Trade Unionism, An Interdisciplinary Reader*, New York, Wiley, 1970.

Gallie, D., *In Search of the New Working Class*, Cambridge University Press, 1978.

Gamble, A. and Walton, P., *Capitalism in Crisis*, London, Macmillan, 1976.

Garaudy, R., *The Turning Point of Socialism*, London, Collins, 1970.

Geare, A. J., 'Final Offer Arbitration: A Critical Examination of the Theory', *Journal of Industrial Relations*, vol. 20, 1978, 378-85.

Gerth, H.H. and Mills, C.W., *From Max Weber: Essays in Sociology*, London, Routledge & Kegan Paul, 1948.

Giddens, A., 'Power in the Recent Writings of Talcott Parsons', *Sociology*, vol. 2, 1968, 257-72.

Giddens, A., *Capitalism and Modern Social Theory: An Analysis of the Writings of Marx, Durkheim and Max Weber*, Cambridge University Press, 1971.

Giddens, A. (ed.), *Positivism and Sociology*, London, Heinemann, 1974.

Gilbert, M., 'Neo-Durkheimian Analyses of Economic Life and Strife:

From Durkheim to the Social Contract', *Sociological Review*, vol. 26, 1978, 729-54.

Giles, W.F. and Holley, W.H., 'Job Enrichment Versus Traditional Issues at the Bargaining Table: What Union Members Want', *Academy of Management Journal*, vol. 21, 1978, 725-30.

Gill, C.G. and Warner, M., 'Managerial and Organizational Determinants of Industrial Conflict: The Chemical Industry Case', *Journal of Management Studies*, vol. 16, 1979, 56-69.

Gill, J., 'One Approach to the Teaching of Industrial Relations', *British Journal of Industrial Relations*, vol. 12, 1974, 247-70.

Giner, S., *Sociology*, London, Martin Robertson, 1972.

Glasgow Media Group, *Bad News*, London, Routledge & Kegan Paul, 1976.

Glyn, A., and Sutcliffe, B., *British Capitalism: Workers and the Profit Squeeze*, Harmondsworth, Penguin, 1972.

Godelier, M., 'System Structure and Contradiction in Capital', *The Socialist Register*, 1967, 91-119.

Godelier, M., 'Structure and Contradiction in Capital', in R. Blackburn (ed.), *Ideology in Social Science: Readings in Critical Social Theory*, London, Fontana/Collins, 1972.

Goldstein, J., *The Government of a British Union*, Chicago, Free Press, 1952.

Goldthorpe, J.H., 'The Social Action Approach to Sociology: a reply to Daniel', *Journal of Management Studies*, vol. 7, 1970, 199-208. 208.

Goldthorpe, J. H., 'Daniel on orientations to work — a final comment', *Journal of Management Studies*, vol. 9, 1972, 266-74.

Goldthorpe, J. H., 'Industrial Relations in Great Britain: A Critique of "Reformism" ', *Politics and Society*, vol. 4, 1974, 419-42.

Goldthorpe, J. H., 'Social Inequality and Social Integration in Modern Britain', in D. Wedderburn (ed.), *Poverty, Inequality and Class Structure*, Cambridge University Press, 1974.

Goldthorpe, J. H. and Llewellyn, C., 'Class mobility: intergenerational and work life patterns', *The British Journal of Sociology*, vol. 3, 1977, 269-302.

Goldthorpe, J.H. and Lockwood, D., 'Affluence and the British Class Structure', *Sociological Review*, vol. 11, no. 2, 1963, 133-63.

Goldthorpe, J. H., Lockwood, D., Bechhofer, F. and Platt, J., *The Affluent Worker: Industrial Attitudes and Behaviour*, Cambridge University Press, 1968.

Goldthorpe, J.H., Lockwood, D., Bechhofer, F. and Platt, J., *The Affluent Worker in the Class Structure*, Cambridge University Press, 1969.

Goodman, J.F.B., Armstrong, E.G.A., Davis, J.E. and Wagner, A., *Rule Making and Industrial Peace*, London, Croom Helm, 1977.

Goodman, J. F. B., Armstrong, E. G. A., Wagner, A., Davis, J. E. and Wood, S. J., 'Rules in Industrial Relations Theory: A Discussion', *Industrial Relations Journal*, vol. 16, 1975, 14-30.

Goodman, J. F. B., and Whittingham, T. G., *Shop Stewards in British Industry*, New York, McGraw-Hill, 1970.

Goodrich, C.L., *The Frontier of Control*, London, Pluto Press, 1975.

Gospel, H., 'European Managerial Unions: An Early Assessment', *Industrial Relations*, vol. 17, 1978, 360-71.

Gospel, H., 'The Disclosure of Information to Trade Unions: Approaches and Problems', *Industrial Relations Journal*, vol. 9, 1978, 18-26.

Grimes, A. J., 'Authority, Power, Influence and Social Control: A Theoretical Synthesis', *Academy of Management Review*, vol. 3, 1978, 724-735.

Halévy, E., *The Birth of Methodism in England*, Chicago University Press, 1971.

Halévy, E., *A History of the English People in 1815*, London, Fisher Unwin, 1974.

Hammer, T. H., 'Relationships Between Local Union Characteristics and Worker Behavior and Attitudes', *Academy of Management Journal*, vol. 21, 1978, 560-77.

Hammond, J. L. and Hammond, B., *The Town Labourer 1760-1832: The New Civilization*, London, Longmans Green, 1918.

Hammond, M., 'Durkheim's Reality Construction Model and the Emergence of Social Stratification', *Sociological Review*, vol. 26, 1978, 713-28.

Harrison, M., 'Participation of Women in Trade Union Activities: Some Research Findings and Comments', *Industrial Relations Journal*, vol. 10, 1979, 41-55.

Hartmann, H., 'Managerial Employees: New Participants in Industrial Democracy', *British Journal of Industrial Relations*, vol. 12, 1974, 268-81.

Heneman, H.G., Jr, 'Toward a General Conceptual Scheme of Industrial Relations: How Do We Get There?', in G.G. Somers (ed.), *Essays in Industrial Relations Theory*, Iowa State University Press, 1969.

Herberg, W., 'Bureaucracy and Democracy in Labor Unions', *The Antioch Review*, vol. 3, 1943, 406.

Herding, R., *Job Control and Union Structure*, Rotterdam University Press, 1972.

Hill, S., *The Dockers: Class and Tradition in London*, London, Heinemann, 1976.

Hill, S., and Thurley, K., 'Sociology and Industrial Relations', *British Journal of Industrial Relations*, vol. 12, 1974, 147-70.

Hinton, J., *The First Shop Stewards' Movement*, London, Allen & Unwin, 1973.

Hobsbawm, E. J., *Labouring Men: Studies in the History of Labour*, London, Weidenfeld & Nicolson, 1964.

Hobsbawm, E. J., *The Age of Capital*, London, Weidenfeld & Nicolson, 1975.

Holland, S., *The Socialist Challenge*, London, Quartet, 1975.

Hollowell, P. G., *The Lorry Driver*, London, Routledge & Kegan Paul, 1968.

Howell, G., *The Conflicts of Capital and Labour Historically and Economically Considered, Being a History of the Trade Unions of Great Britain*, London, Chatto & Windus, 1878.

Howell, G., *Trade Unionism: New and Old*, London, Methuen, 1891.

Hoxie, R., *Trade Unionism in the United States*, New York, Appleton, 1917.

Hughes, J., Trade Union Structure and Government, Research Paper 5, Part 1, Royal Commission on Trade Unions and Employers' Associations, London, HMSO, 1967.

Hughes, J.J. and Brinkley, I., 'Attitudes and Expectations of Skill Centre Trainees towards Trade Unions and Trade Union Membership', *British Journal of Industrial Relations*, vol. 17, 1979, 64-9.

Hunter, F., *Community Power Structure: A Study of Decision Makers*, University of North Carolina Press, 1953.

Husserl, E. G. A., *The Crisis of European Sciences and Transcendental Ethnomethodology*, North Western University Press, 1970.

Hyman, R., *Marxism and the Sociology of Trade Unionism*, London, Pluto Press, 1971.

Hyman, R., *The Workers' Union*, Clarendon Press, 1971.

Hyman, R., *Strikes*, London, Fontana, 1972.

Hyman, R., *Industrial Relations: A Marxist Introduction*, London, Macmillan, 1975.

Hyman, R., 'Pluralism, Procedural Consensus and Collective Bargaining', *British Journal of Industrial Relations*, vol. 16, 1978, 16-40.

Hyman, R. and Brough, I., *Social Values and Industrial Relations*, Oxford, Blackwell, 1975.

Hyman, R. and Fryer, R.H., 'Trade Unions: Sociology and Political Economy', in J.B. McKinley (ed.), *Processing People: Cases in Organizational Behaviour*, London, Holt, Rinehart & Winston, 1975.

Ingham, G.K., *Size of Industrial Organization and Worker Behaviour*, Cambridge University Press, 1970.

Jackson, D., 'Strikes as a category of Group Conflict', Working Paper no. 134, Aston, The University of Aston Management Centre, 1979.

Jackson, M.P., *Industrial Relations: A Textbook*, London, Croom Helm, 1977.

Jahoda, K., Lazarsfeld, P.L. and Zeisel, H.,*Marienthal*, London, Tavistock, 1972.

Jenkins, C., *Power at the Top*, London, MacGibbon and Kee, 1959.

Jenkins, D., *Job Power: Blue and White Collar Democracy*, London, Heinemann, 1974.

Jessop, R., 'Recent Theories of the Capitalist State', *Cambridge Journal of Economics*, vol. 1, 1977, 353-73.

Jessop, R., 'Capitalism and Democracy: the best political shell', in G. Littlejohn (ed.), *Power and the State*, London, Croom Helm, 1978.

Jones, G. P. and Pool, A. G., *A Hundred Years of Economic Development in Great Britain (1840-1940)*, London, Duckworth, 1959.

Jordan, Z. A. (ed.), *Karl Marx: Economy, Class and Social Revolution*, London, Michael Joseph, 1971.

Kahn, L. M., 'Unionism and Relative Wages: Direct and Indirect Effects', *Industrial and Labor Relations Review*, vol. 32, 1979, 520-32.

Kahn-Freund, O., 'The Legal Framework', in A. Flanders and H.A. Clegg (eds), *The System of Industrial Relations in Great Britain, Its History, Law and Institutions*, Oxford, Blackwell, 1954.

Keddie, N., *Tinker, Tailor. . . . The Myth of Cultural Deprivation*, Harmondsworth, Penguin, 1973.

Keenoy, T., 'From the Webbs to Corporatism', Proceedings of the University of Wales Colloquium on Management and Industrial Relations, UWIST, Cardiff, 1979.

Kelly, A., 'Job Satisfaction and the Unionization of the White-Collar

Employee', *Studies*, vol. 67, 1978, 143-63.

Kelsall, R. K., 'Wage Regulation under the Statute of Artificers', reprinted in W.E. Minchinton (ed.), *Wage Regulation in Pre-Industrial England*, Newton Abbot, David & Charles, 1972.

Kerr, C., *Labor and Management in Industrial Society*, New York, Doubleday, 1964.

Kerr, C., 'Industrial Relations Research: A Personal Retrospective', *Industrial Relations*, vol. 17, 1978, 313-42.

Kerr, C. and Siegel, A., 'The Inter-Industry Propensity to Strike – an International Comparison', in A. Kornhauser, R. Dubin and A. Ross (eds), *Industrial Conflict*, New York, McGraw-Hill, 1954.

Kornhauser, A., Dubin, R., and Ross, A., (eds), *Industrial Conflict*, New York, McGraw-Hill, 1954.

Korpi, W., and Shalev, M., 'Strikes, Industrial Relations and Class Conflict in Capitalist Societies', *British Journal of Sociology*, vol. 30, 1979, 164-87.

Laffer, K., 'Industrial Relations, Its Teaching and Scope: An Australian Experience', *International Institute for Labour Studies Bulletin*, no. 5, 1968, 9-26.

Lane, A., *The Union Makes us Strong*, London, Arrow Books, 1974.

Lane, A. and Roberts, K., *Strike at Pilkingtons*, London, Fontana, 1971.

Lawler, E. J., and Bacharach, S. B., 'Power Dependence in Industrial Bargaining: The Expected Utility of Influence', *Industrial and Labor Relations Review*, vol. 32, 1979, 196-205.

Lee, D. J., 'Class Differentials in Educational Opportunity and Promotion from the Ranks', *Sociology*, vol. 2, 1968, 293-312.

Lenin, V. I., 'What is to be done?', in *Collected Works*, vol. 5, Moscow, Foreign Languages Publishing House, 1961.

Lenski, G., 'Social Structure in Evolutionary Perspective', in P.M. Blau (ed.), *Approaches to the Study of Social Structure*, London, Open Books, 1976.

Lerner, S. W., 'The Future Organization and Structure of Trade Unions', in B. C. Roberts (ed.), *Industrial Relations: Contemporary Problems and Perspectives*, London, Methuen, 1962.

Lester, R. A., *As Unions Mature*, Princeton University Press, 1958.

Lester, R. A. and Shister, J. (eds), *Insights into Labor Issues*, New York, Macmillan, 1949.

Levinson, H. M., *Determining Forces in Collective Wage Bargaining*, New York, Wiley, 1966.

Levitas, R. A., 'Some Problems of Aim-Centred Models of Social Movements', *Sociology*, vol. 11, 1977, 47-73.

Lewenhak, S., *Women and Trade Unions: An Outline History of Women in the British Trade Union Movement*, London, Benn, 1977.

Lindop, E., 'Workplace Bargaining: The End of an Era?', *Industrial Relations Journal*, vol. 10, 1979, 12-21.

Little, A. and Westergaard, J., 'The Trend of Class Differentials in Educational Opportunity in England and Wales', *British Journal of Sociology*, vol. 15, 1964, 301-16.

Lockwood, D., 'Sources of Variation in Working Class Images of Society', *The Sociological Review*, vol. 14, 1966, 249-67.

Lockwood, D., *The Blackcoated Worker*, London, Allen & Unwin, 1958.
Lovell, J.C. and Roberts, B.C., *A Short History of the T.U.C.*, London, Macmillan, 1968.
Lozovsky, A., *Marx and the Trade Unions*, London, Allen & Unwin, 1951.
Lukes, S., *Power: A Radical View*, London, Macmillan, 1974.
Lukes, S., *Emile Durkheim: His Life and Work*, London, Allen Lane, 1973.
Lumley, R., *White Collar Unionism in Britain*, London, Methuen, 1973.
Lumley, R., 'A Modified Rules Approach to Workplace Industrial Relations', Working Paper no. 109, Aston, The University of Aston Management Centre, 1978.
Lupton, T., *On the Shop Floor: Two Studies of Workshop Organization and Output*, Oxford, Pergamon Press, 1963.
Luscher, K., 'Time: A Much Neglected Dimension in Social Theory and Research', *Sociological Analysis and Theory*, vol. 5, 1974, 101-17.
McCarthy, M., 'Women in Trade Unions Today', in L. Middleton (ed.), *Women in the Labour Movement*, London, Croom Helm, 1977.
McCarthy, W. E. J., *The Closed Shop in Britain*, Oxford, Blackwell, 1964.
McCarthy, W.E.J. (ed.), *Trade Unions, Selected Readings*, Harmondsworth, Penguin, 1972.
McCarthy, W.E.J. and Parker, S.R., 'Shop Stewards and Workshop Relations', Royal Commission on Trade Unions and Employers' Associations, Research Paper 10, London, HMSO, 1968.
McCormick, B. J., 'Managerial Unionism in the Coal Industry', *British Journal of Sociology*, vol. 11, 1960, 356-69.
McCormick, B. J., *Industrial Relations in the Coal Industry*, London, Macmillan, 1979.
Macdonald, D. F., *The State and the Trade Unions*, London, Macmillan, 1976.
Mack, J., 'The Inequalities of Sex', *New Society*, 8 September 1977, 480-2.
Mackie, L. and Pattullo, P., *Women at Work*, London, Tavistock, 1977.
McKinley, J.B. (ed.), *Processing People: Cases in Organizational Behaviour*, London, Holt, Rinehart & Winston, 1975.
Mallet, S., *The New Working Class*, Nottingham, Spokesman, 1975.
Mann, M., *Consciousness and Action Among the Western Working Class*, London, Macmillan, 1973.
Margerison, C. J., 'What do we mean by Industrial Relations? A Behavioural Science Approach', *British Journal of Industrial Relations*, vol. 7, 1969, 273-86.
Marsh, R. and Pedler, M., 'Unionising the White Collar Workers', *Employee Relations*, vol. 1, no. 2, 1979, 2-6.
Marshall, T.H., *Citizenship and Social Class and Other Essays*, Cambridge University Press, 1950.
Martin, R., 'Union Democracy: An Explanatory Framework', *Sociology*, vol. 2, 1968, 205-20.
Martin, R., 'Edelstein, Warner and Cooke on Union Democracy', *Sociology*, vol. 5, 1971, 243-4.
Martin, R., *The Sociology of Power*, London, Routledge & Kegan Paul, 1977.
Marx, K., *Value, Price and Profit*, New York, Harper & Row, 1954.

Marx, K., *'Selected writings in Sociology and Social Philosophy'*, T. B. Bottomore and M. Rubel (eds), Harmondsworth, Penguin, 1963.

Marx, K., *A Contribution to the Critique of Political Economy*, London, Lawrence & Wishart, 1971.

Marx, K., *Capital*, vol. 1, London, Lawrence & Wishart, 1974.

Marx, K., *Capital*, vol. 3, London, Lawrence & Wishart, 1974.

Marx, K. and Engels, F., *Selected Correspondence 1843-1895*, London, Lawrence & Wishart, 1956.

Maslow, A. H., *Motivation and Personality*, New York, Harper & Row, 1954.

Mayo, E., *The Social Problems of an Industrial Civilization*, London, Routledge & Kegan Paul, 1949.

Menzies, K., *Talcott Parsons and the Social Image of Man*, London, Routledge & Kegan Paul, 1977.

Michels, R., *Political Parties*, New York, Dover, 1959.

Middleton, L. (ed.), *Women in the Labour Movement*, London, Croom Helm, 1977.

Miller, D. C. and Form, W. H., *Industrial Sociology: An Introduction to the Study of Work Relations*, New York, Harper, 1951.

Mills, C. W., *The Power Elite*, New York, Oxford University Press, 1956.

Mills, L., 'The Role of Trade Unions in Strategic Planning', *Long Range Planning*, vol. 11, no. 5, 1978, 78-82.

Minchinton, W.E. (ed.), *Wage Regulation in Pre-Industrial England*, Newton Abbot, David & Charles, 1972.

Mitchell, W. C., *Sociological Analysis and Politics: the Theories of Talcott Parsons*, Englewood Cliffs, Prentice Hall, 1967.

Mommsen, W., *The Age of Bureaucracy*, Oxford, Blackwell, 1974.

Moore, J. C., 'Some Thoughts on Trade Unions', *Journal of Industrial Relations*, vol. 20, 1978, 487-90.

Moore, R., *Pit-Men, Preachers and Politics*, Cambridge University Press, 1974.

Moran, M., *The Union of Post Office Workers: A Study in Political Sociology*, London, Macmillan, 1974.

Moran, M., 'The Conservative Party and the Trade Unions since 1974', *Political Studies*, vol. 27, 1979, 38-53.

Morris, M., *The General Strike*, London, Lawrence & Wishart, 1976.

Mortimer, J. E., *Trade Unions and Technological Change*, London, Oxford University Press, 1971.

Mouzelis, N. P., *Organization and Bureaucracy*, London, Routledge & Kegan Paul, 1967.

Mulvey, C., *The Economic Analysis of Trade Unions*, London, Martin Robertson, 1978.

Mulvey, C., 'The Impact of Unions on Non-Union Wages', Discussion Papers in Economics, no. 32, University of Glasgow, 1979.

Murphy, J. T., *The Workers' Committee: An Outline of its Principles and Structure*, London, Pluto Press, 1972.

Nelson, J. L., and Grams, R., 'Union Militancy and Occupational Communities', *Industrial Relations*, vol. 17, 1978, 342-6.

Neville, P., 'Productivity Bargaining', unpublished undergraduate dissertation, Sheffield University, 1973.

Nichols, T. and Armstrong, P., *Workers Divided: A Study in Shopfloor Politics*, London, Fontana, 1976.

Nichols, T. and Beynon, H., *Living with Capitalism: Class Relations in the Modern Factory*, London, Routledge & Kegan Paul, 1977.

Nicholson, N., 'The Role of the Shop Steward: an Empirical Case Study', *Industrial Relations Journal*, vol. 7, 1976, 15-26.

Nicholson, N., 'Mythology, Theory and Research on Union Democracy', *Industrial Relations Journal*, vol. 9, no. 4, 1979, 32-41.

Nickell, S. R., 'Trade Unions and the Position of Women in the Industrial Wage Structure', *British Journal of Industrial Relations*, vol. 15, 1977, 192-210.

Noble, T., *Modern Britain: Structure and Change*, London, Batsford, 1975.

Offe, C., *Industry and Inequality: The Achievement Principle in Work and Social Status*, London, Edward Arnold, 1976.

Pahl, R.E. and Winckler, J.T., 'The Coming Corporatism', *New Society*, 10 October 1974, 72-6.

Panitch, L., 'The Development of Corporatism in Liberal Democracies', *Comparative Political Studies*, vol. 10, 1977, 61-90.

Panitch, L., *Social Democracy and Industrial Militancy*, Cambridge University Press, 1977.

Pap, M. and Pléy, C., 'Social Class Differences in the Speech of Six-Year-Old Hungarian Children', *Sociology*, vol. 8, 1974, 267-75.

Parker, C. H., *The Casual Labourer and Other Essays*, New York, Harcourt, Brace & Howe, 1920.

Parker, S.R., Brown, R.K., Child, J. and Smith, M.A., *The Sociology of Industry*, 3rd edn, London, Allen & Unwin, 1977.

Parkin, F., *Class, Inequality and the Political Order*, London, Paladin, 1971.

Parry, N. and Parry, J., 'Professionalism and Unionism: Some Aspects of Class Conflict in the National Health Service', *Sociological Review*, vol. 25, 1977, 823-41.

Parsons, T., *The Social System*, Chicago, Free Press, 1951.

Parsons, T., *The Structure of Social Action*, Chicago, Free Press, 1951.

Parsons, T., *Essays in Sociological Theory*, Chicago, Free Press, 1954.

Parsons, T., 'Suggestions for a Sociological Approach to the Theory of Organizations 1', *Administrative Science Quarterly*, vol. 1, 1956, 63-85.

Parsons, T., *Structure and Process in Modern Societies*, Chicago University Press, 1961.

Parsons, T., 'On the Concept of Influence', *Public Opinion Quarterly*, vol. 27, 1963, 37-62.

Parsons, T., *Sociological Theory and Modern Society*, New York, Free Press, 1967.

Parsons, T., *Action Theory and the Human Condition*, London, Collier-Macmillan, 1978.

Parsons, T. and Shils, E.A. (eds), *Towards a General Theory of Action*, Harvard University Press, 1967.

Parsons, T. and Smelser, N.J., *Economy and Society*, London, Routledge & Kegan Paul, 1956.

Partridge, B.E., 'The Activities of Shop Stewards', *Industrial Relations*

Journal, vol. 8, no. 4, 1978, 28-42.

Partridge, B. E., 'An Analysis of the Activities of Shop Stewards', Working Paper no. 66, Aston, the University of Aston Management Centre, 1977.

Pasmore, W.A. and Sherwood, J.J., *Sociotechnical Systems: A Sourcebook*, LaJolla California, University Associates, 1978.

Pedersen, P.J., 'Union Growth and the Business Cycle: a Note on the Bain-Elsheikh Model', *British Journal of Industrial Relations*, vol. 16, 1978, 373-7.

Pedler, M., 'Shop Stewards as Leaders', *Industrial Relations Journal*, vol. 4, 1973, 43-60.

Pelling, H., *A History of British Trade Unionism*, 3rd edn, London, Macmillan, 1976.

Perlman, M. (ed.), *Labor Union Theories in America: Background and Development*, Illinois, Row Peterson, 1958.

Perlman, S., *A Theory of the Labor Movement*, New York, Kelley, 1949.

Pettigrew, A.M., *Politics of Organizational Decision Making*, London, Tavistock, 1973.

Philo, G. and Hewitt, J., 'Trade Unions and the Media', *Industrial Relations Journal*, vol. 7, 1976, 4-19.

Poole, M. J. F., 'A Power Approach to Workers' Participation in Decision Making', unpublished Ph.D. dissertation, Sheffield University, 1969.

Poole, M.J.F., 'The Origins of Trade Unionists' Values: Some Theoretical Inferences', *Sociological Analysis and Theory*, vol. 4, 1974, 47-74.

Poole, M. J. F., 'Towards a Sociology of Shop Stewards', *Sociological Review*, vol. 22, 1974, 57-82.

Poole, M.J.F., 'What are Unions For?', *New Society*, 9 May 1974, 324.

Poole, M.J.F., 'Ideas, Institutions and Economic Development', *Sociological Analysis and Theory*, vol. 5, 1975, 331-57.

Poole, M. J. F., 'A Power Analysis of Workplace Labour Relations', *Industrial Relations Journal*, vol. 7, 1976, 31-43.

Poole, M.J.F., *Workers' Participation in Industry*, London, Routledge & Kegan Paul, 1978.

Popitz, M., Bahrdt, H.P., Jueres, E.A. and Kesting, A., 'The Worker's Image of Society', in T. Burns (ed.), *Industrial Man*, Harmondsworth, Penguin, 1969.

Prandy, K., *Professional Employees*, London, Faber & Faber, 1965.

Prandy, K., 'Professional Organization in Great Britain', *Industrial Relations*, vol. 5, 1965, 67-79.

Prandy, K., Stewart, A. and Blackburn, R.M., 'Concepts and Measures', *Sociology*, vol. 8, 1974, 427-46.

Pribicevic, B., *The Shop Stewards' Movement and Workers' Control, 1910-1922*, Oxford, Blackwell, 1959.

Price, J., *Organised Labour in the War*, Harmondsworth, Penguin, 1940.

Price, R. and Bain, G.S., 'Union Growth Revisited: 1948-1974 in Perspective', *British Journal of Industrial Relations*, vol. 14, 1976, 339-55.

Ramaswamy, E. A., 'The Participatory Dimension of Trade Union Democracy: A Comparative Sociological View', *Sociology*, vol. 11, 1977, 465-80.

Rawls, J., *A Theory of Justice*, Clarendon Press, 1972.

Registrar General, Decennial Supplement, London, HMSO, 1971.

Renshaw, P., *The General Strike*, London, Eyre Methuen, 1975.

Renshaw, P., *Nine Days in May*, London, Eyre Methuen, 1975.

Rex, J., 'Typology and Objectivity: A Comment on Weber's Four Socio-logical Methods', in A. Sahay (ed.), *Max Weber and Modern Sociology*, London, Routledge & Kegan Paul, 1971.

Richardson, R., 'Trade Union Growth', *British Journal of Industrial Relations*, vol. 15, 1977, 279-82.

Richardson, R., 'Trade Union Growth: A Rejoinder', *British Journal of Industrial Relations*, vol. 16, 1978, 103-5.

Roberts, B.C., *Trade Union Government and Administration in Great Britain*, London, Bell, 1956.

Roberts, B. C. (ed.), *Industrial Relations: Contemporary Problems and Perspectives*, London, Methuen, 1962.

Roberts, B. C., Loveridge, R., Gennard, J., Eason, J. V. *et al.*, *Reluctant Militants*, London, Heinemann, 1972.

Roberts, K., Cook, F. G., Clarke, S. C. and Semeonoff, E., *The Fragmentary Class Structure*, London, Heinemann, 1977.

Robertson, N. and Sams, K. I., *British Trade Unionism, Select Documents*, vol. 1, Oxford, Blackwell, 1972.

Robertson, N. and Sams, K. I., *British Trade Unionism, Select Documents*, vol. 2, Oxford, Blackwell, 1972.

Robinson, D., 'Trade Union Recognition and the Case for Goliath', *Personnel Management*, vol. 11, no. 8, 1979, 29-35.

Roethlisberger, F. J. and Dickson, W. J., *Management and the Worker: An Account of a Research Program Conducted by the Western Electric Company, Hawthorne Works, Chicago*, New York, Wiley, 1964.

Rose, E., 'Work Control in Industrial Society', *Industrial Relations Journal*, vol. 7, 1976, 20-30.

Ross, A. M., *Trade Union Wage Policy*, California University Press, 1948.

Ross, A. M. and Hartman, P. T., *Changing Patterns of Industrial Conflict*, New York, Wiley, 1960.

Ross, N. S., 'Organized Labour and Management in the UK', in E. M. Hugh-Jones (ed.), *Human Relations and Management*, London, North-Holland, 1958.

Rowan, R. L., 'The Socio-Economic Environment and International Union Aspirations', *Columbia Journal of Business*, vol. 13, no. 4, 1978, 111-21.

Runciman, W. G., *Relative Deprivation and Social Justice: A Study of Attitudes to Social Equality in Twentieth Century England*, London, Routledge & Kegan Paul, 1966.

Rus, V., 'Influence Structure in Yugoslavian Enterprises', *Industrial Relations*, vol. 9, 1970, 148-60.

Sahay, A., 'The Importance of Weber's Methodology', in *Max Weber and Modern Sociology*, London, Routledge & Kegan Paul, 1971.

Sahay, A., Introduction, in *Max Weber and Modern Sociology*, London, Routledge & Kegan Paul, 1971.

Sahay, A., 'Knowledge, Values and Sentiments', *Sociological Analysis and Theory*, vol. 5, 1975, 289-300.

Salaman, G., *Community and Occupation*, Cambridge University Press, 1974.

Sayles, L. R., *Behavior of Industrial Work Groups: Prediction and Control*, New York, Wiley, 1958.

Sayles, L. R. and Strauss, G., *The Local Union*, revised edn, New York, Harcourt Brace & World, 1967.

Scase, R. (ed.), *Industrial Society: Class, Cleavage and Control*, London, Allen & Unwin, 1977.

Scheler, M., *Die Wissensformen und die Gesellschaft*, Berne, Francke, 1960.

Schmidt, G., 'Max Weber and Modern Industrial Sociology: A Comment on some Recent Anglo-Saxon Interpretations', *Sociological Analysis and Theory*, vol. 6, 1976, 47-73.

Schmitter, P. C., 'Still the Century of Corporatism?', *Review of Politics*, vol. 36, 1974, 85-131.

Schmitter, P. C., 'Modes of Interest Intermediation and Models of Societal Change in Western Europe', *Comparative Political Studies*, vol. 10, no. 1, 1977, 7-38.

Schneider, E. V., *Industrial Sociology*, New York, McGraw-Hill, 1957.

Schumacher, E.F., *Small is Beautiful: A Study of Economics as if People Mattered*, London, Blond & Briggs, 1973.

Schutz, A., *The Phenomenology of the Social World*, North Western University Press, 1970.

Scott, W. H., *Industrial Leadership and Joint Consultation: A Study of Human Relations in Three Merseyside Firms*, Liverpool University Press, 1952.

Scott, W.H., Mumford, E., McGivering, I.C. and Kirkby, J.M., *Coal and Conflict: A Study of Industrial Relations at Collieries*, Liverpool University Press, 1963.

Semmel, B., *The Methodist Revolution*, London, Heinemann, 1974.

Shimmin, S. and Singh, R., 'Industrial Relations and Organizational Behaviour: A Critical Appraisal', *Industrial Relations Journal*, vol. 4, no. 3, 1973, 37-42.

Shirom, A., 'Union Militancy: Structural and Personal Determinants', *Industrial Relations*, vol. 16, 1977, 152-62.

Shister, J., 'The Direction of Unionism, 1947-1967: Thrust or Drift?', *Industrial and Labor Relations Review*, vol. 20, 1967, 578-601.

Shuchman, A., *Co-determination: Labor's Middle Way in Germany*, Washington, Public Affairs Press, 1957.

Silverman, D., 'Formal Organizations or Industrial Sociology: Towards a Social Action Analysis of Organizations', *Sociology*, vol. 2, 1968, 221-38.

Simpson, W., *Labour: the Unions and the Party*, London, Allen & Unwin, 1973.

Singh, R., 'Systems Theory in the Study of Industrial Relations: Time for a Reappraisal?', *Industrial Relations Journal*, vol. 7, 1976, 59-71.

Singh, R., 'Theory and Practice in Industrial Relations', *Industrial Relations Journal*, vol. 9, 1978, 57-64.

Skelley, J. (ed.), *The General Strike*, London, Lawrence & Wishart, 1976.

Smith, R. L. and Hoplins, A. H., 'Public Employee Attitudes Towards

Unions', *Industrial and Labor Relations Review*, vol. 32, 1979, 484-95.

Somers, G.G. (ed.), *Essays in Industrial Relations Theory*, Iowa State University Press, 1969.

Sorge, A., 'The Evolution of Industrial Democracy in the Countries of the European Community', *British Journal of Industrial Relations*, vol. 14, 1976, 274-94.

Sorge, A., 'The Cultural Context of Organization Structure: Administrative Rationality, Constraints and Choice', in M. Warner (ed.), *Organizational Choice and Constraint: Approaches to the Sociology of Enterprise Behaviour*, Farnborough, Saxon House, 1977.

Sorge, A. and Warner, M., 'The Societal and Organizational Context of Industrial Relations: A Comparison of Great Britain and West Germany', Discussion Paper nos. 78-83, Berlin, International Institute of Management, 1978, 1-21.

Spinrad, W., 'Correlates of Trade Union Participation: A Summary of the Literature', *American Sociological Review*, vol. 22, 1960, 237-44.

Spoor, H., *White Collar Union: Sixty Years of NALGO*, London, Heinemann, 1967.

Stark, W., *The Sociology of Knowledge*, London, Routledge & Kegan Paul, 1958.

Stenning, R., 'Industrial Relations, Multinational Corporations and Trade Union Response', *Anglian Management Review*, vol. 2, 1978, 2-16.

Strauss, G., 'Union Government in the U.S.: Research Past and Future', *Industrial Relations*, vol. 16, 1977, 215-42.

Strauss, G. and Warner, M., 'Symposium Introduction on Research on Union Government', *Industrial Relations*, vol. 16, 1977, 115-25.

Sturmthal, A. (ed.), *White-Collar Trade Unions: Contemporary Developments in Industrial Societies*, Illinois University Press, 1966.

Tannenbaum, A. (ed.), *Control in Organizations*, New York. McGraw-Hill, 1968.

Tannenbaum, F., *The Labor Movement*, New York, Pitman, 1921.

Tannenbaum, F., *A Philosophy of Labor*, New York, Knopf, 1952.

Tawney, R.H., *The Webbs in Perspective*, London, Athlone Press, 1953.

Taylor, R., *The Fifth Estate: Britain's Unions in the Modern World*, London, Routledge & Kegan Paul, 1978.

Terry, M., 'The Emergence of a Lay Elite?: Some Recent Changes in Shop Steward Organization', Discussion Paper no. 14, University of Warwick, Industrial Relations Research Unit, 1978.

Therborn, G., *Science, Class and Society*, London, New Left Books, 1976.

Therborn, G., 'Working Class Ideology and Working Class Action: What is Wrong with the Best Sociology of Class', *Acta Sociologica*, vol. 19, 1976, 199-203.

Thompson, E. P., *The Making of the English Working Class*, London, Gollancz, 1963.

Thompson, E. P., *William Morris, From Romantic to Revolutionary*, London, Merlin Press, 1977.

Thompson, E.P., *The Poverty of Theory and Other Essays*, London, Merlin Press, 1978.

Tivey, L. (ed.), *The Nationalised Industries since 1960*, London, Allen & Unwin, 1973.

Touraine, A., 'Towards a Sociology of Action', in A. Giddens (ed.), *Positivism and Sociology*, London, Heinemann, 1974.

Tracy, L. and Peterson, R. B., 'Differences in Reactions of Union and Management Negotiators to the Problem Solving Process', *Industrial Relations Journal*, vol. 8, 1978, 43-53.

Trades Union Congress, *Annual Report*, London, TUC, 1970 and 1976.

Trotsky, L., 'Marxism and Trade Unionism', in T. Clarke and L. Clements (eds), *Trade Unions under Capitalism*, Glasgow, Fontana/Collins, 1977.

Tunstall, J., *The Fishermen*, London, MacGibbon & Kee, 1962.

Turner, B. S., 'The Structuralist Critique of Weber's Sociology', *British Journal of Sociology*, vol. 28, 1977, 1-16.

Turner, H. A., 'Trade Union Organization', *Political Quarterly*, vol. 27, 1956, 57-70.

Turner, H.A., *Trade Union Growth, Structure and Policy: A Comparative Study of the Cotton Unions*, London, Allen & Unwin, 1962.

Turner, H. A., 'The Royal Commission Research Papers', *British Journal of Industrial Relations*, vol. 6, 1968, 346-59.

Turner, R. (ed.), *Ethnomethodology*, Harmondsworth, Penguin, 1974.

Van Doorn, J.A.A., 'Sociology and the Problem of Power', *Sociologia Nederlandica*, vol. 1, 1962/3, 3-47.

Walker, J. M., and Lawler, J., 'Dual Unions and Political Processes in Organizations', *Industrial Relations*, vol. 18, 1979, 32-43.

Walker, K.F., 'Towards Useful Theorising About Industrial Relations', *British Journal of Industrial Relations*, vol. 15, 1977, 307-16.

Walton, R. E. and McKersie, R. B., *A Behavioral Theory of Labor Negotiations: An Analysis of a Social Interaction System*, New York, McGraw-Hill, 1965.

Warner, M., 'An Organizational Profile of the Small Trade Union: A Composite Case Study', *Industrial Relations Journal*, vol. 3, no. 4, 1972, 51-64.

Warner, M. (ed.), *The Sociology of the Workplace*, London, Allen & Unwin, 1973.

Warner, M., review of H.A. Clegg, *Trade Unionism under Collective Bargaining* in *British Journal of Industrial Relations*, vol. 15, 1977, 297.

Warner, M., (ed.), *Organizational Choice and Constraint: Approaches to the Sociology of Enterprise Behaviour*, Farnborough, Saxon House, 1977.

Warr, P. B., Bird, M. and Hadfield, R. W., 'Some Characteristics of Foremen in the Iron and Steel Industry', *Occupational Psychology*, vol. 40, 1966, 1203-14.

Wearmouth, R. F., *Methodism and the Trade Unions*, London, Epworth Press, 1959.

Webb, S. and Webb, B., *Industrial Democracy*, London, Longmans Green, 1897.

Webb, S. and Webb, B., *The History of Trade Unionism*, London, Longmans Green, 1902.

Webb, S. and Webb, B., *Methods of Social Study*, London, Longmans Green, 1932.

Webb, T., 'Jobs in Jeopardy and the Trade Union Response', *Personnel*

Management, vol. 11, no. 7, 1979, 28-31.

Weber, M., *The Theory of Social and Economic Organization*, New York, Oxford University Press, 1947.

Weber, M., *The Methodology of the Social Sciences*, Chicago, Free Press, 1959.

Weber, M., *Economy and Society*, New York, Bedminster Press, 1968.

Wedderburn, D., and Crompton, R., *Workers' Attitudes and Technology*, Cambridge University Press, 1972.

Wedderburn, K. W., *The Worker and the Law*, Harmondsworth, Penguin, 1971.

Weekes, B., Mellish, M., Dickens, L. and Lloyd, J., *Industrial Relations and the Limits of Law: The Industrial Relations Effects of the Industrial Relations Act, 1971*, Oxford, Blackwell, 1975.

Weir, D., 'Radical Managerialism: Middle Managers' Perceptions of Collective Bargaining', *British Journal of Industrial Relations*, vol. 14, 1976, 324-38.

Welton, H., *The Trade Unions, the Employers and the State*, London, Pall Mall Press, 1960.

Westergaard, J. H. and Resler, M., *Class in a Capitalist Society*, London, Heinemann, 1975.

Whelan, C.T., 'Orientations to Work: Some Theoretical and Sociological Problems', *British Journal of Industrial Relations*, vol. 14, 1976, 142-58.

Wigham, E., *What's Wrong with the Unions?*, Harmondsworth, Penguin, 1961.

Wigham, E. L., *Trade Unions*, London, Oxford University Press, 1969.

Wigham, E. L., *Strikes and the Government*, London, Macmillan, 1976.

Wilson, J. H., *The Relevance of British Socialism*, London, Weidenfeld & Nicolson, 1964.

Winckler, J.T., 'The Corporate Economy: Theory and Administration', in R. Scase (ed.), *Industrial Society: Class, Cleavage and Control*, London, Allen & Unwin, 1977.

Withers, G. A., 'Social Justice and the Unions: A Normative Approach to Cooperation and Conflict Under Interdependence', *British Journal of Industrial Relations*, vol. 15, 1977, 322-37.

Wood, S.J., 'The Radicalisation of Industrial Relations Theory', *Personnel Review*, vol. 5, 1976, 52-7.

Wood, S.J., 'Ideology in Industrial Relations Theory', *Industrial Relations Journal*, vol. 9, no. 4, 1979, 42-56.

Wood, S.J. and Elliott, R., 'A Critical Evaluation of Fox's Radicalisation of Industrial Relations Theory', *Sociology*, vol. 11, no. 1, 1977, 105-24.

Wood, S.J., Wagner, A., Armstrong, E.G.A., Goodman, J.F.B., and Davis, J.E., 'The "Industrial Relations System" Concept as a Basis for Theory in Industrial Relations', *British Journal of Industrial Relations*, vol. 13, 1975, 291-308.

Woodward, J., *Industrial Organization: Theory and Practice*, London, Oxford University Press, 1965.

Wrong, D. H., 'Some Problems of Defining Social Power', *American Journal of Sociology*, vol. 73, 1968, 673-81.

Zimmerman, D.H., 'The Practicalities of Rule Use', in J.T. Douglas (ed.), *Understanding Everyday Life: Toward the Reconstruction of Sociological Knowledge*, London, Routledge & Kegan Paul, 1971.

Index of names

Index of subjects